EFFECTIVE SECURITY
MANAGEMENT

EFFECTIVE SECURITY MANAGEMENT
Fourth Edition

Charles A. Sennewald, CMC, CPP, CPO

An Imprint of Elsevier
www.bh.com

Amsterdam Boston Heidelberg London New York Oxford
Paris San Diego San Francisco Singapore Sydney Tokyo

Recognizing the importance of preserving what has been written, Elsevier prints its books on acid-free paper whenever possible.

Library of Congress Cataloging-in-Publication Data

Sennewald, Charles A., 1931–
    Effective security management / Charles A. Sennewald. — 4th ed.
        p.   cm.
    Includes bibliographical references and index.
     ISBN-13: 978-0-7506-7454-6 ISBN-10: 0-7506-7454-7 (alk. paper)
        1. Private security services — Management.   2. Industries — Security measures.
    3. Retail trade — Security measures.   I. Title.
    HV8290.S46   2003
    658.4'7 — dc21
ISBN-13: 978-0-7506-7454-6
ISBN-10: 0-7506-7454-7

British Library Cataloguing-in-Publication Data

A catalogue record for this book is available from the British Library.

The publisher offers special discounts on bulk orders of this book.

For information, please contact:
    Manager of Special Sales
    Elsevier
    200 Wheeler Road
    Burlington, MA 01803

For information on all Butterworth-Heinemann publications available, contact our World Wide Web home page at: http://www.bh.com

10 9 8 7 6 5 4

Printed in the United States of America

*To my family,
who, close behind FAITH,
is my most precious possession*

CONTENTS

PREFACE

When I first positioned myself in front of a portable electric typewriter to write the original version of this book back in the 1970s, there were relatively few books in and for the industry. For the most part they were "nuts and bolts" texts, dealing with such specific protection areas as hospital security, hotel security, office building security, industrial security, and sources of information.

At the same time, national seminars and other training forums sponsored by such professional organizations as the American Society for Industrial Security, to name but one, similarly focused on the "how-to" of security, such as how to improve facility security through the integrated use of state-of-the-art technology with a smaller staff.

Those kinds of books and training programs were professionally done and certainly welcome. In fact, they were indispensable in the ever-growing protection industry. However, little attention was being paid to the administrative, managerial, and supervisorial aspects of our industry.

We were becoming highly skilled protection technicians but remained aloof and insensitive to the principles and practices of good management. Security executives, as a group, had fallen behind—had become less than "whole" executives in comparison to others in the corporate structure. Men and women in other organizational and career disciplines, such as finance, marketing, production, research, and human resources, were regularly being exposed to management development trends, but for a number of reasons Security Managers were not. One reason was that we were too busy keeping up with racing security technology. Another reason was that we were too busy with important investigations and too absorbed with the so-called emergencies and crises that rightfully belong in the Security Department's arena. Still another reason was that security executives are of a disciplined and hard-set mentality, stemming in part from military or other public sector organizational experience, such as the police—organizations in which people performed because they were told to perform.

It was at this time and in this vacuum that I chose to focus on what was, in my judgment, the greatest need in the industry—better management. I had personally seen so many abuses that to me the need simply cried out.

Some of these management abuses were truly tragic, some were idiotic, and some were hilariously funny. The common denominator was ignorance. I wrote *Effective Security Management* with the hope that through education and awareness, abuses would subside, and Security Managers would favorably compare with other managers regarding modern attitudes and practices in management.

The field of security management has certainly improved its image since the first edition of *Effective Security Management* was published. Security management is increasingly viewed as a professional area within a company's or an institution's management framework. I would like to think that this book, in some small way, had a part in the growth, development, and enhancement of the security profession and its managerial practices.

This fourth edition remains a basic introduction to the principles of management applicable to Loss Prevention and Security Departments. I believe it's still in keeping with the practical, real-life approach to the subject. My friend and colleague Jim Broder's valuable material on risk management and security surveys remains in this work, as does Geoff Craighead's insightful contribution on computers and security management. These two well-known security professionals are now joined by another talented expert, Karim Vallani, known for his work on crime and statistical analysis. The three honor me with their contributions.

John Sanger at Cahners Publishing Company was kind enough to give permission to reprint his material on managing the organization, which serves as the introduction. This material describes succinctly the purpose of my book—so well, in fact, that I have included it with few changes.

I have again included my "Jackass Management Traits" at the end of this book, material I created for and that originally appeared in the Protection of Assets Manuals published by the Merritt Company in Santa Monica, California. These fun, tongue-in-cheek caricatures may indeed be the most important part of the book, because it is all very well and good to understand organizational principles and management techniques, but if a manager does not know how to manage and supervise the employees, this learning will be all for naught.

I hope that the fourth edition of *Effective Security Management* will continue to be an effective tool in preparing students as well as practitioners for the exciting and demanding challenges offered in our industry today.

Charles A. "Chuck" Sennewald, CMC, CPP, CPO

Introduction

MANAGING THE ORGANIZATION

What is management? What functions do managers perform? Although these are complex questions that will be explained in more detail throughout this book, we still need a fundamental idea of what management is and what a manager does before much of the material will be meaningful. Let us start, therefore, with an exploration of what management is. Then we will explore the functions of management.

MANAGERIAL ACTS

If we were to follow a Security Manager about all day and list on a sheet of paper everything that he or she does as a manager, the list would probably look somewhat as follows:

- Talks to employees
- Gives directions to lower-level supervisors
- Dictates letter
- Establishes loss prevention goals
- Plans new loss prevention programs
- Hires new security officer
- Reads mail and reports
- Attends meeting
- Makes decision about new alarm equipment

Note that these activities are either physical or mental in nature. The physical activities revolve around the concept of communications. The manager is either telling someone something verbally or in writing, or he or she is receiving a communication via the written or spoken word.

The mental activities, however, cannot be observed directly, but we know through his or her communication that the manager must ponder and make decisions—a mental activity. The ultimate objective of both physical and mental activities is to create an environment in which other individuals willingly participate to achieve objectives.

MANAGERIAL FUNCTIONS

Management functions are categorized differently by different managers. Generally, though, there are five identifiable functions.

Planning

Every manager must, to some extent, make plans. These vary from immediate tasks to long-range objectives, from simple to involved, and from departmental to companywide impact. A manager, for example, may plan the work for tomorrow, decide when vacations will start, determine which security systems will be purchased next month, or determine the department's objectives during the next 5 years. Planning is nothing more than looking ahead, a vital function performed by every manager. Determining future activities necessarily involves a conceptual or mental look ahead and a recognition of needed future actions—whether they be tomorrow or next year. It involves looking forward, conceptualizing future events, and making decisions today that will affect tomorrow.

If future events could be determined with accuracy, then a plan of action could be developed to accomplish the objectives of the organization under the conditions that the future would bring. The future, however, is not certain, and, at best, forecasting future events is a game of educated guessing. Therefore, the manager estimates or forecasts that one of several possible conditions will exist at some given future time. A manager's future planning actually consists of developing a series of plans, some of which will be put into effect, depending on the conditions existing at that future time.

Planning is not a function reserved exclusively for top management. To the contrary, it is one of the functions that every manager performs, regardless of his or her location in an organization. The higher the level of management, the more time spent planning.

Organizing

Managers must organize—organize people, organize materials, organize time, and organize jobs. Through organizing, the manager is creating an environment that will be conducive to achieving the organization's objectives. Organization consists of the following:

1. Determining what activities need to be done
2. Grouping and assigning these activities to subordinates
3. Delegating the necessary authority to the subordinates to carry out the activities in a coordinated manner

When you, as a manager, direct work, establish goals, and affix authority relationships, you are performing organizing functions in addition to the previously discussed planning functions. Before you can organize, you must plan. Neither planning nor organizing is clearly or separately discernible, but both are intermixed in the overall management function.

Directing

In addition to planning and organizing, a manager must succeed in directing the activities of others. This managerial function deals directly with influencing, guiding, or supervising subordinates in their jobs. Directing cannot be performed alone. It must be executed with planning and organizing.

When directing employees in their tasks, the manager's communication is a planned and organized one. An unplanned or disorganized directive is useless.

Coordinating

Few tasks can be undertaken without coordinating the efforts of several people—inside and outside the organization. A typical security program may require coordinating the efforts of the Personnel Department, the contract guard company, the Shipping Department supervisor, and the local police department.

It is the manager's job to ensure that the various tasks are scheduled and implemented in an efficient and economical manner. As with the other functions of a manager, it is difficult to separate out the activity of coordinating. It, too, is part of the composite that includes planning, organizing, and directing.

Controlling

Whenever people are joined together in some common undertaking, some form of control is necessary. Orders may be misunderstood, rules may be violated, or objectives may unknowingly shift. Whatever the reason, it seems that the larger the number of individuals concerned, the greater the probabilities that inappropriate action (or no action) will be taken.

Controlling merely consists of forcing the tasks that have been undertaken to confirm to prearranged plans. Thus, planning is necessary for control. As with the other functions of management, controlling is not performed independently. That it cannot exist alone is immediately apparent when we realize that managerial control consists of preconceived and planned acts that must have been organized. Likewise, employees must be directed and activities coordinated for control to exist.

SUMMARY OF MANAGEMENT FUNCTIONS

The management process, therefore, is not a series of separate functions (planning, organizing, directing, coordinating, controlling) but a composite process.[1]

If you have any doubts about the composite aspect of these functions, consider this:

- A plan is a course of action—an organized scheme for doing something. Planning without organization, therefore, is impossible. A plan, to be a plan, must be known and communicated.
- To effect communication of the plan, some directions must be given and some coordination must occur.
- To control is to verify something by comparing it with a standard (the plan) and taking action if necessary.

THE SUCCESSFUL MANAGER

The manager's job is to create an environment conducive to the performance of acts by others to accomplish personal as well as company goals. Managers should be able to inspire, motivate, and direct the work of others.

Characteristics

A truly definitive list of characteristics for a successful manager would be impossible to develop. The list that follows includes some of the desirable characteristics, however:

1. A manager should be able to think clearly and purposefully about a problem.

---

[1] Many management professionals refer to this process by the acronym PODSCORB: *P*lanning, *O*rganizing, *D*irecting, Staffing, *C*oordinating, *R*ecord keeping, and *B*udgeting. Later chapters in the book will cover each of these functions in detail—Author's Note.

2. A manager should be able to express himself or herself clearly. A manager's chief physical act is communicating. The best conceived idea is worthless if it cannot be communicated.
3. A manager must possess technical competence. He or she does not necessarily have to be a technician. Rather, the manager should possess the technical ability to enable him or her to manage effectively.
4. A manager should possess the ability to think broadly. Broad comprehension is necessary to see the effect of each proposed action on the whole organization.
5. A manager should be a salesperson. Selling an idea—convincing others of its worth—is one of management's tasks. Selling a plan of action is a vital part of communication and motivation.
6. A manager should possess moral integrity. Both superiors and subordinates should have implicit confidence in the manager and his or her actions.
7. A manager should be emotionally stable. He or she should keep personal feelings out of business problems.
8. A manager should possess skill in human relations and have insight into human motivation and behavior. This enables the manager to lead, not drive, the subordinates.
9. A manager should possess organizational ability. A logical, ordered process is invaluable to achieving established goals.
10. A manager should be dynamic—a characteristic trait of leaders.

Leadership

Leadership is a quality that inspires others to perform. It is that quality in a manager's personality that enables him or her to influence others to accept direction freely or willingly.

A good leader is not necessarily a good manager, but an effective manager must have many of the qualities of a good leader. A leader must be able to recognize each of the follower's needs to motivate him or her through these needs.

The following are some general qualities that good leaders exhibit:

1. The desire to excel. A leader is never content with second best. He or she must always be first. The leader must be a self-starting individual who is willing to engage in long hours and hard work to achieve success.
2. Sense of responsibility. A leader is not afraid to seek, accept, and faithfully discharge responsibility.
3. Capacity for work. Good leaders are willing to accept the demands of success—long hours and hard work.

4.   Feel for good human relations. Leaders study and analyze their followers, trying always to understand them and their problems. The ability to understand their fellow workers is probably the most important single characteristic of good leadership.
5.   Contagious enthusiasm. Good leaders should impart this contagious enthusiasm to their associates.

Obviously, these are not the only qualities of good leadership. Intelligence, character, integrity, and other similar traits are also important.

TIME MANAGEMENT

Everything we have discussed so far involves time. Time management may well be the most difficult of all of your management tasks.

Time management consultants often refer to the 80/20 rule, which reflects their discovery that people tend to spend about 80% of their time on tasks that produce 20% of the results. Too many people work diligently on low-value activities. These activities may make you feel good and give you a sense of accomplishment, but they are not significantly productive.

Time Management Tips

Here are some general hints on managing your time:

1.   Figure out what time of the day you are most productive and make sure that you schedule important work during those hours. If, for example, you are a "morning person," schedule less productive tasks for the afternoon.
2.   Keep a detailed log of how you spend your time. You will quickly see when and how you waste time and you will probably be able to spot your most productive hours if you are not already aware of them. If the log shows a lack of self-discipline, create new time management habits.
3.   Write a fairly rigid schedule for yourself, and stick to it until it becomes habit.
4.   Keep a calendar, preferably covering a week at a time, so you can always see what you have to do.
5.   Do similar tasks at one time; for example, do all of your telephoning or all of your letters at one time.
6.   Relegate the small or routine tasks to your least productive hours. (This is the time to write letters and make phone calls.)
7.   Get someone else to do work you do not absolutely have to do. If your secretary or assistant can perform the task, delegate it.

8. Use downtime—when you are riding a train or waiting for a flight —to do certain routine or easy tasks such as reviewing a memo, figuring your expense account, reading the morning mail, or reading trade journals.

9. Resist the urge to handle the mail as soon as it arrives. Save it for the less productive time that you have scheduled.

10. Control paper. Keep your records simple and look for ways to streamline.

11. Keep things where they belong and keep them in logical places.

12. Eliminate unnecessary meetings.

13. Establish a time for planning—"quiet time"—and handle only true emergencies during that time if they arise.

14. Try to make your first hour at work your most productive hour.

15. Attach priorities to tasks. Do not spend more time on a project than it is worth.

16. Jot down notes of things that need to be done. Do not try to do them immediately.

17. Use your notepad for notes—do not attempt to rely on your memory for important information.

18. Keep unscheduled and social visits to a minimum.

19. When someone brings you a problem, expect them to have a suggested solution in mind.

20. Do a job right the first time so you do not have to do it again.

Time management gives managers more time to manage.

John Sanger

I

GENERAL SECURITY MANAGEMENT

1

General Principles of Organization

The structural framework of an organization is a vehicle for accomplishing the purposes for which a company or a department is established. That skeleton, the organizational structure itself, does not think, has no initiative, and cannot act or react. However, it is absolutely essential in the work environment. A sound organizational framework facilitates the accomplishment of tasks by members of the organization—people working under the supervision of responsible managers.

A hospital, for example, is organized for the purpose of providing health care services. A subunit of that master organization, the Security Department, is organized for the purpose of protecting that health care environment. Organization, then, is the arrangement of people with a common objective or purpose (in a manner to make possible the performance of related tasks grouped for the purpose of assignment) and the establishment of areas of responsibility with clearly defined channels of communication and authority.

ORGANIZATION PRINCIPLES

In the design of a sound organizational framework there are six widely accepted principles:

1. The work should be divided according to some logical plan.
2. Lines of authority and responsibility should be made as clear and direct as possible.
3. One supervisor can effectively control only a limited number of people, and that limit should not be exceeded. (This principle is called "span of control.")
4. There should be "unity of command" in the organization.
5. Responsibility cannot be given without delegating commensurate authority, and there must be accountability for the use of that authority.
6. All efforts of subunits and personnel must be coordinated into the harmonious achievement of the organization's objectives.

Because each of these principles has a meaningful application within a security organization, it will be helpful to elaborate on them.

Logical Division of Work

The necessity for the division of work becomes apparent as soon as you have more than one person on the job. *How* the work is divided can have a significant impact on the results at the end of the day. The manner and extent of the division of work influence the product or performance qualitatively as well as quantitatively. The logical division of work, therefore, deserves close attention.

There are five primary ways in which work can be divided:

1. Purpose
2. Process or method
3. Clientele
4. Time
5. Geography

Purpose

It is most common for work to be divided according to purpose. The Security Department could be organized into two divisions: a Loss Control or Loss Prevention division (its purpose being to prevent losses) and a Detection division (its purpose being to apprehend those who defeated the efforts of the prevention unit).

Process or Method

A process unit is organized according to the method of work; all similar processes are in the same unit. An example in security might be the alarm room operators and dispatchers or the credit card investigators unit of the general investigative section.

Clientele

Work may also be divided according to the clientele served or worked with. Examples here would be the background screening personnel, who deal only with prospective and new employees; store detectives, who concentrate on shoplifters; or general retail investigators, who become involved with dishonest employees, forgers, and other criminal offenders.

Division of work by purpose, process, or clientele is really a division based on the *nature* of the work and consequently is referred to as "functional." In other words, the grouping of security personnel to perform work divided by its nature (purpose, process, or clientele) is called *functional organization.*

For many organizations, the functional organization constitutes the full division of work. Security, however, like police and fire services in the public sector, usually has around-the-clock protective responsibilities. In addition, unlike its cousins in the public sector, it may have protective responsibilities spread over a wide geographic area.

Time

At first glance, the 24-hour coverage of a given facility may appear relatively simple. It might be natural to assume there should be three 8-hour shifts, with fixed posts, patrol, and the communication and alarm center all changing at midnight, 8:00 A.M., and 4:00 P.M. However, a number of interesting problems surface when a department begins organizing in this fashion by time:

- How many security people are necessary on the first shift? If a minimum security staff takes over at midnight and the facility commences its business day at 7:00 A.M., can you operate for 1 hour with the minimum staff or must you increase coverage prior to 7:00 A.M. and overlap shifts? (There are hundreds of variables to just this type of problem.)
- If you have two or more functional units, with some personnel assigned to patrol and others assigned to the communications and alarm center (in another organizational pyramid altogether), who is in command at 3:00 A.M.? The question of staff supervision confuses many people. (See Chapter 5 for a detailed discussion of staff supervision.)
- How much supervision is necessary during facility down-time? If the question is not *how much*, then how is *any* supervision exercised at 3:00 A.M.?
- If there are five posts, each critical and necessary, and five persons are scheduled and one fails to show, how do you handle the situation? Should you schedule six persons for just that contingency?

These and other problems do arise and are resolved regularly in facilities of every kind. Organizing by time, a way of life for security operations, does create special problems that demand consideration, especially if this approach to the division of work is a new undertaking for a company.

Geography

Whenever a Security Department is obliged to serve a location removed from the headquarters facility, and one or more security personnel are assigned to the outlying location, there is one major issue that must be resolved: To whom do the security personnel report—to security management back at headquarters or to site management (which is nonsecurity)?

The real issue is: Should nonsecurity management have direct supervision over a security employee who has technical or semitechnical skills that more often than not are beyond the competence or understanding of nonsecurity management personnel?

In defining the type of authority an executive or supervisor exercises, a distinction is generally made between *line* and *staff* authority. Although these terms have many meanings, in its primary sense, line authority implies a direct (or single line) relationship between a supervisor and his or her subordinate; the staff function is service or advisory in nature.

Security personnel should only be directly supervised by security management. Site management may provide staff supervision, providing suggestions and assistance, but these should be restricted to such matters as attention to duty, promptness in reporting, and compliance with general rules. Detailed security activities fall outside the jurisdiction of such a manager.

Nonsecurity management should not have line authority (direct supervision) over security, not only because of the issue of professional competency but also because site management should not be beyond the "reach" of security. Site management would indeed be "out of reach" if the only internal control, security, were subject to its command. Site management would be free to engage in any form of mischief, malpractice, or dishonesty without fear of security's reporting the activities to company headquarters.

Clear Lines of Authority and Responsibility

Once the work has been properly divided, the organization takes on the appearance of a pyramid-like structure, within which are smaller pyramids, as illustrated in Figure 1.1. Each part of each pyramid defines, with exactness, a function or responsibility and to whom that function is responsible. One can easily trace the solid line upward to the Security Manager or Security Director who is ultimately responsible for every function within the security organization.

Not only is it important to have this organizational pyramid documented, normally in the form of an organizational chart, but also it is essential that security employees have access to that chart so they can see exactly where they fit into the organization pattern, to whom they are responsible, to whom their supervisor is responsible, and so on right up to the top. Failure to so inform employees causes unnecessary confusion, and confusion is a major contributor to ineffective job performance.

In addition, the organizational chart is a subtle motivator. People can see themselves moving up in the boxes; in order for goal-setting to be successful, one must be able to envision oneself already in possession of one's goal.

Finally, the apparent rigidity of boxes and lines in the organizational chart must not freeze communication. Employees at the lowest layer of

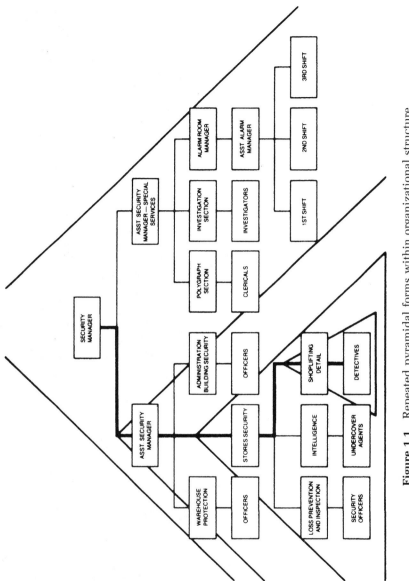

Figure 1.1 Repeated pyramidal forms within organizational structure.

the pyramid must feel free to communicate directly with the Security Manager without obtaining permission from all the intervening levels of supervision.

Span of Control

There is a limit to the number of subordinates who can be supervised effectively by one person, and that limit should not be exceeded. The limit ranges from a maximum of five at the highest level in the organization to a maximum of twelve at the lowest level. The greater the degree of sophistication of the interactions between supervisors and subordinates, the narrower is the optimal span of control. However, this very important principle is in jeopardy as we have entered into the twenty-first century because of the growing trend of "flattening" the organizational pyramid—that is, having fewer supervisors and/or supervisors with expanded responsibilities. This trend increasingly presents an operational dilemma that must be addressed by each organization.

Exceeding the limits of span of control is really no different from spreading oneself too thin in some nonwork environment, such as school. If a student carries a full academic load of core subjects, becomes involved in student government, goes out for varsity football, is engaged to be married, belongs to the military reserve, and works 20 hours a week in a convenience store, it is likely that some of these activities will not receive the attention they deserve and few, if any, will be done with excellence.

Slipshod, undisciplined, and poorly executed security work is an almost inevitable consequence of violating the organizational principle of span of control.

Unity of Command

The fourth principle, that of unity of command, means that an employee should be under the direct control of *one and only one* immediate superior (Figure 1.2). This principle also dictates that a task or function

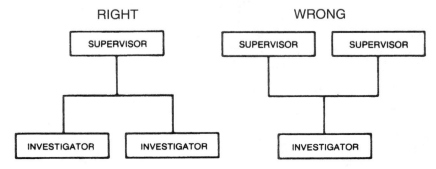

Figure 1.2 Unity of command.

requiring the action of two or more people must also be under the direct control of one supervisor.

Violations of the principle of unity of command are not usually found in the design of the organization but occur more by accident than design during special events or other nonroutine occasions that bring out more company executives than usual. The security officer or agent who is given conflicting orders by several superiors becomes confused, inefficient, and angry.

One cannot successfully serve two masters. This is discussed further in Chapter 5.

Responsibility, Authority, and Accountability

The fifth principles of organization is all too frequently violated by the manager or executive who gives a subordinate the responsibility to do a task but holds back the authority needed to discharge such responsibility effectively. A prime example of this is the case in which individuals are given the job of supervising a unit and are told that the unit is their responsibility and that they will be measured by how well they perform in that assignment. However, the new supervisors then discover they do not have the right (authority) to select the applicant of their choice to fill a vacancy; they discover that disciplinary matters are decided by their superiors (and their subordinates know this). They soon find that their plans, suggestions, and ideas are replaced with those of their boss, and, thus they become totally frustrated. They have a job and yet they do not.

The true art of delegation requires giving responsibility with commensurate authority and then holding the employee fully accountable for the use of that authority. *If*, in the previous example, new supervisors had the authority to hire, discipline, and implement their own ideas; did so without exercising good judgment; and could not be corrected or trained to use their authority properly, then they should be stripped not only of the authority but of the responsibility as well. The employee must be given *both* responsibility and authority and be held accountable for both.

Perhaps the major reason why so many managers violate this principle is that they are unwilling, sometimes subconsciously, to allow subordinates to carry out the responsibilities delegated to them. The reason for this unwillingness, ironically, is that the manager knows that he or she is ultimately responsible. The manager knows it is true that you cannot *completely* delegate responsibility. This may seem confusing and sound like double-talk, so let us approach the problem from a different angle:

a.   The head of the security pyramid, the Security Manager or Security Director, is the only one accountable for the organization, the Security Department. The Security Manager's reputation grows brighter in the department's successes and suffers in its failures. Almost invariably, this manager rose to the top because of his or her proven ability and track record. In other words, his or her method of doing things has proven, over the stretch of time, to be successful. That is why the manager has this position.

b.   The Security Manager or Security Director cannot do the entire security job alone and needs people to help get it done. Depending on the scope of the job, the Security Manager may need anywhere from 2 to 300 people. Ideally, if every person on the team thinks and acts exactly as the Security Manager does, he or she would ensure continued outstanding personal success.

c.   The manager understands, however, that no one else thinks and acts exactly as he or she does. The manager may reason that the next best thing, then, is to do the thinking for all the key people, make the decisions for them, and have them run the organization in his or her image. The Security Manager holds the authority, and when things go wrong—and they will—he or she will probably severely criticize the party who failed. This manager has not really delegated responsibility and authority. Ironically, when things go wrong the Security Manager will point out to company management the employee who failed and in so doing will have someone to *share* the responsibility with, because ultimately it is the Security Manager's responsibility.

d.   In contrast to the situation described previously, the manager may open up the organization to other talented people. Within the broad guidelines the Security Manager sets as a leader, those key people will have genuine responsibility. They will be accountable, and they will respond positively to that accountability. When things go wrong—and they will—the party who failed will judge himself or herself critically. This manager *has* truly delegated responsibility and authority. Ironically, he or she will take full responsibility for failure, because it *is* ultimately and rightfully the manager's responsibility.

Coordination to Meet Organizational Goals

Theoretically, if the first five principles just discussed were adhered to, everything would function smoothly. In practice such total harmony is rare if not impossible. Human frailties such as jealousy over assignments and promotions, elitism in some subunits, friction between supervisors, the historic poor reputation of certain subunits or assignments, and more tend to compromise efficiency.

How then does management coordinate the efforts of the various subunits and personnel? Or better, what can management do to *attempt* to coordinate all units and personnel into the harmonious achievement of the department's goals? The answer is to establish a sound security training program and good departmental communication.

Both training and communication are dealt with in separate chapters (Chapters 9 and 13, respectively). The emphasis in both cases should be on educating employees about the organization and its objectives; defining the importance of each subunit's contribution to the whole; developing organizational pride and individual security employee self-esteem; creating a sense of security unity and identification within the company as a whole; and, finally, developing a climate wherein the individual employee includes organizational goals within his or her own personal goals.

WHERE SECURITY FITS IN THE ORGANIZATIONAL STRUCTURE

The Changing Role of Security

In the past five decades the security function has climbed up from the depths of organizational existence, from dank and smelly basement offices to the heights of executive offices and a place in the sun. Despite some major downsizing, corporate mergers, and the growing emergence of facilities management and technology replacing some security personnel, security is now viewed as a critical part of most organizations today with security professionals reporting directly to senior management if not the chief executive officer. This has become even more common since the tragic events of September 11, 2001.

When I entered this industry there was no such thing as a Vice President of Security. There was no place for security practitioners in senior management. Today, many security professionals hold the office of vice president because the importance of the security function is now recognized in the private sector.

Why this ascent? Before September 11, 2001, the ever-increasing contribution security made to the organization's objectives, principally profit, had earned corresponding increased recognition from top management. Subsequent to September 11, it was crystal clear that risks and threats of global terrorism, heretofore viewed as "overseas problems," were now no longer vague or unlikely but rather a genuine reality. Over time, security, as a profession, made the transition from a burdensome and obligatory liability to a vital and integral component of American business and industry here on the ground in the United States.

Another reason for the growing recognition of security's importance is the increasing prevalence of crime in our society. A number of socioeconomic factors, along with political and cultural conditions, have combined to create a social climate of complacency toward deviant or antisocial behavior. As a result, more and more deviant behavior occurs, particularly attacks against property (theft) and attacks against persons on premises (with the resultant specter of civil litigation), until the point is reached at which the magnitude of the problem far transcends the limited prevention ability of public law enforcement. The burden of crime prevention more than ever before falls on the private sector.

In an address to the International Association of Chiefs of Police, Richard W. Velde, Administrator of the Law Enforcement Assistance Administration, stated:

> The criminal justice system, and particularly our nation's police, do perform a rather narrow function that is largely a responsive one that follows the commission of crime. There are constitutional and statutory responsibilities in all the states that define the role of the police force and essentially they say that police are not in the crime prevention business.[1]

Without question, a large number of firms and even entire industries would fail today without their own internal security organizations. This is true aside from terrorist threats. Imagine the position of a major credit card company without its Security Department. Who would coordinate and track the criminal abuse of that credit privilege across the country, or indeed, around the world?

Security's Contribution to Profits

Security contributes to company or corporate profits by reducing or eliminating preventable losses, including those caused by criminal behavior. Consider the retail industry, for example. A major chain with sales of $1 billion might realize a 3% net profit as well as a 3% inventory shrinkage (these figures are quite realistic). This firm, then, realizes $30 million in profits and $30 million in losses, or lost profit. If the Security Department through its efforts and programs can reduce the inventory shrinkage by just one half of 1%, profits would rise $5 million!

Where else can management find such opportunities to increase profits? The cost of raw materials cannot be reduced; they are becoming scarcer and more expensive. The cost of labor cannot be reduced; labor's demands are only going up. The costs of so-called fixed expenses such as rent, utilities, and insurance cannot be reduced; they are all rising. Because losses are so enormous, their reduction is in the hands of protection professionals who manage corporate and divisional security organizations.

To Whom Does Security Report?

With increased recognition of the need for security within the whole spectrum of company activities, all of which affect directly or indirectly the

---

[1] Velde, Richard W., quoted in *Private Security: Report of the Task Force on Private Security.* (Washington, DC: National Advisory Committee on Criminal Justice Standards and Goals, 1976), p. 19.

"bottom line" of business (profits), came increased responsibility, and with increased responsibility came commensurate authority. To provide the Security Manager with that necessary authority, the entire security organization has moved up in the organizational pyramid to report directly to senior management, usually a senior or executive vice president. That senior executive delegates a portion of his or her authority to the Security Chief, who can then exercise what is known as *functional* authority.

Reporting directly to an officer places the security executive either at the top of middle management or bottom of upper management. The most dynamic people in the firm are now his or her peers. Figures 1.3 and 1.4 illustrate the place typically held in the organizational chart by a Security Director in manufacturing and a Vice President of Loss Control in a retail organization, respectively.

The Difference Between Corporate and Company Security

Although the word *corporate* is sometimes used to describe a firm's central authority, the word more accurately refers to that small holding organization that owns a number of firms. A conglomerate is a combination of a variety of individual companies, each with its own executive team, its own goals, its own volume, and its own profit performance. The financial results of each of the companies in a corporate structure (or conglomerate) are, for the sake of simplicity, forwarded to the corporate organization at the very top of the pyramid.

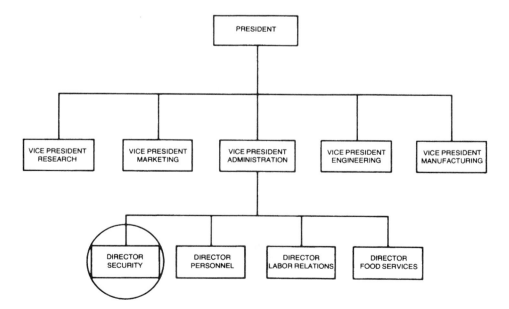

Figure 1.3 Example of manufacturing firm's organization.

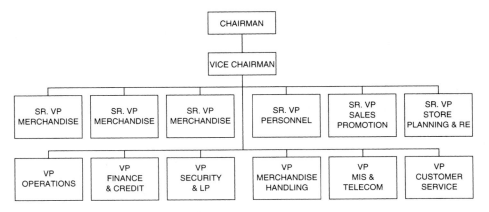

Figure 1.4   Example of retail company organization.

Many corporations have a Corporate Security Director who maintains a purely staff relationship with the individual Security Directors in charge of protection in the various companies within the corporate family (Figure 1.5). The corporate director's job is as follows:

1.   Establishes corporate security policies that serve as guidelines for divisional (company) security operations
2.   Serves as an advisor and counselor to divisional senior management in terms of his or her assessment of how effectively divisional security is functioning
3.   Serves as an advisor and counselor to each division's Security Director, giving the division director support in terms of professional expertise, advice, encouragement, and constructive criticism
4.   Serves as a central clearinghouse and information center for all divisions within the corporation, disseminating important information about the corporation and industry as a whole
5.   Provides for those few but important security services needed by the relatively small corporate organization comprised of, as a rule, top-ranking executives in the company

Corporate Security Directors have other functions, such as maintaining liaison with top officials in the public sector and participating in trade and professional association activities. But the real thrust of these corporate security jobs is one of counsel. If the corporate director has a security staff, it is usually quite small. This individual simply does not have direct accountability for the performance of the divisions; however, certainly if divisions demonstrate a consistently poor performance in security activities over a prolonged period, it will indeed reflect on the corporate director.

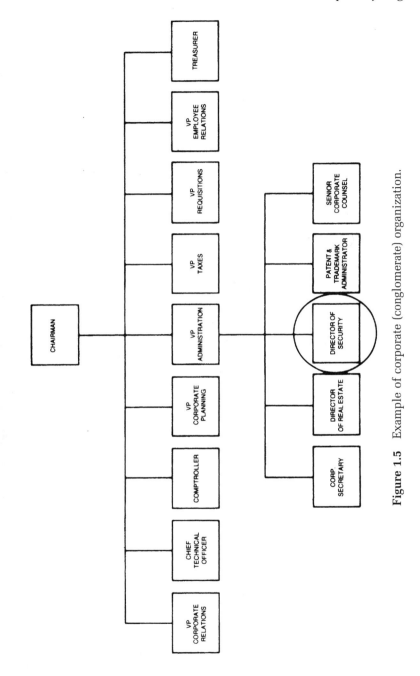

Figure 1.5 Example of corporate (conglomerate) organization.

On the other hand, the divisional or company Security Director (or Security Manager, or whatever the head of the Security Department may be called) is directly accountable for the activities and results of the security organization. Throughout this text, when I refer to the Security Director, unless otherwise specified, I am talking about the divisional or company director (or Vice President of Security), not the corporate person.

SUMMARY

Organization is the arrangement of people with a common objective in a manner that groups related tasks, establishes areas of responsibility, and defines lines of communication and authority.

There are six basic principles of organization: (1) logical division of work (according to purpose, process, clientele, time, or geography); (2) clear lines of authority, visible on the organizational chart as a pyramidal structure; (3) limited span of control; (4) unity of command; (5) true delegation of responsibility and authority, with attendant accountability; and (6) coordination of efforts through training and communication.

Within the company or corporate organizational structure, security in recent years has shown a sharp vertical movement, an ascent primarily attributable to international terrorist threats, rising crime, and increased recognition of security's contribution to profits. The Security Director now commonly reports to a member of senior management.

In the corporate or conglomerate structure, the Corporate Security Director serves generally in a staff relationship both to higher management and to the individual company Security Directors. In this text, discussion of the Security Director's or Security Manager's role refers to the security function in the individual company rather than that of the corporate organization.

REVIEW QUESTIONS

1. Explain the five methods of dividing work.

2. Discuss the problems that may arise in organizing work by time.

3. Give two reasons why nonsecurity management should not have line authority over security employees.

4. What is meant by span of control?

5. Explain the principle of unity of command.

6. Discuss the relationship between responsibility and authority. Give an example in which a manager has given a subordinate responsibility without commensurate authority.

7. How does security contribute to the company's profits?

2

Organizational Structure

The organizational structure of a department within a company reflects the six organizational principles discussed in Chapter 1, including:

- Logical division of tasks or responsibilities
- Clear lines of authority and responsibility within the department specifically and within the organization generally

The department's organizational structure is two-dimensional in its formal representation, as illustrated in Figure 2.1. On the *horizontal* plane it indicates the division of areas of responsibilities; on the *vertical* plane it defines levels of authority or rank. In the illustration shown, responsibility for security under the Security Manager has been divided into two areas, with an Assistant Manager for Loss Prevention and an Assistant Manager for Investigations. The horizontal division defines areas of responsibility for each Assistant Manager, whereas the vertical chart indicates that they are of equal rank, each reporting directly to the Security Manager. Similarly, Loss Prevention responsibilities are divided among the officers in charge of the Computer Room Detail, General Facility Protection, and Credit Cards and Accounts Receivable. The organizational chart indicates this separation of duties and shows the relationship of each officer in charge of these subdivisions to the officers under them and to the Assistant Manager and Security Manager above them.

The organizational structure of one company's Security Department will differ in widely varying degrees from that of another company, *even within the same industry*. This is true for several reasons. First, each organizational structure reflects how the particular Security Director and management above him or her perceive departmental and company priorities. The formal pattern will also be influenced by individual personnel. Finally, the structure is and must be fluid, or highly changeable, to meet the ever-changing character of most private enterprise operations.

THE INFORMAL ORGANIZATION

It is revealing to compare the formal organizational structure outline in Figure 2.1 with the informal organization in Figure 2.2, which illustrates how the typical organization might really work. The conspicuous difference

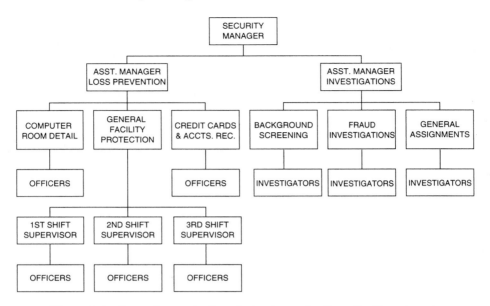

Figure 2.1   Formal organizational structure of a Security Department.

between the two organizations is that, in the informal organization—the *real* organization—five supervisors report directly to the Security Manager, not just two. In addition to the two Assistant Managers, there are the supervisors in charge of the Computer Room, Credit Cards and Accounts Receivable, and Background Screening. Reasons behind such a change in structure are many. They might include any of the following:

1.   Physical protection of the Computer Room and of the Credit Cards and Accounts Receivable areas logically belong under the Loss Prevention banner, but that Assistant Manager has limited interests and talent, favors the area of general facilities protection, and as a consequence has literally abrogated the other two functions.

2.   The supervisors of those two areas of responsibility do not accept the Assistant Manager for Loss Prevention as their immediate superior and look instead to the Security Manager, who permits this condition.

3.   The Security Manager has little confidence in that Assistant Manager's ability but is unable to fire the individual, with the result that he or she informally brings those sensitive units under his or her own wing.

4.   The Security Manager has great difficulty in delegating authority in sensitive areas to subordinates; consequently he or she tends to personally exercise direct authority over most activities.

5.   The Security Manager regards such areas of activity as "toys" and violates the organizational structure because he or she enjoys "playing" these games.

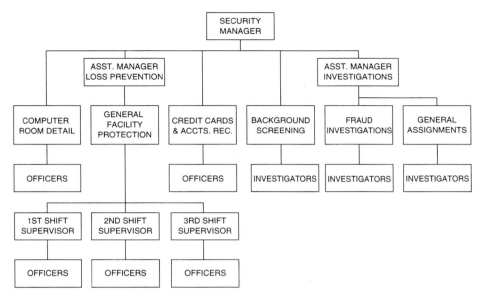

Figure 2.2   Sample *informal* organizational structure of a Security Department.

6.   There is a personal relationship between the Security Manager and those supervisors on that second level of supervision, a friendship that interferes with the organizational integrity.

All such possible explanations—and there are many more—could also, of course, explain why the supervisor in charge of the Background Screening Unit also reports directly to the Security Manager instead of to the logical immediate superior.

Another major factor in the changing dynamics of organizational structure is company (and, therefore, departmental) growth. As an example, one major retail chain had 11 stores in 1961, all located in Southern California. Sixteen years later there were 45 major department stores and two clearance centers in five states with other stores scheduled to open. Obviously, the structure of the Security Department was far removed from what it had been 16 years earlier. During that period the department experienced at least a dozen reorganizations. Contrast this flexibility with, for instance, a municipal police department with a relatively stable city population. Few, if any, major departmental reorganizations would be expected to occur during the same period.

Budgetary considerations also play an important role in the organizational design. Consider again the organization illustrated in Figure 2.1. The chart indicates a total of six supervisors at the third level reporting directly to the two Assistant Managers. What would happen if the department's new budget were to allow only four supervisors at that level? How would the organization be changed?

A number of variations are possible. The Computer Room detail might be combined with the Credit Cards and Accounts Receivable area into one unit or detail called the *High-Risk Detail*, under one supervisor; similarly, the Background Screening unit might be combined with the General Assignments unit for investigations. Such horizontal shrinkage may or may not serve the best interests of the organization; however, budgetary restrictions may make such changes inevitable.

Whatever the changes required by growth or budget, the point of organization remains the same: to serve the interest of the department in getting its job done through an intelligent division of tasks and the establishment of clear lines of authority. This applies to the small organization as well as the larger one. There will be fewer vertical levels of authority or rank and a simpler division of responsibilities on each horizontal plane in a small department, but the *purpose* of organization and the approach to organizational structure are identical.

As I have already indicated, the structure is two-dimensional. In the ideal situation, achieving a viable organization involves three steps: (1) identify the departmental objectives, (2) identify the various tasks and divide them into logical work units, and (3) identify the levels of leadership necessary to achieve the task. All that remains is to "fill in" the boxes with appropriate personnel.

This is the ideal. Unfortunately, it does not normally work that way. As a rule, people—the employees to be put into the boxes—are already aboard. Thus the two-dimensional plan of organizational design becomes complicated by the introduction of what might be called a third dimension—the personnel. The results are almost invariably bad because the design tends to lean toward personnel considerations. Expressed in another way, there is a tendency to build jobs and organizations around people, rather than identifying qualified talent and placing them in the jobs defined by a plan of organization. This is true because, for policy or personnel reasons, the Security Manager in charge of a department for the most part has no choice but to make the best possible use of existing, in-house personnel. It is easier to change the organization than it is to change the individual.

The reality of organizational structure, then, is inevitably a compromise between a pure design, based on the best possible horizontal and vertical layout, and existing security department employees. For this reason the typical organizational chart must be suspect.

The organizational chart is suspect in another significant way; it clearly defines reporting lines, or "chain of command," when, in reality, numerous informal reporting lines may exist. This aspect of organizational life clouds the levels of authority, taking from some and adding to others. In this respect the three-dimensional aspect of the organization acquires an almost sinister air in terms of who really is whose boss and who really can tell whom what to do—and who is meddling in areas outside their arena of responsibility.

SUBUNIT STRUCTURES

In addition to the departmental organizational structure, both formal and informal, the security administrator should be aware of the existence of interdepartmental or subunit structures at lower levels within his or her own organization. The number and size of these ministructures will be related to the size of the department. These structures will tend to have the same characteristics as the formal organization—that is, horizontal divisions (of tasks) and vertical levels (of authority).

Singling out the General Facility Protection division of our example department, consider the security officer's level on the second shift. To begin with, the second shift will probably represent the top of the nearly invisible hierarchical structure of security officers assigned to that division; the officers lower on the totem pole will be assigned to the least desirable shift, the first shift. The organizational structure of that second shift is shown in Figure 2.3.

In the absence of the Shift Supervisor, or Sergeant, the officer assigned to patrol assumes leadership (in this example only). The Main Gate Officer assumes leadership for exterior protection, and the Main Lobby Officer is responsible for all security activities of an internal nature.

On the exterior protection side of this organizational pattern is a typical example of a "pecking order" or vertical line of authority; on the interior protection side, by contrast, all officers except the relief officer are of equal rank. In the latter case, the absence of the Main Lobby Officer could result in a struggle for position in the line of authority.

As a rule, such ministructures or organization exist although they have never been agreed on by management, never been reduced to writing or charts, and in some cases never even been understood. Obviously, then, it is important for the Security Manager to be sensitive to the existence of such informal "structures" at the lowest levels of the organization to maintain overall organizational integrity and harmony.

Consider this: How many times does a new supervisor, especially one who is not intimately familiar with the organization and its personnel, come onto the scene and commence changing operations and personnel around— and meet stubborn resistance? From an administrative point of view the consequences of putting a lieutenant over a captain are clearly understood. The same is true at the bottom of the organizational ladder; these employees have their own "captains" and "lieutenants," even if they were not officially appointed as such.

Sensitivity to such organizational facts of life not only avoids disharmony—a negative advantage—but also can be highly productive in terms of organizational performance. If a superior officer or manager wants to ensure that something is done in the absence of the Shift Supervisor, he or she goes to the Patrol Officer. If, instead, the manager bypasses the Patrol Officer and goes to the Main Lobby Officer, the job may not be done properly.

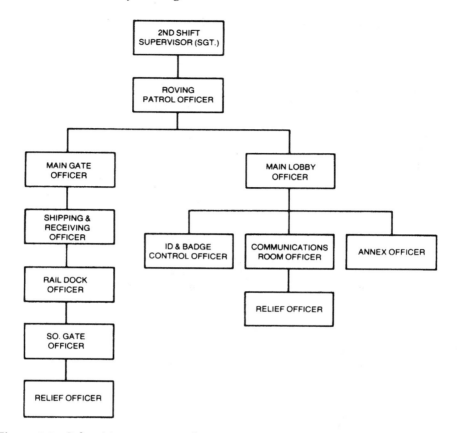

Figure 2.3   Subunit's structure within Security Department's organizational structure. Such ministructures may exist without official departmental recognition or planning.

There's no question that one key to supervisorial or managerial success is the ability to identify informal leaders and then use them for the organizational cause.

CORPORATE CULTURE

So-called corporate culture is another aspect of the informal organization. Such "culture" is more philosophical than structural, yet it can dramatically affect operations. It has many faces, is very real, and, if ignored, could cause the new and unsuspecting security executive problems that can be a career threat. Some examples of rules emanating from the "corporate culture" are as follows:

- Every salaried employee (including security personnel) is expected to be in the workplace 2 hours earlier than line employees, that is, expected to work at least a 10-hour day.
- Certain categories of employees are considered exempt from organizational rules. A specific example here is a physician in a health care facility who ignores rules governing parking or the use of designated employee doors.
- "Executives" are expected to make an *appearance* on Saturday mornings, even though no one works. It's the *appearance* that is mandated, culturally. If one ignores this, he's not a "team player."
- Corporate culture might include where power is centered. If the power, for example, is vested in Human Resources, their interpretation and administration of organizational rules can frustrate the conscious and well-directed efforts of the security program. To ignore or challenge that power source could be equivalent to seeking a career change!
- Certain levels or categories of employees are "above suspicion" or are exempt from being interviewed by security personnel. Only a high-ranking senior executive may interview or question such employees.

Then, of course, there's a myriad of petty forms of corporate culture that have no specific impact on security's responsibilities, such as wearing dark suits (like a company uniform) or all executives driving certain vehicles such as BMWs or sport-utility vehicles.

The point of all this is there indeed is an invisible dimension to the organizational chart. The totality of that structured, informal subunit and corporate culture creates a dynamic, living, functional organization.

SUMMARY

Organizational structure, then, as applied to a Security Department, is a valuable and necessary management tool to organize tasks and people in an intelligent, meaningful, and responsible structure to meet and successfully discharge the security function in any company.

This structure is ideally two-dimensional, defining responsibilities (horizontal) and lines of authority (vertical). In practice, the structure will be affected by a third dimension: personnel. This dimension is reflected in the influence of the individual Security Manager, the necessity of using existing personnel, and the presence of invisible interdepartmental structures.

The organizational structure, finally, is not and should not be rigid, because it must be capable of adapting to budgetary considerations, changing goals, and evolving company size and growth.

REVIEW QUESTIONS

1.   What does the *horizontal* plane of an organizational chart represent? The *vertical* plane?

2.   Why does the organizational structure of one Security Department differ from that of another, even within the same industry?

3.   Discuss four reasons why the *informal* organization may differ from the *formal* organization.

4.   What are the three steps in achieving a viable organizational structure?

5.   Explain how personnel form the "third dimension" of organizational design.

3

Security's Role in the Organization

THE PROTECTIVE SERVICE ROLE

The singularly most conspicuous role of the Security Department in any organization is that of protector or guardian—protecting the company's property, product or merchandise, assets, equipment, reputation, and employees. This responsibility is not limited to just the company's assets and employees. It extends to nonemployees as well, be they guests, patrons, customers, or any other form of invitee on company property. Put another way, the Security Department is the guardian of all property and all people on company property.

That protective role constitutes a service to the organization; thus, the Security Department's function is one of service. The value of such service is better measured by what does *not* happen than by what does. For the company to operate over a given period of time without a payroll hold-up; major burglary; significant disappearance of inventory, equipment, or documents; or a rape, mugging, or assault in the parking lot (or parking structure—both of which are inherently dangerous areas), stairwell, or anywhere else on company property is indicative of the security function's effectiveness in its guardian role. The posture of the guardian role is one of prevention—prevention of crime and prevention of losses by means of a strategy and philosophy of denying the criminal the opportunity to succeed. In keeping with that posture, some organizations have abandoned the name Security Department in favor of Department of Loss Prevention or Loss Control. I prefer the latter because each incident we fail to prevent mocks our effectiveness, whereas no one expects us to "control" *everything!*

Stated another way, security could easily be identified as a *protective service of prevention and control.*

It is beyond the scope of this text to discuss in detail all of the individual protective duties with which a Security Department will become involved. The specific responsibilities of any department will be adapted to the specific organization—its buildings and contents, its operations, its assets, its personnel, its interaction at all levels with the public, and its general environment as well as the organization's reputation. Nevertheless, the role of security normally involves common elements, among which the following can be included:

- Arrests and causes prosecution of all persons committing a criminal attack on or against company property, equipment, supplies, products, goods, and/or other assets
- Designs and implements physical controls of the facility
- Administers and conducts access controls to the facility, including identification badge program
- Conducts preemployment and postemployment screening
- Monitors control of Department of Defense (DOD) classified documents and information
- Maintains liaison with local, state, and federal law enforcement authorities
- Monitors control of company proprietary information
- Administers vehicular access and parking controls and secures the parking environment
- Prevents or otherwise reduces crime by maintaining a "security presence" and high visibility through such activities as patrolling company property in distinctively marked vehicles (if vehicular patrol is required) and wearing distinctive apparel, although not necessarily military-type uniforms
- Administers company's lock and key control program
- Conducts security indoctrination and training
- Investigates all criminal activity committed on company premises or against company interests, including attacks against persons
- Administers executive protective program
- Conducts financial stability or due diligence investigations of potential vendors, merger candidates, and so forth
- Coordinates special protection arrangements necessary during or as a result of riots, natural disasters, strikes, explosions, and so forth
- Coordinates or assists in Disaster Preparedness and Response programs
- Designs and conducts security/loss prevention vulnerability surveys
- Contracts for and administers outside security services such as professional consulting services, guard services, undercover agents, shopping services, certain investigative services, polygraph services, armored transport services, document destruction, and so forth
- Provides emergency courier and escort services as needed
- Acts as adviser and in-house consultant to senior management on all security-related matters

This extensive list by no means exhausts the possible protection services that will fall on a given Security Department as it responds to particular situations. What the previously listed menu does suggest is the general purpose of the security function in any organization: to protect the company (people and assets) against attack or loss.

Within security's protective role, there are a host of subroles that are often neglected or unrecognized by security management. These subroles may be divided into three service categories:

1. Special Services
2. Educational Services
3. Management Services

SPECIAL SERVICES

The Security Department's objectives are designed to contribute to the achievement of company goals. Company executives, who provide vital leadership for company goal achievement, have personal goals that are difficult to separate from company goals. More often than not, their goals *are* company goals. Service, then, to the "company" and service to management should be synonymous, for what is good for the executive team is good for the company and vice versa. All demands for protective service, whether clearly related to the work environment or of a peripheral nature involving senior management, require attention.

The security management that understands the reasonableness and logic of providing the broadest possible range of special services moves the security function more closely to the mainstream of the business and makes a more significant contribution to the overall success of the company. A sampling of special services follows.

Executive's Home Security Survey

The executive who wishes to "harden" his or her home, installing protective measures against criminal intrusion and attack, has the choice of calling the police for advice, hiring an outside security consultant, attempting to select appropriate defenses personally, or calling on the company's security staff. The latter is recommended—providing, of course, that the staff has the expertise to achieve the desired degree of security.

The homes of executives are far more attractive targets for burglary than those of the average employees, and it makes good sense to take extraordinary precautionary measures.

In one recent case, a personnel executive's rented home in the hills of Southern California was burglarized several times in the same number of weeks. The question of increasing protection or asking for company security advice never crossed the executive's mind until total frustration set in. On the occasion of each burglary, the home was entered and ransacked while the executive was away, with no evidence of forcible entry. On each occasion the police came to the home and conducted their investigation, usually a surface examination of the physical premises and a documentation of pertinent facts surrounding the loss. The police and the executive theorized that a friend of the former tenants was still in possession of the house key and was responsible for the crimes. The former tenants had moved out of state, and the identity of the friend was unknown.

Based on that theory, the executive purchased a manual burglary alarm and attached it to the door. If entry was made through the door, the alarm would sound, and a subsequent examination of the device would indicate it had been activated.

The home was again burglarized and the alarm was not activated. The executive at this point was distraught over the dilemma. He finally turned to his own company for assistance, and there, at his home, the security investigator within minutes located the point of entry used by the burglar—the louvered glass windows over the kitchen sink. The security executive temporarily secured these windows and the similar windows over the breakfast nook and advised the executive of two alternative methods to secure those windows permanently. The executive was never victimized again. The simple technique of removing the screen and then removing the louvered window panes one at a time, and later replacing them, had escaped the notice of police, literally as well as figuratively.

Executive home surveys will also examine the possible use of digital or central station alarming, inventory of valuable personal properly (which includes recording serial numbers, photographing, videotaping, and/or marking), and establishment of emergency procedures and exterior lighting, to name but a few of the areas of concern, depending on the person and properties to be protected.

It should be noted that if company funds are expended to safeguard executives and the company wants the tax advantage of such expenditure, an outside independent security consultant must approve, recommend, or otherwise agree such protection costs are necessary and reasonable.

Investigative Assistance

Sooner or later the whole spectrum of investigative skills can be used in peripheral service—from tracing the license plate of a hit-and-run driver who sideswiped an executive's car, to tracking the source of an obscene letter sent to an executive's home, to locating (in cooperation with police) the runaway daughter of an executive. Such investigative service need not be limited to executive or senior management problems; someone in middle management or a key supervisor in the company could have a problem that senior management feels is deserving of company attention.

Bodyguard/Escort Service

So-called bodyguard duties constitute another dimension to the variety of special services the security organization can provide. Such service could be any of the following:

1. Serving as an executive's chauffeur, temporarily or permanently
2. Serving as escort for the dignitaries who are guests of the firm
3. Serving as escorts for company executives visiting locations deemed hazardous
4. Serving as escort for members of executives' families
5. Intermingling with guests at special social functions
6. Escorting couriers or messengers
7. Serving as courier

Emergency Service

Most Security Departments run a 24-hour-a-day operation from either an alarm room, security operations room, or desk. Because of that 24-hour telephone capability, the department can offer company management a unique emergency service, as follows: Every member of management participating in the emergency plan provides the department with a data card or electronic file that lists the name, sex, and date of birth of the executive and his or her entire family; their home address and phone number, with directions how to reach the home; the address and phone number of any summer or second homes and directions how to reach those residences; the names and phone numbers of family physicians and dentists; local police department's address and phone number; local fire and rescue department's names and numbers; local ambulance data; local hospital and emergency service data; insurance agent's identity and number; description and license numbers of family vehicles; and identity of people to call (family, neighbors, or friends) in the event of an emergency. The data card, computerized or manual, is maintained in the 24-hour operational room. When an executive is traveling, he or she calls in a supplement to the file, listing his or her itinerary with phone numbers.

The emergency service becomes a clearinghouse for processing emergency messages, dispatching emergency services, notifying appropriate people of problems, and expediting the flow of such information. Certainly the executive or a member of his family can call the police, fire department, rescue squad, and so forth directly and perhaps faster than routing the call through the Security Department. On the other hand, youngsters at home alone or domestic employees could be at a loss as to whom to call. Even an executive's wife might choose to call the Security Department before calling

the police if her husband is traveling—for example, if she became fright-
ened and felt a prowler was on the property. A call from the company's Security Department reporting to the police that a prowler was on the property
of an executive's home would, in all probability, receive a quicker response
than the wife calling the police herself.

There are a number of clear advantages to this type of service, still
relatively unheard of and rare, but a growing function in the future of
service-minded Security Departments throughout the country.

EDUCATIONAL SERVICES

An increasingly important and relatively new role for the Security Department is that of trainer and educator. As the private sector assumes more and
more responsibility for law and order on private premises, there is an
increasing need to educate employees and nonemployees alike on the necessity and objectives of security.

A striking example of the need for employee security education is in
the retail industry. Retailers, including food, drug, department, chain, discount, specialty stores, and independents, lose billions of dollars each year
to dishonest employees. Part of that loss is directly attributable to the fact
that the employee is ignorant of the company's security efforts and capabilities to detect dishonesty.

Every day, new or relatively new employees "discover" clever methods
to misroute or deliver merchandise or funds into their personal possession,
unaware of the fact that the ingenious scheme has been attempted and
detected thousands of times before. Because they have not been properly
educated, they contrive for unwarranted advantages in total ignorance, dam-
aging their employer and exposing themselves to the tragic consequences of
detection, termination, and prosecution—all for the want of a security
induction or awareness program for new employees.

The hospitality industry provides another good example of the
need for employee training and education. Programs that teach employees
how to recognize the signs leading up to alcohol overindulgence
and the proper use of force are critical issues today. Time was when
such issues were of little regard. Bouncers just threw out drunks
(often times, literally). Today, in our litigious society "Door Hosts"
or "Hosts" are held to a higher standard of conduct in terms of how
they eject a patron; careless attention to protocol in these circumstances
invites lawsuits. Hence, today, specific training programs, including videos,
are used as training tools.

Who is to conduct such training sessions? Experience tells us that the
most effective presentations about the security function are made by security personnel. They know what they are talking about, and their expertise
is apparent. A security presentation by a training officer or member of man-

agement lacks the same degree of conviction or credibility. Security must, therefore, assume the role of trainer/educator.

New employee induction programs are but one of a number of educational activities in which the Security Department is involved.

General Security Programs

Whereas the induction training addresses itself to the new employee and the consequences of dishonesty, the general security programs are aimed at creating an appreciation and understanding of the Security Department's objectives as they relate to the specific industry they serve. Thus, in retailing, the whole mix of problems—including shoplifting, credit card frauds, hide-in burglars, counterfeit passers, and quick-change artists—can be an interesting, informative, and educational experience for employees, who leave such sessions with a deeper insight into the problems and with ideas as to what they can do in the future to prevent them.

Supervisory Training Sessions

New supervisors (not security supervisors), while undergoing a new set of directions aimed at assisting them in their new responsibilities as leaders, should be exposed to security problems that are peculiar to supervisors. What can and what should supervisors do under certain circumstances? What are their limitations? What are the company's expectations of supervisors under a variety of security conditions, such as the discovery of a break-in or major loss?

Again, as in the programs listed previously, the best trainer is a security professional.

Employee Self-Protection Programs

Perhaps the most dramatic and best-attended employee self-protection programs are rape prevention sessions, using one of the quality commercial films or videocassettes available today. Employees are impressed that the Security Department is concerned about the protection of female employees and not only the more business-related security activities.

Other employee self-protection programs, such as kidnapping prevention for executives, protection of personal property and home for regular (nonexecutive) employees, and basic self-defense, are all programs the Security Department possibly could offer, even on an optional basis, to employees of the company.

This type of educational service demonstrates that the security organization cares about the company's employees. Consequently, the service tends to build a foundation of respect and support for the department's main objectives of protecting the company.

Unit or Departmental Presentations

Another important educational service role that the Security Department plays is in giving security presentations to various company units or departments. If a particular company unit—regardless of its organizational function or composition—wishes to hear from the Security Department, then the department should respond with a message aimed at that particular group. Housekeeping, Engineering, Purchasing, the Faculty Club, Merchandising Managers, the Youth Council—any group within the work environment—is worthy of the Security Department's time and attention. (Sometimes it is necessary to cultivate an interest in security among the company's departments.)

The objective of each presentation, regardless of the audience, is twofold. First, the Security Department should educate the group on the role and importance of the security function in the whole enterprise. This should be done in an entertaining and intriguing way; the description of the security organization and its assignments can be liberally sprinkled with actual "war stories" that fascinate those not connected with the world of security. The second part of the objective is to point out to whatever group is being addressed how its role, contribution, or responsibility ties in with the security and protective efforts of the company or institution. In that way, the group can identify with and relate to the security organization.

The educational efforts all strive to bridge the gap between the Security Department and the rest of the organization. The gap has been an accepted fact for too long; indeed, it has served to isolate security from the rest of the organization. Unfortunately, that isolation or insulation has bred distrust and fear of the security function—a function that must, if it is to be truly effective, have the understanding, trust, and support of all employees of the organization.

MANAGEMENT SERVICES

For the Security Department to make the maximum contribution to the organizational goals, security personnel (particularly at the managerial level) should achieve visibility as company management representatives as well as security management representatives. Specialists, as important as they may be, make limited contributions. Those who demonstrate interest in company problems and affairs, and who serve on various committees not specifically formed for pure protection purposes, play an additional, new role in the organization. They provide the company with a managerial support or service always in demand in organizational life.

This new dimension in security's role must be sought out and cultivated, because the Security Department has traditionally been content to limit its activities, and sometimes its image, to that of "company policeman." Organizational management, as a consequence, is accustomed to looking beyond the Security Department for general problem-solving counsel and assistance.

SUMMARY

Security is primarily a protective service of prevention, most conspicuously engaged in such general protective activities as access control, cargo protection, building security, investigation of criminal activities, inspections, and enforcement of company rules.

Security can and should also provide many related services. *Special services* might include executive protection, bodyguard service, special investigations, and emergency services. Security should be actively engaged in *educational services*, bringing security awareness to new and established employees and to supervisors whose responsibility must include loss prevention. Wherever possible, the effective Security Department will seek out ways to expand its role, making its presence felt in a positive way, as a general problem-solving arm of *management services.*

REVIEW QUESTIONS

1.   Explain the statement, "The value of the Security Department's service is better measured by what does *not* happen than by what does."

2.   Briefly stated, what is the general purpose of the security function in any organization?

3.   Give four examples of special services that the Security Department might provide to company management.

4.   Describe how the Security Department might set up and operate an emergency service for the benefit of company management.

5.   What are two objectives of the Security Department in making presentations to other company units or departments?

4

The Director's Role

Definitions of titles in the world of private-sector security are not as clear as those in the public sector. There is little confusion over the position of the Chief of Police within the Police Department or his or her status within the municipal government. On the other hand, the private sector tends to be rather indiscriminate in the use of the title Security Director. Too frequently the Security Director is, in fact, a Security Manager. There is a difference between the two. The easiest way to differentiate between them is to consider to whom they report. A director is ranked at the highest level of middle management and ordinarily reports to a member of senior management such as the company president or a vice president (VP). Some Security Directors are vice presidents and, as such, are part of the lower levels of senior management, more often than not reporting to a senior VP or executive VP, if not the President or Chief Executive Officer (CEO). Irrespective of where he or she is positioned in the overall hierarchy, that person is in a key leadership position.

The effective Security Director should have a track record of success in handling people and problems. He or she will be a dynamic, results-oriented individual with a high level of personal integrity. The director should have the ability to develop organizational plans, to evaluate personnel and their assignments, and to provide direction (including new approaches where necessary) to the security function.

Although all of the Security Director's activities come under the single umbrella of management, it is possible to examine each of the important component parts or roles of that directorship. The director is

- Leader
- Company executive
- Executive with high visibility
- Executive with a broad profile
- Innovator
- Counselor and advisor (in-house security consultant)
- Trainer
- Contemporary professional
- Goal setter and strategic planner

THE SECURITY DIRECTOR AS A LEADER

The Security Director provides leadership to the management of the security organization. Note that the director does not directly manage the department; he or she provides leadership for the manager and management team. Providing leadership means setting the right climate, pointing out directions, suggesting alternative solutions to problems, and encouraging and nurturing the growth of subordinates. The Security Director might be likened to the motion picture director. A fine film is a reflection of the director's talent, but the director is rarely in the film—so it is with the Security Director. He or she brings out the best of his or her people's talent, and they perform.

The most difficult aspect of the leadership role is to refrain from making operating decisions. This is when the delicate art of good management skills comes to the fore. If the Security Director has selected and developed his or her team properly, if he or she has given them real responsibility (and they understand this), if he or she has established a climate of confidence and professionalism, and if he or she has motivated them, then his or her direction and suggested alternatives will allow subordinates the courage, wisdom, and confidence to make decisions. The Director must have the courage, wisdom, and strength to let subordinates make their own decisions and their own mistakes.

AS A COMPANY EXECUTIVE

The Security Director, as a company executive, identifies with and is accepted by senior and middle management as part of the company's management team. He or she should not be viewed narrowly as a unique security specialist but rather as an effective executive (first) in the security field (second). The Security Director should not have the reputation or image of simply being the company policeman.

Too many security executives tend to be company isolationists out of the mainstream, sticking closely to the Security Department. Too many find excuses to avoid attending upper- and middle-management developmental programs that are designed to enhance a wide range of managerial skills. Wise is the Security Director who engages in those company activities that comparable executives attend. Such involvement and/or attendance puts the security executive in a one-on-one contact with company peers, which can result in meaningful relationships throughout the greater organization.

The Director's demeanor, deportment, grooming, and attire should be equivalent to that of other executives in the company (and that includes no tie-tacks that are miniature handcuffs).

AS AN EXECUTIVE WITH HIGH VISIBILITY

High visibility means just that: a Security Director who is well known in and out of the company and who is seen frequently. Ideally, the Director should be an interesting and effective speaker who is sought after to make presentations. The advantages of a popular Security Director over an unpopular one should be obvious in terms of creating good will toward the security organization and its objectives.

In addition, the Security Director should be visible—and available—to all the security ranks. He or she should make every effort to meet new security personnel, irrespective of their assignments, and seize every opportunity to chat with security people. That kind of visibility and the reputation of meeting and talking with every security employee pays off in terms of employee motivation. It makes for a Security Director who is deemed "approachable." Such approachability enhances loyalty, provides for sources of information that otherwise would never be forthcoming, and creates a healthy climate of well-being and "security" within the security organization.

AS AN EXECUTIVE WITH A BROAD PROFILE

A broad profile means that the Security Director has interests in and contributes to other areas of the business beyond the security function. Such exposure and activity not only enhance the executive image but have other rewards as well. One benefit is that the Security Director has the opportunity to meet, talk to, and work with people in the company whom he or she might never meet otherwise. Conversely, these people have the opportunity to meet and exchange ideas with the Security Director. The experience can be mutually rewarding and positive—good for them and good for the company (let alone the Security Department).

As an example of the Security Director's involvement in other areas of the business beyond security, in one large company the Security Director takes part in two different activities: college campus recruiting for company management trainees and the company's Supervisory Training School for first- and second-level supervisors.

The Security Director's responsibilities have nothing to do with campus recruiting and vice versa. However, the company's approach to recruiting is to use interested and qualified middle-management personnel as campus recruiters. This brings to the recruiting effort a diversified range of experience and talents, functioning within the selection guidelines designed by the Human Resources executive who is an expert in campus recruiting.

As a result of this approach to recruiting, there are young men and women moving up throughout the company today whom the Security

Director initially selected. What do you imagine their respective attitudes are about security people in general and the Security Director in particular? As time goes by, these people will move into ever more important levels of responsibility, and security needs friends—the more the better.

At an in-house Supervisory Training School, the Security Director lectures on the subject of discipline and the disciplinary process. Attendance at the Supervisory Training School, a 3-day program that ranks among the top in-house supervisory training programs in the industry, is highly coveted throughout the company. The program is meaningful and inspiring. Attitudes are changed. Skills are learned. Concepts open minds and eyes. In most cases the students are grateful for the experience and grateful to the lecturers who gave them new insight and understanding of important leadership skills.

What is the beneficial consequence? One particular company had 49 separate facilities located in five states, and the Security Director could not go to a facility without former "students" waving or coming up to greet him. Those relationships continue to foster greater acceptance and recognition of the Security Department.

AS AN INNOVATOR

The Security Director is constantly charged with the responsibility of finding new ways to do the job—better, less expensive ways—and thus he or she must be an innovative, flexible administrator. The term *creative security* is apt because the very phrase sparks one's imagination. "Is there a better way?" should be the Director's continual question. Innovation means experimentation and risk. Time was when security tasks tended to become entrenched, routine and safe, tried and true, with a tendency to discover a successful formula for solving a problem and then sticking with it. However, with the advent of September 11, 2001, those old wraps are off! Like magic, resistance to change has melted away overnight in favor of thinking "outside the box."

An excellent example of an innovative approach to a communication problem in a widely dispersed security organization before the advent of e-mail was the adoption of a telephone prerecorded message system. Each day every agent dialed the appropriate number at his or her appointed time to receive the Security Message of the Day; for example, the Salt Lake City agent called each day at 11:15 A.M. Rocky Mountain Time. The messages might be instructional (explaining a company procedure and how security could inspect for compliance), informative (reporting results of the department's activities, such as a major forger arrested), warning ("Be alert for counterfeit money orders bearing numbers L21344566 through 5699, with greasy feel around the indicia"), or motivational ("Keep up the outstanding work; all inspections were received prior to report deadline").

The implementation of this daily communication tool solved a long-standing problem of disseminating information to the entire organization in a timely manner. Formerly, especially if the information was urgent, headquarters personnel would undertake the long and tedious task of trying to reach all members of the department by telephone. When agents were not in, messages left for them tended to become garbled and misunderstood. The innovative program not only transmitted the message to everyone each day but also ensured that all received the same message. Today, e-mail and the fax can similarly be used to reach security employees who are dispersed geographically or otherwise difficult to communicate with. Today's challenge is to use the computer as an innovative communication tool.

Another creative approach to a security problem in one retail organization was the shift away from total reliance on theft detection to a rigorous loss prevention program. This shift was in answer to the staggering problem of an unacceptable inventory shrinkage figure. More arrests simply were not the answer to reducing losses. There had to be a better way than the traditional store detective and investigator approach.

Thus, because of innovative leadership at the Security Director's level, this company's "Red Coat" security program was born—a retail security program aimed at preventing shoplifting and other thefts instead of detecting them after the fact. Highly visible security personnel, dressed conspicuously in bright red blazers with gold emblems, have the job of discouraging, deterring, and preventing theft. If an act of theft is in progress or just completed, they attempt to "burn" it out—to discourage the thief by making him or her aware that the conduct has been observed and he or she is under surveillance. If "burning" does not work, then, and only then, is an arrest made.

This program has balanced out to a remarkably successful prevention-to-apprehension ratio of 25:10. It took courage to launch such a radically different approach to retail security in the face of long-standing tradition, but there was a better way!

AS A COUNSELOR AND ADVISOR (IN-HOUSE SECURITY CONSULTANT)

Because of his or her wisdom and years of security experience, the Security Director's role as counselor and advisor is an invaluable one to the company. Indeed, in the last decade, which saw a plethora of downsizing and corporate mergers, there has been a gradual transition in which many Security Directors ended up with either no or minimal staffs. By default they became "in-house security consultants." In reality, today we have top security executives who continue to serve as Director, Director *and* In-house Consultants, or In-house Consultant, depending on the Security Department's configuration and mission. In recognition of this new role, the International Association of Professional Security Consultants (IAPSC),[1] the premier professional society for security consultants, added a new membership classification to accommodate Security Directors/consultants who are still employed by corporations. The reader should bear in mind this in-house consultant role is not the mainstream or most common characterization of the Security Director's role.

It is interesting to point out how frequently security management seeks the Security Director's advice on routine operational problems. More often than not, they ask advice to "test" or compare their solutions against the Director's solutions. This is good, as long as the Director does not succumb to the temptation of grabbing the reins and requiring management to include him or her in the problem solving and decision making.

The role is to give advice, suggest alternatives, and help solve problems. He or she gives the benefit of experience and judgment to the Security Manager and staff. Occasionally, when a particularly difficult problem is under discussion and no answer has been developed for comparison with the Director's, the Director may hit on a solution that is immediately recognized by the Security Manager and his or her staff as the solution and consequently is adopted. In this kind of situation, the Director did not force his or her will on the subordinates; the climate was one of mutual and open exchange. The Director's involvement was participatory in nature.

Of course, the Director can decide to make all the decisions and solve all the problems. Some do or at least approve each and every decision. However, once the Director does this, he or she steps down into the role of the subordinate (the Security Manager under the Director in a large department). The Security Director is no longer directing but is now actively involved in operations. On the other hand, the Director sometimes will be called on to solve a problem. In these circumstances he or she will interject himself or herself into the decision-making process and force his or her will if necessary. However, these situations, especially the latter, should be rare.

The Security Director is also seen as the consultant to company management in matters of policy, construction planning, special events, emergency and disaster planning, executive protection, executive problems (such as the earlier reference to the executive's daughter running away from home), and a host of other situations in which the Director's good counsel is sought.

AS A TRAINER

The Security Director's attitude about the importance of the training and development of every security employee sets the climate for the department. If he or she is supportive of an aggressive, structured training program

---

[1] www.iapsc.org

within the organization, then that is what he or she will get. If the Director is lukewarm about training and feels that it takes away time that is necessary to get the job done, he or she will end up with a fragmented, ineffective program. The Director's role as a trainer deserves as much consideration as his or her other roles. It is certainly the one role that has an impact down through every level of the Security Department, with the obvious end result of improved performance.

With respect to the organization generally, the Security Director's role as trainer is primarily one of a climate-setter. With respect to the staff, particularly the Security Manager or Assistant Director, however, his or her role is very functional. The Director must personally train, guide, and develop his or her immediate subordinate, with the objective of preparing that manager to take over the directorship at the earliest possible date. One reason is that there is no one else who can do it. Second, there is a moral responsibility to the subordinate to help him or her grow vertically. Third, there is a moral responsibility to the company to develop talent that can function in the Director's absence. Finally, effective management dictates that a replacement be ready so that the Director can move vertically to assume more responsibility—for example, Corporate Security Director or Vice President of Loss Prevention, a position that has the same rank but with a larger division within the corporation, or a more advanced position with another company.

The training of the manager does not terminate at some fixed point in time. It is ongoing in nature and more often than not it lasts for several years. The development of this Manager (or Assistant Security Director) to be prepared to move into the Director's shoes may be one of the most important training responsibilities the Director has. However, just as the Security Director must develop and train his or her own staff, so too must the Director contribute to the training and education of all company employees in matters relating to security and loss prevention. The input of the Security Director with the Training Department on induction programs for new employees, general security or loss prevention awareness programs, and special campaigns or promotions can make the difference between a very credible production and a program that is flat and ineffective.

AS A CONTEMPORARY PROFESSIONAL

Being a contemporary professional means that the Director keeps abreast of the security industry—familiar with current case law affecting the industry, new and improved technology and systems, current trends, and the general state of the art of security as well as the art of management. To accomplish this the Director must subscribe to and read trade journals; participate in local, regional, or national security associations; attend seminars to hear peers and see new products; and freely communicate and exchange ideas with contemporaries on a regular basis. The Director who is not current with changes in our society in such areas of concern as the rights of disabled Americans, as reflected in the Americans with Disabilities Act (ADA), and the growth of concern over sexual harassment, cannot be "contemporary" or in step with the times. With the passage of time comes change, and the Director must be aware of and respond to that change, irrespective of his or her personal likes and dislikes about such change. He or she must overcome the tendency of resisting change and make it a professional goal to be contemporary.

The importance of this professional role is better understood when one recognizes that the subordinate Security Manager and Security Technician are normally absorbed in the operating demands of their jobs and may be less free than the Director to stay abreast of the vast array of information and data pertinent to our ever-changing world.

The contemporary professional is constantly involved in developmental and educational programs. How can one be considered professional unless he or she is growing in his or her selected profession? This growth comes from broadened experiences coupled with new concepts, strategies, and tactics made known through some form of institutionalized educational process. Education in the security industry is not limited to the novice. Many security training and educational programs are specifically designed for experienced practitioners, supervisors, and managers.

Contemporism, as such, also includes comparing the organization to others, or "benchmarking," that is, asking what the Security Department of Company A is doing compared to one's own organization. This comparison could cover every conceivable facet of operation, from orientation programs for new employees to handling trespassers. Put another way, has Company A discovered, invented, or adopted a new or better way to do the job, and if so, should we consider doing that? Have we become too set in our ways or should we change too? Can we build on what they are doing and do it better? No one company or executive knows it all, all the time. There's nothing wrong with copying someone else's successes if it enhances and improves your own organization or performance. Benchmarking is simply a structured way of comparing programs or operations systematically, that is, comparing apples to apples.

AS A GOAL SETTER AND STRATEGIC PLANNER

Establishing objectives and setting goals for the organization is an important aspect of the Security Director's job. Who else could do it? If senior management sets security goals, then there is no need for a Director. A subordinate cannot establish departmental objectives and tell the Director the strategy to achieve those objectives.

Goals obviously set directions, provide challenge, and should require genuine effort to be achieved. Goals too easily achieved are not real goals. For example, if one departmental goal for the coming year is to have 100% of the department's supervisors graduate from the company's Supervisory Training School, and only 10% (representing two or three people) have yet to go when that goal is set, then this is not a real goal. It is simply one of many things to be done on an ongoing basis. A goal must be an objective—an accomplishment that requires stretch—that you must work at constantly to achieve.

Goals, which must be quantitative or qualitative in nature, could include replacing personnel with hardware to reduce payroll dollars, converting a predetermined number of units to a new access control program within a specified time frame, reducing specific losses by a set percentage, improving a certain measurable skill of security personnel such as firing range scores, or designing and implementing a new Programmed Learning program for major disasters.

One method of identifying and achieving goals is called strategic planning. Simply stated, there are three parts to such planning:

1. A clear understanding and good articulation of the department's mission as exemplified in the department's Mission Statement.
2. A detailed description of the most important issues the department anticipates facing. One example might be the theft of proprietary data, which is the work product of Research & Development (R & D).
3. A set of action plans that should enable the department to move forward.

The ultimate goal of good strategic planning is to lay out specific long-range plan objectives and then devise short-term action plans to meet each major objective (or goal). For example, if the long-range plan includes the objective of having a new investigative unit that specializes in computer-related offenses, the short-term plan that would eventually lead to that objective would be various steps including (1) writing job descriptions for these new people, (2) hiring qualified personnel, (3) developing the training program, (4) writing the policies and procedures on how they will function/perform, (5) working with Human Resources to develop a performance measurement instrument unique to that work, (6) developing the forms and reports that might be required for that work, (7) budgeting for the new department, and so forth all aimed at the targeted date of implementation.

In addition to the major roles described previously, the Director should wear a number of other hats that can be significant. He or she may be the departmental "Court of Last Appeal," "father confessor," listener, financier, departmental defender on a white horse, taskmaster, politician, professor, and intelligence expert. He or she must be purer than Caesar's wife, and, finally, he must be a gentleman, or, as the case may be, she must be a lady.

THE NEW SECURITY DIRECTOR

To be appointed the new head of security in a long-established organization, even if coming up through the ranks; to come into an established organization from outside the company; to be transferred from another area of the business to head up a newly created security organization; or to arrive on the company scene from outside for the purpose of setting up a program are difficult situations indeed. The new head of security is unknown and unproved (in that position), and most people are suspicious of the unknown.

How can this natural suspicion of "the new man" be overcome? The answer is for the new Security Director to come in with the lowest possible profile. He or she should look and listen and speak when spoken to, except when asking necessary questions. He or she should have a pleasant manner and be concerned initially with the people in his or her pyramid. Such concern must be sincere and warm. In private chats with each subordinate, he or she will learn much without going out to seek it.

The new Security Director should be very conservative in terms of making changes, unless such change is badly and conspicuously needed. In that case, he or she should allow the change to be made but not in his or her own name. The Security Director should allow the credit to go to a subordinate. People will suspect that the new manager is behind the change anyhow and quietly admire his or her style. The new manager should not threaten to "clean house," make sweeping changes, bring in "qualified" help, or in any way forecast change; to do so tenses up the organization and prolongs the period needed for assimilation into the environment. It is never wise for the new director to criticize his or her predecessor, if there was one. If criticism is due, it will naturally come from below. The new person should listen to the criticism and be prudent in his or her responses. A neutral response is best; then the Director should move the conversation on to positive statements about the future.

If a problem or question arises to which the new Security Director does not know the solution or answer, he or she should say so. Just because he or she is the chief does not mean he or she knows everything. The Director should ask subordinates for their advice and/or opinions.

This low-keyed, low-profile, nonthreatening approach—which even helps take some of the butterflies out of the new Director's stomach because he or she is not trying to prove anything—will buy time, and time is the new Director's ally. Changes will occur, of course, because the new Director is there to ensure protection for the company, and that means his or her style, philosophy, and strategy will come into play with the passage of time.

Loud noises and quick movements not only frighten animals and infants but they frighten adults too.

SUMMARY

The Security Director is commonly one who reports to a member of senior management; the head of Security reporting to someone at a lower level is more properly called a Manager. Within the Security Department the Director's role is that of leading rather than operational decision making. (The Manager of a smaller department will inevitably have more direct involvement in operations.) In the leadership role, the mark of a good Director or Manager is the ability to delegate responsibility and commensurate authority.

Outside of his or her own department, the effective Security Director should be a highly visible company executive, a part of the management team with interests that go beyond security. In his or her relationship with security staff the Director will be an innovator, counselor, trainer, and goal setter and strategic planner.

The Security Director moving into a new company or position will advisedly seek a lower profile initially than the one just described previously. He or she will seek not to force events and people but to lead with patience and example.

REVIEW QUESTIONS

1.   What is the distinction between a Security Director and a Security Manager?

2.   Give an example of how the Security Director may be involved in other areas of the company beyond security.

3.   What are the reasons why the Security Director should prepare his or her subordinate to take over the responsibilities of the Security Director?

4.   List three ways the Security Director can keep abreast of developments in the security industry.

5

The Security Supervisor's Role

Supervision is comprised of many factors, including (but not limited to) hiring, training, discipline, motivating, promoting, and communicating. Each of these factors is a specific skill unto itself. Rather than grouping all of these skills under the single heading of "Supervision" or "The Security Supervisor's Role," each is examined individually. This chapter deals with the supervisor and his or her relationship with those higher and lower in the organizational structure, his or her responsibilities, and the general principles of supervision. Subsequent chapters are concerned more specifically with those factors intrinsic to supervision.

In the smaller department the Security Manager may be directly involved in supervision, and the comments in this chapter on the supervisor's role would obviously apply to the Manager.

One popular definition of supervision is the task of getting others (subordinates) to get the job done, the way management wants it done, when management wants it done—willingly. Willingness, of course, is the key aspect of this definition. We are interested in enlightened supervision, not the kind of supervision used to oversee the slaves on the plantations of years ago, the slave labor programs of Hitler's regime, or even some of the penal and correctional institution's work programs of today. Historically, such autocratic methods, by and large, do get the job done—but not always at the time or in the manner desired. In a free society the most difficult part of the supervisor's task is to get the job done willingly.

The supervisor's job, then, is to get other people to accomplish tasks, which means they must perform. Performance is the ultimate responsibility and goal of supervision. Everything revolves around job performance—execution at the line level. The supervisor's performance (his or her supervisory skills) is reflected in the performance of those who work for him or her.

THE SUPERVISOR AS AN INSPECTOR

There is an old adage that says, "Employees don't do what you expect, they do what you inspect." More often than not that is true, not because they do not want to or do not care to perform their tasks but simply because of human frailty. That same element of human failure is not limited to line employees; it can be traced to every level of every organizational structure right to the top. From the top down, therefore, each "supervisor" must inspect the work of his or her subordinates. The Director inspects the Security Manager, the Manager inspects the middle managers, the middle managers inspect their supervisors, and the supervisors inspect their subordinates. When that inspection process breaks down, for whatever reason, tasks break down, deadlines are missed, and other tasks are temporarily neglected and eventually forgotten. It is a source of amazement to all levels of management that functions, tasks, duties, reports— all assumed to be taking place with regularity—have "slipped through the cracks" and disappeared from organizational life, all because the inspection process failed.

On the other side of the coin, inadequate inspection frequently surfaces when a change in supervision reveals tasks or reports that are religiously accomplished but that no longer serve their original purpose. Often, no one seems to know who started the tasks or what they were intended to accomplish.

The inspection need not, and should not, be a negative process wherein the supervisor tries to find errors or omissions and then criticizes. That managerial style creates a climate of resentment, defensiveness, and hostility. One can always find fault.

The most effective managerial style in the inspection process is to find those tasks that are done properly, acknowledge and give credit for good performance in such areas, and then point out deficiencies in an objective fashion. Most employees want to do a good job. Most failures, as already indicated, are the result of human frailties and not of malicious design. Consequently, when performance deficiencies are pointed out objectively, they are usually received with some embarrassment on one hand and an expression of genuine desire to improve on the other.

To be effective, this critical process of performance inspection must be consistent, continuous, constructive, and tailored to the individual employee.

THE SUPERVISOR AND THE INDIVIDUAL EMPLOYEE

Because every employee is different, the supervisor must deal on an individual basis with each subordinate. Every human being on the face of the earth is different. The differences are manifested not only in observable physical features, fingerprints, and DNA but also in how each individual responds to external stimuli; how the individual perceives things; and his or her beliefs, fears, aspirations, and needs. Such human differences mean that different people require different handling. Some may require more supervision than others may. Some respond to persuasion and some to command. Some want to set goals and some want goals set for them. Some are uncomfortable around authority figures and some are at ease. Sensitivity to employee differences is one characteristic of a good supervisor.

SUPERVISORY AUTHORITY

A supervisor must have commensurate authority to carry out his or her responsibilities. If a supervisor is told he or she has the responsibility of 10 security officers to protect the facility between 4:00 P.M. and midnight and at the same time is told that any disciplinary action against any one of those 10 will be handled by the next level of supervision, then he or she has been denied the necessary tools or stripped of the necessary authority to carry out this responsibility. Such conditions, which do indeed exist, make a mockery of organizational integrity and turn what should be legitimate supervisors into "straw bosses" or lackeys. The supervisor represents management and must be given the necessary authority to make that representation meaningful. If, for any reason, appropriate authority cannot be vested in a supervisor, it will still be necessary to have some form of "lead person" in charge.

The supervisor—with his or her officers, agents, investigators, or whatever their titles—should have not only the necessary authority to discipline but should also have some input in the selection of assignment to his or her unit. The supervisor should be heard when his or her people are considered for promotion; must have authority to require additional training; must have the authority to communicate to his or her people, including sending instructions, memos, and so forth; and must have the freedom to measure his or her people's performance without interference.

The issue of a supervisor's need to measure his or her people's performance without interference is even larger than the one of disciplinary rights. Here is a typical case: The supervisor is obliged to evaluate the performance of his subordinates on an annual or semiannual basis. He follows directions in terms of completing the personnel form prepared for each employee. (A sample Employee Performance Evaluation form is provided in Appendix A.) He marks the various boxes that represent rating factors such as "submits reports in a timely manner" and finally makes an overall evaluation as "Above Standards." He submits his evaluations. Two weeks later he is called before his superior or the Human Resource office and is advised that his rating of "Above Standards" of Officer X is too high. The rating should be "Meets Standards." Although there are no flaws or inconsistencies in the various factor-ratings with the overall rating, the supervisor is instructed, for whatever reason, to reduce the rating to the next lower (or he might be instructed to raise the overall rating to the next higher).

The previously mentioned problem is frequently a point of concern in any discussion of supervisory training and practice. Those raising the question say, "I don't want to get into trouble with anyone, so I changed the rating, even though I felt my evaluation was correct. What should I have done, or what should I do next time?"

For the responsible supervisor, the answer is clear. If he or she is convinced that the evaluation is not incompatible with the firm's definition of standards and the evaluation is not inconsistent with his or her other evaluations, then the supervisor should seek to support his or her own rating. If, after sufficient discussion, the supervisor is still asked to change that rating, he or she may have no alternative but to make the change as requested. In such circumstances, the supervisor should indicate on the evaluation form that the rating is not his or her own.

If a supervisor is not capable of disciplining, then he or she should not be a supervisor. By the same token, if the supervisor is incompetent to evaluate the performance of subordinates, he or she should not be a supervisor. If it is a question of skills in disciplining or evaluating performance, then it is incumbent on management to provide the necessary supervisorial training to develop such skills—not to take that authority away.

THE SUPERVISOR AS THE "IN-BETWEEN" MAN

The supervisor is the vital link between the employee and security management. The supervisor represents management's needs and views to those below and at the same time has the responsibility of representing the needs and views of his or her people up to management. Failure to discharge this function objectively and faithfully, in a timely manner, can have disastrous results. The supervisor who, being closest to the scene, is aware of sentiments, grievances, or problems but who does not inform management fails twofold. First, such a supervisor fails his or her subordinates by not carrying the message to management. The condition, whatever it may be, is allowed to continue, fester, and/or grow, to the disservice of his or her subordinates in terms of morale, accidents, or turnover, depending on the problem. Second, this supervisor fails management by withholding information that could provide them with answers, explanations, or decisions to resolve the issue.

This intermediary status is usually well understood by line personnel. It makes sense. However, that status can easily serve as a crutch for the weak supervisor, providing an excuse to shirk responsibility so that all distasteful duties or assignments or decisions that may be unpopular are passed off (even if they are his or her own) with the disclaimer, "Management wants it this way." The weakness is apparent: This supervisor wants to be popular all the time. Fortunately, that kind of supervisory weakness cannot be concealed for too long.

THE SUPERVISOR'S SPAN OF CONTROL

Span of control, which is the number of employees a supervisor can manage, depends on a number of factors. One important factor is the individual supervisor—his or her skill level in handling people and ability to delegate responsibility. Another factor is the job description of his or her subordinates. Field investigators with relatively sophisticated assignments require more attention from the supervisor than a uniformed staff assigned to one location on one shift. In the former case, the proper span of control might be 6 and in the latter, 12. Long-standing and widely accepted span of control standards suggest the following ratios of supervisor to employees:

Ideal 1 : 3

Good 1 : 6

Acceptable 1 : 12

These numbers represent spans of control under normal operating conditions on an ongoing basis. However, under certain circumstances (for a relatively short period of time and with a homogenous group) one leader could handle up to two dozen employees.

ONE BOSS

The principle of unity of command is the classic or traditional way of saying that every employee must report to only one superior. Find a situation in which a person is being directed by more than one superior and you will find that subordinate coping with conflicting instructions and confusion, resulting in diluted performance.

Consider the frustrations experienced in one actual situation by the Chief of Campus Police for a group of adjacent private colleges in Southern California. In that position the Chief was responsible to five college presidents, each of whom had his own particular point of view. In one incident, a group of students had gathered off campus in a neighboring county for a Friday afternoon "thank God it's Friday" (TGIF) party. The Sheriff's Department of that county arrived on the scene and took this large group of students into custody for possession and consumption of alcoholic beverages. One student slipped away, advised the Chief of Campus Police of the events, and stated that the Sheriff's officers were calling in buses to transport the students to the county jail.

At the scene the Campus Chief discussed the matter with the officer in charge and convinced him the interests of justice would be best served if he would release the students to the Chief, who in turn would process them through their respective college student court systems. The Sheriff's office could see the wisdom of avoiding the booking hassles and subsequent difficulties of proving in the county court just which student was doing what (there were close to 100 students).

The Chief of Campus Police escorted all the students back to his office and had them line up for identification purposes. He then submitted lists to three different college student courts. The courts, as expected, levied substantial fines and built up the coffers of the student body fund and justice prevailed—at least the Chief thought so initially.

The outcome of all this was that one college president expressed warm appreciation for the Chief's intervention, which had saved the school from what would have been certain unfavorable publicity at the hands of the local press and most of all for the avoidance of criminal booking records for his students. However, one of the other college presidents took exception to the Chief's intervention. His position was that the students sooner or later had to assume responsibility for their conduct. They had been warned about assembling at that particular location for "beer busts" before, and, therefore, they should have experienced the full consequences of their conduct.

The point is that this Security Director could have lived with either position had he worked for either president, but he worked for both. His job was to serve both, and obviously he could not please both. The employee, then, who has more than one supervisor can find himself or herself in an unworkable situation. The organization must follow the principle of unity of command to avoid such counterproductive conditions.

AUTOMATIC SHIFTING IN THE LINE OF COMMAND

There are necessary and legitimate exceptions to the principle of unity of command. Two situations that require another supervisor are:

1. In emergencies
2. When the failure of a ranking employee to take command would jeopardize the department's objectives or reputation

As an example of number one, imagine that a uniformed security officer, immediately following a natural disaster such as an earthquake, is approached by a security investigator (who is in an entirely different departmental pyramid or line of command but has rank over the guard). The investigator instructs the security officer to run to the side of the building and cut off the gas supply. The officer cannot refuse this shifting in supervision, in view of the circumstances.

For an example of number two, imagine that a uniformed security officer on a parking control assignment for a major event has been instructed by his supervisor to deny access to one reserved parking lot. A supervisor other than the officer's, because of his mobility and overview of the parking and traffic conditions, reaches the opinion that the growing traffic congestion can only be relieved by routing traffic into the empty lot—not to relieve the congestion could have serious repercussions on the event itself. The supervisor, knowing he or she is accountable for the decision, can command the security officer to let the cars in.

Such direct orders out of the normal chain of command are invariably given under a time pressure, that is, a decision and action must be immediate. The consequences of delaying action to locate the proper supervisor could be serious if not grave.

Such automatic shifting in the line of command, always of a short duration, requires full understanding on the part of all department members at all levels. Such shifting does not violate the principle of unity of command; rather, it enhances and supports the principle by having a rule and understanding of the exception. Exceptions add credence to rules.

FUNCTIONAL OR STAFF SUPERVISION

Although every employee has his or her own supervisor, there are numerous occasions and conditions in which the employee must perform at a time or location outside the immediate control of this supervisor. An example would be an alarm operator and alarm serviceperson working the graveyard shift. Their supervisor works the day shift. By agreement, the graveyard watch commander, in another pyramidal structure within the Security Department, assumes functional (or staff) supervision over these two security employees. As a functional supervisor the watch commander has responsibility for a limited degree of supervision but not complete control.

There are two aspects to this functional supervision. The first is that the watch commander in all probability has no technical competence in alarm operations or servicing, so he or she cannot give commands that would interfere with performance. This means his or her supervision is limited to such things as promptness, following general orders applicable to all personnel, and demeanor on the job.

The second aspect of functional supervision is that it is essentially advisory in nature. The functional supervisor can discuss problems with the subordinate, make suggestions, point out mistakes, but—and this is most important—he or she lacks authority to take disciplinary action. Certainly he or she can cause disciplinary action by reporting the problem to the subordinate's supervisor; that supervisor can take the corrective action, but the staff supervisor cannot.

SUPERVISORY TRAINING

Perhaps the most common shortcoming in the security industry is the failure to properly prepare and equip new supervisors with the tools to discharge their important responsibilities. A line employee on Friday may become a new supervisor on Monday, with no distinguishable difference in the eyes of former peers.

It is better to give the new supervisor a week off with pay and have him or her sit in the library studying books on the fundamentals of supervision than to put this individual in his or her new assignment immediately. If the new supervisor is off for a week and the employees believe he or she is attending some special training just for supervisors, they see their former peer, on his or her return, through entirely different eyes.

The library trip, of course, is a barely acceptable alternative in the absence of what should really happen. Ideally, the new supervisor, before taking command, should attend a workshop, seminar, or training session for new supervisors. If an in-house program is not available, the new supervisor should be sent to a commercially conducted program, from which there are many to choose in most communities.

The problem in this area is the false assumption that because a person was an outstanding investigator or officer, he or she will make a good supervisor. That simply does not follow automatically. A new supervisor must master an entire new set of skills that have absolutely nothing to do with investigative ability. Such skills must be learned; they are not inherited and do not come into play automatically on promotion. New supervisors are often quick to discover that they are ill prepared for their new responsibilities. They are sensitive to their deficiencies and lack confidence in handling problems and people. Subordinates are very quick to sense this absence of confidence, and some will not be at all sympathetic but will capitalize on the apparent weakness to their own advantage—especially those who jealously believe they should have received that promotion.

If, for a variety of reasons, it is impossible to send the supervisor to a training program immediately or to the library, the next best thing is to arrange for his or her attendance at a later date. Subordinates, knowing the new boss will indeed be attending special training in the near future, will respond in a more supportive posture than in the complete absence of training.

SUMMARY

Supervision has been defined as the task of getting work done how and when management wants it done—willingly. Performance is the ultimate goal of supervision.

The effective supervisor will best ensure the performance of his or her subordinates by constant inspection. He or she will be sensitive to individual employee differences in providing both criticism and encouragement. This supervisor must have the authority (both in discipline and in employee evaluations) to carry out his or her responsibilities. As the man-in-the-middle between management and the employee, the supervisor should play an active part in the process of communication both upward and downward.

Important principles of effective supervision are limited span of control and unity of command. The latter principle (no employee can serve two bosses) is not violated by functional supervision, which is exercised over employees only temporarily under a supervisor's control. Functional supervision is both limited and advisory in nature.

A good employee does not necessarily make a good supervisor. Effective security management will provide adequate training for new supervisors. Training inspires confidence in both the supervisor and those who will serve under him or her.

REVIEW QUESTIONS

1. Define supervision. What is the ultimate responsibility and goal of supervision?

2. Explain how you would handle the situation if you were asked by a superior to change your rating of a subordinate's performance.

3. In what way is the supervisor "the vital link between the employee and security management"?

4. What are two factors influencing a supervisor's effective span of control?

5. Give two examples of legitimate exceptions to the principles of unity of command.

6

The Individual Security Employee

Relatively little instructive material is available concerning the individual security employee's role, contribution, or importance in the overall security function. The truth of the matter is that the good reputation of the Security Department and the successful achievement of the department's objectives are, ultimately, the result of the employee's execution of the job. Poor performance equals poor reputation. Good performance equals good reputation. Excellent performance equals excellent reputation.

Regardless of how knowledgeable security management may be, the line employee's performance is the measurement of success. This performance has two dimensions: (1) application of skills and (2) general conduct. Specific skill development, skill levels, and execution of skills are the subject of many texts and are not our concern here. Rather, we examine the issue of conduct, not only because it has been touched on so lightly within the industry but also because, in its critical importance, conduct frequently transcends skills. Thus if a security administrator had to choose between good skills but poor conduct and poor skills but good conduct, more often than not he or she would choose the latter.

Conduct, then, plays a significant role in the Security Department's general reputation. The company that Security serves expects exemplary conduct of its security force. Security Management must demand exemplary conduct. Line employees will respond to such expectations and demands if they know and understand what the standards of conduct are. It is a truism that most employees will do what management wants *if they know what management wants.*

In the absence of any generally circulated or official standards of conduct in the security industry,[1] the following is submitted.

---

[1] For additional discussion of this subject, see *Private Security: Report of the Task Force on Private Security.* (Washington, DC: National Advisory Committee on Criminal Justice Standards and Goals, 1976), especially Standard 3.2, "Conduct of Security Personnel."

STANDARDS OF CONDUCT

1. Security employees are habitually courteous and attentive to those seeking assistance, reporting conditions, or lodging complaints.
2. Security employees are punctual and expeditious in the discharge of their duties.
3. Security employees conduct themselves in a just and objective manner, treating all with equal reasonableness.
4. Security employees consistently exhibit a spirit of cooperation with all and do not allow personal feelings to interfere with their work.
5. Security employees conduct their personal and business life in an exemplary fashion that is above reproach in terms of stability, fidelity, and morality.
6. Security employees have a cheerful and positive approach to their work.

Today these standards may sound idealistic if not old-fashioned, but if they are adopted and followed the end results will have a favorable impact on a department's reputation.

Courtesy

Courtesy starts at home, granted, but the development of courtesy on the job starts with mutual respect for fellow security employees. One cannot be expected to respect one's associates unless one respects oneself first. Security management's responsibility in this area is to ensure that the employee has dignity—dignity in pride in his or her uniform, workplace, and personal responsibility in work. Standards set in these areas have a definite influence on an employee's assessment of his or her worth and sense of self-esteem.

Issuing or permitting the use of shabby uniforms, for example, takes away from a person's sense of pride. High standards for uniforms, on the other hand, automatically instills self-pride and, hence, self-respect. Old and inadequate office equipment and furniture in poor condition have a demoralizing effect, whereas equipment and furniture in fine condition make employees feel valuable to the organization. Of course, the knowledge that each day's work is important and contributes to the overall success of the department is most necessary. The trouble is that many employees do not understand or see that their daily contribution is significant, usually because management has not bothered to tell them.

When an employee works within a climate that fosters feelings of self-worth, the employee will normally feel that his or her coworkers are also important and worthy of respect. Respect and courtesy will radiate beyond the Security Department—*if they are part of an understood standard of conduct.*

The emphasis on "if they are part of an understood standard of conduct" is important because of the nature of the security business, particularly those types of security organizations that are heavily engaged in the detection and apprehension of criminal offenders, like shoplifting agents in a retail Loss Prevention Department. Frequent, regular contact with offenders or violators often is a negative experience and tends to harden the security officer, just as it tends to desensitize law enforcement officers in the public sector. Unless courtesy is demanded under all circumstances, it may be practiced within the organization but may not be demonstrated consistently outside the organization.

Of the six standards suggested, courtesy is the most conspicuous. Courteous behavior is not restricted to personal contacts; telephone courtesy, or its absence, also stands out. A great deal of security business is conducted over the phone, and employees in the security organization, including clerical workers, must understand the importance of telephone courtesy. Everyone, including scoundrels, needs and likes to be treated with courtesy.

Responsibility

Standard number two speaks to "punctual and expeditious" performance. The individual who is not punctual is not a responsible person — to be late for duty, to be late with reports, and to be late with assignments reflect a lack of responsibility. Such a person is expressing the attitude, "I don't really care about what's happening." Children lack responsibility; maturity is a factor in assuming responsibility. Children are impatient and soon weary of details. Concern for details, including time, is another measure of responsibility and maturity.

Webster's New Collegiate Dictionary defines the word *expeditious* as "characterized by or acting with promptness and efficiency." For the department to have a reputation of being prompt and efficient, every member must be prompt and efficient. Much security work involves reporting facts (details). A lackadaisical approach, an absence of concern over details, and unnecessary delays reflect negatively on an organization. Every security employee must be punctual, attentive, and accurate. Company as well as security management relies on the security employee's sense of responsibility.

This may seem self-evident. Responsibility is a question of self-discipline, and the setting of standards imposes self-discipline.

Due Process

Standard number three requires that security employees act "in a just and objective manner, treating all with equal reasonableness." Essentially this means respecting the rights of others. To be other than just or to be subjective, particularly in the enforcement aspects of security work, is to give more rights to some and to deny the rights of others. Such conduct is intolerable in the public sector as evidenced by many appellate court decisions restricting law enforcement, as well as by the public outcry over public and political scandals, such as Watergate, which brought down a president. As of this writing, the courts have not yet reached down into the private sector with binding restrictions in terms of our enforcement activities, but that is not to say that they will not. At the time of this writing we in the private sector are not obliged to "Mirandize" people we interview or interrogate, but abuses could change that.

Respect for the rights of others is more a state of mind than the sort of behavior that can be legislated. Security professionals can create the proper state of mind through standards of conduct expected of their employees.

The obligation of *due process* is very important in an organization, such as a large retail store, that takes scores of people into custody every month of the year. To be objective and treat each one equally is often a challenge, especially when confronted with violence as well as verbal abuse. However, it is both practical and humane to treat all suspects with respect; after all, once they have been apprehended the victory is already won. There is no need to harass or further embarrass them, to be verbally abusive, or to gloat over their misfortune in having been caught. Even in the face of vile verbal attacks, members of the staff should impassively and objectively go about their business of completing reports and related tasks with an air of quiet dignity that evokes nothing but respect from onlookers, from management on the scene, and from the police who arrive to assist.

A store detective with an abiding respect for the rights of others is a store detective with the smallest ratio of false arrests. Some may say the smallest false-arrest ratio is purely skill-related; in truth, however, the best detective not only has masterful skills but he or she is also sharply tuned into the consequences of a questionable arrest—consequences not only regarding exposing the store to possible civil liability but also regarding the mental trauma and anguish of the innocent person. The best detectives are sensitive to human rights. Insensitive detectives tend to be rash. They will gamble, will act on instinct, and will take the word of another rather than what they know through their own senses. Insensitive detectives, and all other classifications of security personnel, can become sensitive through adoption of standards of conduct.

Cooperation

A reputation of willingness to work with and for others—to serve and assist—materially contributes to the department's good image. Far too many departments attempt to find reasons not to do a job or reasons why they cannot. From the Security Director down to the newest employee with the most limited responsibilities, the watchword should be "Why, certainly"— assuming, of course, that the requested service is possible and not contrary to the best interests of the organization and that there is no specific rule against it.

For example, the lobby desk officer may not have facilities to store briefcases. The officer could easily refuse a request from a visiting dignitary to watch a briefcase. However, if he or she says, "Why, certainly" and places the case behind the desk for 15 minutes, a most favorable impression is created. It is the spirit of cooperation that counts. The VIP would not ask unless there was a need, and he or she would not ask a particular person unless he or she believed that person was responsible. A response of "No" or "I can't" is hardly helpful.

The more Security can do as a service, the more important the entire operation becomes and the more company management will look to Security for such service. For example:

Executive: Could you spare a security officer to pick up a visitor at the airport? The taxis are on strike, you know.

Security: Sure. I'll take care of it.

Public Relations Officer: Could you have one of your officers help out at the entrance to the special event? We need another pair of hands to collect the passes—we're afraid of gatecrashers.

Security: Why, certainly.

Employee (to security patrol in the parking lot): Could you call on your radio and ask for a tow truck to come out here? I think my battery is dead.

Security: Sure. I'll take care of it right away.

Every member of the department should be coached to look for ways to serve instead of looking for ways not to. If you develop that spirit and attitude in the security organization, the department's reputation will be enhanced.

Personal Integrity

Standard of conduct number five states: "Security employees conduct their personal and business life in an exemplary fashion that is above reproach in terms of stability, fidelity, and morality." The terms *above reproach* and *exemplary fashion* are very broad but hint of such qualities as self-respect, honesty, cleanliness, and fair play—qualities of universal appeal. Let us consider some of these standards as they relate to the security officer's job.

Self-Respect

As discussed earlier in this chapter, self-respect means dignity and pride in oneself and what one does. An individual's sense of pride and self-respect is mirrored in the way he or she walks, dresses, holds the head, looks others in the eye, and executes assignments. A security employee who takes pride in his or her reputation and work will perform in an exemplary fashion.

Honesty

Honesty here refers to the smallest corners of our character, areas such as the tendency to exaggerate. Honesty in words as well as deeds is required of every security professional at every level.

Security people are subjected to more temptations than perhaps any other career field—an "occupational hazard" of a sort. Only a strong conviction of what is right and what is wrong can provide the necessary strength to resist the temptations. More often than not it is the little things that test people. Everyone has heard others say, "If I ever steal, it's got to be worth it—say $5 million!" The truth is that most of these people would not really have the courage to commit a substantial theft but might take something small and unnoticeable, like a can of soda from the refrigerator in the employees' lounge or a pad of Post-it Notes from the supply room.

Cleanliness

An individual's personal habits can be pleasant to others or can be loathsome and offensive. Most security people are highly visible, and their contact with other company employees or the public must be positive. People notice other people. Dirty fingernails, earwax, nose hairs, and body odors are all correctable.

Stability

Consistency in action and reaction is most important. The luxury of being moody cannot be permitted in the security organization. A moody security officer at the front lobby desk would not last long.

Excitability is another unacceptable characteristic in a security employee's makeup. Being moody, being excitable, or having a tendency to lose one's temper are types of mental peaks and valleys that detract from exemplary conduct.

Fidelity

Fidelity means the careful observance of duties as well as loyalty. A loyal security employee is steadfast and true, dedicated to the organization. To complain about departmental policies, procedures, assignments, or personnel is not disloyalty but lacks the true ring of fidelity. However, a legitimately channeled and righteous complaint does not take away from one's loyalty. There is a fine line between what can be called a "positive" complaint and a merely negative one. Perhaps the difference lies in the manner in which the complaint is made. I can immediately call to mind a supervisor with years of faithful and loyal service whom I considered absolutely dedicated to the organization. This man rarely complained, but when he did, it was always very quietly stated, upward.

Dissatisfaction on the job does reflect in one's performance. This obviously suggests that poor or questionable job performance could be an indicator of unhappiness and dissatisfaction. Dissatisfaction erodes loyalty. It must be identified and dealt with as early as possible in a very upfront, open, and honest manner. If the source of dissatisfaction cannot be corrected or explained satisfactorily and the employee is still not happy, he or she should be advised that the organization cannot change to accommodate him or her. The employee must adapt to the organization; if the employee cannot, he or she will remain dissatisfied. If the employee remains dissatisfied it will affect performance and his or her work record. In view of that, it should be pointed out to the employee that under such circumstances the honest thing to do is to change organizations, for the employee's best interest as well as the organization's.

Morality

The security officer must observe the highest of standards in terms of right or proper conduct. Because of the high visibility of security personnel, employees in that capacity with questionable or low moral standards attract attention. Once a poor reputation is established, it is difficult, at best, to reverse.

The poor reputation of individual officers impinges on the department's reputation; however, the real threat or hazard, from the administrator's point of view, is compromise. Once just one security employee is compromised, the organizational objectives are compromised. To cause personal, then organizational, compromise by sexual behavior is commonplace in intelligence, political, and organized crime strategy today. To treat so-called sexual freedom lightly in the security context would be naive and counterproductive.

There are obvious limitations on security management's influence on employees' standards of morality. Management cannot dictate what movies they can or cannot see, what books they should or should not read, what websites should be avoided, or what personal relationships would or would not be acceptable. What management can do is to discourage improper conduct by (1) setting high standards, (2) ensuring that every security employee knows those standards, (3) educating the employees about the hazards of compromise, and (4) discouraging fraternization with company employees. How effective those actions prove depends a great deal on the effectiveness of the organization's employee selection and screening processes.

Attitude

Of all the characteristics or virtues one brings to the job, none, including educational achievement, can exceed that of attitude. Attitude determines a person's conduct and bearing toward others and their reaction to him or her. Good attitude produces good reaction; bad attitude produces bad reaction. Attitude is contagious. It is a key ingredient in success or failure.

Take a security employee exemplifying the other five standards of conduct—one who is courteous, punctual, objective, cooperative, and above reproach—and imbue that employee with a cheerful and positive attitude and you will have the finest security employee. The department's reputation is a reflection of that composite.

SUMMARY

The Security Department's performance ultimately depends on the performance of the individual security employee. That performance is measured by conduct as well as by specific job skills.

Standards of conduct for the security employee should emphasize basic *courtesy* toward fellow employees and others, even in the handling of transgressors; *responsibility* in carrying out duties; *fairness and objectivity,* respecting the rights of others; a spirit of *cooperation;* personal *integrity,* both on the job and in personal life; and a cheerful, positive *attitude.*

Security employees who exemplify these standards enhance the reputation and the effectiveness of the security function.

REVIEW QUESTIONS

1.   What can management do to foster feelings of self-worth among security employees?

2.   Explain the concept of due process.

3.   What would you include in your own "Standards of Conduct" for security employees?

II

SECURITY PERSONNEL MANAGEMENT

7

Hiring Security Personnel

Hiring new security employees is one of the most important functions and responsibilities of security management. This is true whether the employer is a proprietary security department or a security service company. The real magnitude of that responsibility is best appreciated in light of the old adage about sending a fox to guard the hen house. Hence, great care and attention is required to avoid hiring that fox. The standards of care and attention applied in hiring security applicants must far exceed those used for other applicants. The hiring standards in terms of effort, care, and attention must be higher for security applicants, and the very standards set for the applicant, as an individual, must be higher than for other employees.

An applicant should meet the following minimum standards, which apply to the lowest entry-level position, typically a uniformed security officer:

1. The security applicant must be free from any physical or emotional disorder or handicap that would preclude meeting predetermined performance standards. (Note the term "predetermined performance standards." Obviously there are those individuals who are physically handicapped or challenged that can perform adequately, if not more capably, in some security assignments. Assignments such as access control and alarm monitoring immediately come to mind.)
2. The security applicant must demonstrate responsibility, maturity, and honesty through a verifiable history of prior employment and/or pursuit of education.
3. The security applicant must not have a conviction of any crime involving moral turpitude.

Most states now license security officers. However, each state has set a standard, as it pertains to a criminal conviction, that is too low: Security officers must not have suffered a felony conviction. These low state standards suggest that anyone with a lesser conviction (misdemeanor or petty crime) is okay or is otherwise suitable for security employment and licensing. There are several reasons why this suggestion is mistaken:

1. Many felonious acts are intentionally reduced to misdemeanors to accommodate the judicial process.

2. Excluded evidence may result in the conviction of a lesser but included offense.
3. Many so-called misdemeanors would become felonious if not interrupted or intercepted (the perpetrator is caught or arrested).
4. The felony cut-off by licensing states is probably an arbitrary and expeditious solution to an awesome workload in a relatively high-volume, high-turnover industry being processed by an underfunded, short-handed state staff.

Moral turpitude, not the felony conviction, must be the standard in the security industry. *Moral turpitude* is best defined as any act characterized by a violation of trust or an act contrary to justice, honesty, or good morals. Answer the following questions:

- Would you hire a man convicted of indecent exposure (an exhibitionist) to work as a security guard in a summer camp for girls? That offense is not a felony. It's only a misdemeanor!
- Would you hire a woman convicted of shoplifting a blouse from a department store as a store detective? That offense is not a felony. It's only a misdemeanor!
- Would you hire a man convicted of filing a false crime report as a security employee? Such falsification is not a felony!
- Would you hire a person convicted of a misdemeanor—involuntary manslaughter committed while driving intoxicated—with two other convictions for drunk driving? Would you hire him or her as a security driver of an armored truck? No felonies here!
- Would you hire a hospital security officer who has been convicted of peeking in bedroom windows at night, a "Peeping Tom"? That's a misdemeanor!
- Would you hire a man or woman convicted of possession of and smoking marijuana, a misdemeanor, as a security officer for the university?
- Would you hire a man caught and convicted of fondling another man's private parts in a public toilet—a misdemeanor—and place him in a position of trust to safeguard highly valuable proprietary data?

I considered including in this work excerpts from *Security Letter Source Book*[1] reflecting state-by-state licensing requirements for uniform security officers but concluded it serves no useful purpose here because, in my view, the various states license more for revenue than for screening and qualifying candidates.

The security industry has a grave responsibility to those it serves. It must set higher standards than state licensing bodies. After all, it is the

---

[1] McCrie, Robert D. *Security Letter Source Book.* (Newton, MA: Butterworth-Heinemann, 1993).

employer who ultimately is accountable for its service and the employees who provide that service—not the state! What if a given employer has no security executive or policy or program with respect to hiring security employees? They exist. Indeed, I personally know of one state's Department of Education that had no security executive to establish and monitor policies regarding hiring security officers for their statewide school system. Each school, independently and unilaterally, could hire whomever they pleased without a background investigation. One school hired a security aide who had served prison time for sexually molesting a school-aged child. Within weeks after being hired as a security employee for a high school he removed a student from campus and sexually assaulted her. That state agency failed its responsibility to ensure the safety and security of its students! As a consequence of that failure the state was successfully sued.

How we avoid placing the fox by the chicken coop is amplified later in this chapter in the section on conducting background investigations of applicants. We must not only be concerned about the negative aspects of hiring the unsuitable or undesirable candidate, but we must also want to create a hiring process that will help find people who are intelligent and well groomed, who have a sense of purpose and well-being, who are motivated to achieve, and who, by their membership in the department, will help establish a reputation of quality service.

HIRING

Hiring is a step-by-step process that eventually leads to the applicant's acceptance of a job offer. These steps are as follows:

- Recruiting
- Initial interviewing
- Secondary interviewing
- Selection of best candidate
- Background investigation of applicant
- Job offer

Recruiting

Entry- or First-Level Positions

A direct approach in advertising an existing vacancy is usually desirable. This openness can include information such as company name, the fact that it is an equal opportunity employer, location of job, uniform benefits (or requirements), starting salary, minimum requirements, and the fact that the position is an entry-level job. As a rule the Human Resources Department of the company administers the recruiting activity; however, they look to the individual managers for direction. Within the limitations of company policy, the Human Resources Department strives to meet the manager's wishes. Policy restrictions such as "No salary quotations in newspaper advertising" would obviously have an impact, although not an adverse one, on the degree of openness in advertising.

The issue of advertising salary is quite controversial. The salary question must be answered at some point, and it will indeed be a factor in the applicant's decision. Just as the company is in the market for new employees, the applicant is shopping for a new employer. Based on certain data available in the newspaper ad (or whatever the medium may be), the applicant selects prospective employers. How many used automobile advertisements in the newspaper go unanswered because the seller withheld the price of the car?

In addition to newspaper ads, entry-level security applicants may be solicited by posting announcements on bulletin boards in the security administration or criminal justice departments of local community colleges. If a college does not have a security or criminal justice program, the opening may be posted with the school's placement office. College students constitute a great reservoir of manpower for entry-level positions—sometimes with, but more frequently without, career intentions. They are quick to learn and are usually willing to work those shifts or hours considered least desirable.

Nonentry-Level Recruiting

The recruiting approach for skilled, technical, and managerial personnel is different from that for entry-level positions. Rather than the direct, open approach, the "blind ad" technique is recommended. Such advertisements are designed to attract career or professional people. Advertisements must appeal to and solicit their specific talents; for example, the copy might read, "Major banking firm's Security Department accepting applications for position of Fraud Investigator. Applicants must have minimum five years' credit fraud and/or forgery investigative experience."

Some candidates reading such an ad will say to themselves, "That's me. I qualify." If they are in the market for a change or a new job, they will respond. The blind ad is simply one in which the company's identity is not revealed. Instead, interested parties are directed to submit their resumes to a post office box number or to some other third party.

The unidentified advertisement permits the company to prescreen candidates and interview on a highly selective basis. It also allows some time for at least a preliminary background investigation into the candidate's qualifications before the initial interview. This is the key to the two opposing types of recruiting techniques. The entry-level positions require rather broad, general qualifications that are possessed by a greater segment of the labor market. Such applicants select their employers. In the advanced positions in the department, on the other hand, the company is seeking specific candidates with specific skills. The organization knows exactly what it wants, and it will select the future employee.

Finally, skilled, technical, or managerial candidates will be filling far more sensitive positions in the security organization than will entry-level candidates. For this reason, far greater care must be exercised in the selection of advanced candidates.

Initial Interviewing

An applicant's first contact with the company should be with the Human Resources (Personnel) Department. Even though the applicant has submitted a resume of background and experience, the application for employment with the company should be formalized and documented by the completion of the company's standard job application form.

Every applicant's first interview should be with a professional human resource interviewer who will review the data on the application, making any corrections and clarifications as appropriate. This initial personnel interview is not for the purpose of selection or making an employment decision. Rather, it is an official preliminary, preparing the applicant for the coming interview with the security representative.

The applicant is then escorted or sent to the Security Department with the employment application, preferably sealed, for the real job interview. (Many applicants look on the personnel interview as a nuisance and are anxious to talk to the person they believe has the authority to make a hiring decision—the security official.)

Following the interview, the security representative will make notes on the reverse side of the application form concerning the impressions he or she has made. The security interviewer must, however, be properly trained in those laws specifically pertaining to hiring practices, both at the federal and state level, that prohibit discrimination against applicants based on sex, age, race, or creed. For example, the notation on a female candidate's application that "mother-in-law baby-sits" could be construed as gender discrimination should the applicant not get the job. (Would the interviewer ask a male applicant if he would have trouble getting to work because of baby-sitting problems?)

The question of discrimination becomes particularly important when an applicant is rejected. Any subsequent claims of discrimination in hiring practices will then be processed and administered by the Human Resources Department. It is the Human Resources Department that has the expertise and resources to handle such problems efficiently, not the Security Department. For this reason, it is ill advised to bypass the Human Resources Department and talk privately to possible candidates about employment opportunities.

The Interview

The purpose of the interview is for the interviewer to determine if there is a match between the interests and qualifications of the applicant and the needs of the department. This can only be achieved on a personal, one-on-one basis.

Before the commencement of the interview, the interviewer should study the written application in private. It is disconcerting for the applicant to sit in silence watching the interviewer pore over the application. Likewise the interviewer will find it difficult to concentrate on the application with the applicant staring at him or her. As the interviewer reviews the application, he or she should make a mental note of two or three highlights that will be explored in some depth during the interview. Throughout the questioning, the interviewer should feel free to refer to the application but should not make the too frequent error of repeating to the applicant the same data presented on the application.

For example:

Interviewer: I see that you worked for Mason Glass Works for three years as an investigator.

Applicant: Yes, sir.

Such an exchange does nothing to help determine whether the applicant offers the qualifications desired. It is better to give the applicant a chance to provide that information in his or her own words. For example:

Interviewer: Tell me a little about your experience at Mason Glass Works.

Applicant: Okay. I joined them as a trainee when I graduated from State U, on a special projects assignment . . . mostly compiling statistics for department manpower and budget projections. Six months later an investigator position came up and I got the promotion. I was assigned to background investigations while I was there.

This exchanging gives the interviewer some meaningful information to consider and explore further. For example, the next question might ask the applicant how much time it took to complete a typical background check. Put another way, one should question the answers.

The Seven Interviewing Rules

Rule #1: Ask open-ended questions that cannot be answered with a yes or no.

Rule #2: Probe the answers.

Rule #3: Do not signal the answers you are looking for in your question.

Here's an example regarding the #3 rule: The question "Did you ever have to fill in for a supervisor and have people report to you?" is a signal to the applicant that the interviewer considers some supervisory experience very important. Naturally, the applicant will tell the interviewer what he or she wants to hear: "Oh, yes, a number of times the Special Agent in Charge had to go out of town and I took over the Screening Section."

Rule #4: Ask motivator-type questions that tend to give the applicant a chance to provide revealing answers.

For example:

Interviewer: Think of a time while at Mason's when you really felt good . . . a time you consider a real highlight of your time there.

Applicant: I think the high point of my time there was when the section's Special Agent in Charge was obliged to return to the Midwest on a personal leave . . . death in the family and some estate problems . . . and I was appointed acting supervisor during his absence. To think the Director had that much confidence in me, well . . . I really felt good about that.

Now the interviewer can probe that answer with the question, "Why would the Director's expressing confidence in you make you feel so good?" Probably the reply would be something to the effect, "I'd worked hard and wanted more responsibility and the Director felt I could handle it."

The original motivator-type question has revealed the following: The applicant responds to recognition, is an achiever, and seeks increased responsibility. These are very important factors to look for in the recruiting process of the department.

Rule #5: Ask the applicant what he or she likes to do most on the job. Most applicants do not have a chance to even consider what they would like to do. It is often surprising how wide a variety of talents and skills can surface in response to such a question.

Rule #6: Do not waste precious time "selling" your company or department. By the time the applicant gets there, he or she is convinced of the desirability of the job, although the applicant may have a few questions he or she would like answered.

Rule #7: At the conclusion of the interview, give the applicant a date that he or she can go by. For example, "I'd like to have you talk with my boss Friday afternoon." Or, "Our interviewing concludes on Friday. After that we will make our final selection. You can expect our decision no later than next Wednesday."

Most applicants are keyed-up and nervous before and during the early stages of the interview. In the security profession, which includes interrogation responsibilities, these factors make applicants emotionally vulnerable to the experienced supervisor or manager. As the level of professionalism in security rises, it is to be hoped that all employment interviews will be handled in a sensitive and empathetic fashion.

Secondary Interviewing

The primary or initial interviewer in the Security Department is the person who will be the new employee's supervisor. If this supervisor has meaningful responsibility in his or her assignment, and if he or she is to conduct meaningful employment interviews, then the supervisor should make the selection. Why, then, should there be a secondary interview?

The secondary interview should essentially be a consultative arrangement between supervisor and manager. The supervisor should understand that he or she will decide whom he or she wants out of all the applicants. However, management must provide a climate wherein the supervisor not only wants to extend the courtesy of having this selected applicant meet the manager but also sincerely wants the input, opinion, and concurrence of his or her superior. Admittedly, this is a fine balance. However, if the climate is right, the manager can actually reject an applicant with the supervisor's total concurrence and support.

Ideally, the arrangement should go something like this:

Supervisor: Out of six applicants I found a guy I really like and think he'll do the job. Before I go back to Human Resources, I'd like the benefit of your thinking. I think you'll agree, but who knows, maybe you'll see something I missed. Can you talk to him?

Manager (following the secondary interview): Your candidate has very impressive credentials and I think you made a good choice.

Or:

Manager: Your applicant has impressive credentials and I believe he'll be a good man. But did you realize the guy is quite inflexible in terms of transfers or promotions out of town due to his mother's health and her dependence on him? How would his inflexibility affect you?

If the information about the dependent mother strikes the supervisor as news, the supervisor might very well reconsider the selection. On the other hand, the supervisor might decide to hire the applicant anyway and modify the developmental strategy for the applicant somewhat, knowing his restrictions are probably of relatively short duration. The point is that the purpose of the secondary interview is to confirm the interviewer's choice and/or to apprise the interviewer of additional data to consider. This is not to say that the secondary interviewer should be powerless to override the other interviewer's choice, because under some unusual circumstances such authority may very well have to be exercised.

The secondary interviewer may also be instrumental in selecting one of two good candidates. This happens when the interviewer has narrowed the field down to two and cannot decide which one is preferred.

Selection of Best Candidate

If the interviewer understands the job function for which he or she is recruiting and knows precisely what job qualifications are necessary (in terms of acquired skills, experience, education, and temperament and personality) and if the interview is conducted in an objective manner, then one candidate should stand above the rest. The goal is one of objectivity; the problem is subjectivity. Too frequently the best candidate is not selected because of bias on the part of the interviewer. This is not the proper textbook to delve into the problems of personal bias, but it is important to observe that the professional manager must recognize that personal bias exists and tends to distort decisions. Overcoming such bias can be an exciting challenge.

To discipline oneself in the interviewing and selection process to look for the candidates with the best qualifications, regardless of their color, age, sex, hair style, complexion, weight, shoe size, and so forth, will assuredly contribute to the selection of the best candidate.

Background Investigation of Applicant

The purpose here is to emphasize how critical the screening effort is in selecting security applicants. The management team that fails to turn over every reasonable stone in clearing a candidate reflects a negligent if not derelict staff. The key word in that statement is *reasonable.* To subject one security applicant to a thorough neighborhood check may be a reasonable way to expose a reputation of excessive drinking, child neglect, or other unsavory personal habits, but with another applicant that same strategy may not be deemed necessary or reasonable. Before we review the various screening strategies, let us first look at what we are obliged to accomplish in this background investigation/screening process. We should, if at all possible, satisfy ourselves with the answers to the following questions:

1. Is the applicant really who he or she says he or she is?
2. Does the applicant really have the work experience that is claimed? For the length of time that he or she claims?
3. Does the applicant have the education that is claimed?
4. Does the applicant possess the skills that are claimed?
5. Is the applicant financially stable or does he or she have a history of credit problems?

6.   Is the applicant's apparent good character genuine or does he or she have a criminal history?

7.   What kind of reputation did the applicant have on prior jobs or in his or her neighborhood?

How does the Security Department (or security service company) reasonably satisfy themselves that they have the answers? They do this by a combination of the following:

1.   Careful examination of the applicant's application for employment, looking for unanswered questions, erased answers, answers that were struck out or otherwise changed, gaps in the history of employment, and answers or statements that demand explanation, for example, "Have you ever been convicted of any crime other than a minor traffic offense?" *Answer:* "Yes." Or, "Reason for leaving job." *Answer:* "Quit" or "Terminated." A simple, inexpensive, intelligent, and direct way to gather information is by asking the candidate questions and asking for explanations. The answers could very well disqualify an applicant right then and there or provide direction for a subsequent investigation that could disqualify an unacceptable (below standards) applicant.

2.   Telephone calls to former employers to verify dates of employment, reason for leaving, reputation, type of work, salary, and rehireability. There are those skeptics who will say former employers won't divulge information over the phone, and in some cases that's true, but the skilled and professional investigator more often than not can obtain some of the desired information.

3.   Computerized or manual referencing to negative databases in compliance with the Fair Credit Reporting Act, for example, the United States Mutual Association (USMA) (see Chapter 23); Equifax, Experian, or Trans Union for credit data; or other various Internet online services.

4.   Neighborhood checks, that is, actually going to the immediate neighborhood and talking to local residents.

5.   Checks of local and/or state criminal records that are legally available, including court records.

6.   Requiring applicants to take the so-called paper and pencil tests, which are essentially psychological survey instruments that have the capability of identifying attitudes that suggest that the applicant is unsuitable for employment.

7.   If time permits, written communication to former employers, schools, training centers, and so forth, seeking verification of information claimed on the application.

8.   If military service is claimed, requiring evidence of such service by way of documentation, for example, DD Form 214 or discharge form.

The enlightened security administrator is fully cognizant of the fact that security employees, like police officers, are expected to serve and perform in a manner above reproach. Like officers in the public sector, if the security officer in the private sector is discovered in any form of misconduct or criminal behavior, that's deemed reprehensible! It is all the more reprehensible if that propensity for misconduct was open to discovery, but due to mismanagement it was not sought! That kind of managerial/operational failure is precisely what "negligent hiring" civil lawsuits are all about.

Job Offer

Once the applicant has been chosen and screening is completed, we have come full circle—back to the Human Resources Department. The selected candidate's application and the interviewer's comments are reviewed by the Human Resources representative and interviewer. The salary and starting date are agreed on and the matter is then left in Human Resources' hands. They will make the job offer. If for any reason there is a problem with the starting date or salary, the representative will serve as the intermediary until the matter is resolved. This is an important service that shields the Security Department from what can be a disagreeable or unpleasant dialogue.

SUMMARY

An organization is people, and the performance of the Security Department will benefit from care and attention to personnel selection.

Recruiting activity will be adapted to the job level, with open ads recommended for entry-level positions. Blind ads, followed by more detailed screening, will be used for higher level positions.

Interviewing is the heart of personnel selection. After the initial screening by the Human Resources Department, the primary interview should be conducted by the supervisor for whom the selected candidate will work. Questions should require meaningful answers (not signaled in the question) and should be designed to allow the candidate to reveal as much of himself or herself as possible. A secondary interview by the Security Manager is advisable, not to overrule the supervisor but advisory in nature.

If the interviewing process is based on clear knowledge of the job function and the qualities necessary for its performance, the selection of the right candidate is often expedited. Above all, that selection must be based on objective, not subjective, criteria.

Background investigation and screening before the final job offer is critical because of the responsible and sensitive role played by the security officer.

REVIEW QUESTIONS

1. What are the six steps in the hiring process?

2. Name the seven interviewing rules.

3. Besides newspaper advertising, what is another method of soliciting applicants for entry-level positions?

4. Discuss the differences in the approach to recruiting for a nonentry-level position versus an entry-level position.

5. What does "sending a fox to guard the hen house" mean?

6. Name three ways to "screen" or otherwise verify an applicant's background.

8

Job Descriptions

The very underpinnings of the Security Department's organizational structure are the job descriptions. Indeed, Newman and Warren,[1] in their discussion on clarifying job specifications, state "If an organization is *designed properly,* we have a series of job descriptions." There is a direct relationship between the strength and effectiveness of an organization and the quality of job descriptions. Quality here can be defined in terms of:

- Accuracy in and completeness of describing each job classification in the department
- The matching of applicants/candidates to the job description
- The individual employee's understanding of the department expectations, as expressed in the job description
- The department's ability to design its training efforts to support the job descriptions, or, put another way, to match the training to the job descriptions
- Performance evaluations based on the job descriptions
- Job descriptions that currently reflect those tasks necessary for the larger organization (i.e., the Security Department) to achieve its stated objectives

Thus the job description has life; it is a living, viable document that dictates success or, conversely in its absence, that allows a climate of confusion, shoddy work practices, vague and subjective performance evaluations, and organizational disharmony. Believe it or not!

Let's analyze the quality factors listed previously.

ACCURACY AND COMPLETENESS IN DESCRIBING THE JOB

An accurate and complete definition should leave no questions as to the nature of the work and the expectations of management. Compare the following undesirable and desirable job descriptions first for a background investigator.

---

[1] *The Process of Management,* 4th ed. (New York: Prentice-Hall, 1977).

Undesirable

"The background investigator is responsible for those activities that either disprove or validate the information submitted by an applicant for employment."

Desirable

"The background investigator's responsibility is to validate the truthfulness of an applicant's statements, and to determine his or her suitability for employment, which would include:

1. Confirming previous positions by contacting former employers, supervisors, or personnel executives. Such contact would verify dates of employment, reason for termination (if available), general evaluation of applicant, and whether or not the applicant would be considered rehireable
2. Conducting personal interviews with the applicant's neighbors, landlord, and so forth to determine the general reputation in his or her social setting
3. Conducting a credit check to ensure the applicant is financially responsible
4. Conducting a search of Department of Motor Vehicle records to determine the applicant's accident or citation history, if any
5. Conducting a search of those available court and/or criminal records that could reflect former criminal activities that the applicant denies"

MATCHING APPLICANT TO THE JOB

Once we have an accurate and complete description of the assignment, we should be able to identify those qualifications necessary or desirable to discharge the task. Those qualifications then become the hiring criteria or standards for that job. If the department has 10 such positions, then all 10 employees have at least a "floor" of similar minimum qualifications. Furthermore, the Human Resources Department, which frequently does the initial recruiting and screening of applicants, has clear goals in terms of what the Security Department is looking for in a given position.

Undesirable

1. No qualifications are listed in the job description.
2. Vague or overgeneralized qualifications, for example: "Applicants must possess a degree from an accredited college or university and three

years' comparable experience." Degree in what? If the job description is for background investigation, would a degree in astronomy be suitable? What's comparable experience?

Desirable

1. "Applicants must have a baccalaureate degree in Security Administration, Criminal Justice, Administration of Justice, Law, Accounting, or a degree in some relatively comparable discipline in which research and investigation is the primary thrust of the career for which it is designed."
2. "Applicants must have a minimum of three years' investigative experience. Experience in personnel administration may be substituted on the basis of two to one for two of the three investigative years of experience for this position in background investigations. Experience in credit reporting may be substituted on a one-for-one basis as long as the candidate meets the educational requirements."

EMPLOYEE'S UNDERSTANDING OF THE JOB

Many times I have discovered employees who didn't even know what a job description was! Just imagine the difference in a given employee's attitude as well as in performance if presented with the description of the company's expectations for performance (as spelled out previously, for example, in the detailed duties of the background investigator).

One of the great pities in organizations is the gap between line performance and management's expectations. The pity is the gap itself—the employee's perceptions of management's expectations are different from what, in fact, management expects! This is not confined to the lowest level of the organization; that gap can, and does in many organizations, go all the way up to middle and senior management.

Here's the test of tests: If the organization has not been keen on or sensitive to the importance of job descriptions, have employees in a given job classification write out what they believe management expects of them in their job. At the same time, have the supervisor write down what he or she expects of those subordinates—in detail. More often than not, there will be just on paper a wide variance of perceptions. Is there any question then that performance variances exist? This results in recriminations, fault-finding, resentment toward management for not recognizing good performance (when management doesn't see that "good" performance as truly good), and so forth.

MATCHING TRAINING TO JOB DESCRIPTION

More security organizations than ever before are engaged in their own training of staff. Earlier, much training was so-called *on-the-job training*, which
was usually sketchy at best (see more on training in Chapter 9).

Even where we find in-house or proprietary security training, there's a
tendency to approach it generically. In other words, all investigators are
trained in the art of interviewing and interrogations, but the finite application is missing. Certainly all investigators (e.g., fraud specialists, forgery specialists, dishonest employee investigators, freight claims investigators, "due
diligence" investigators) need training and retraining on interviewing. What
about applying the principles of interviewing, as an example, to the specifics
of a given investigator's daily work? More specifically, there should be a
special interviewing workshop for background investigators, in which they
role-play gathering information from a landlord or a neighbor—this really
makes the training activity productively meaningful. After all, gaining the
confidence of and encouraging an applicant's neighbor to share information
is quite different from interviewing an employee who witnessed another
employee roll a company forklift.

The Security Training Officer, or outside training firm working with the
security executive, should build the programs on and around the department's job descriptions. It only makes sense.

PERFORMANCE EVALUATIONS BASED ON JOB DESCRIPTIONS

An employee's performance and management's reaction to that performance, that is, disciplinary action if substandard or rewards (including
promotions) if outstanding, have their roots in the job description (or at
least should have).

Example: Harry is assigned to the Background/Screening Detail as an
investigator. He doesn't think that job is as exciting as others and when not
pressed with his own work he has slipped off and climbed into the parking
lot tower apprehending several teenagers for stripping parts from cars and
pilfering their contents. As laudable as those arrests are, Harry cannot be
rewarded for that action because it *wasn't his job,* either by assignment or
by job description. Every employee has to be held accountable for his or her
performance per the job description. Otherwise chaos creeps in.

Another example: Joelle conducted a background investigation on a
prospective manager and reported that there was no derogatory information
that would preclude his appointment. Within weeks that new manager is
identified, confidentially, as having a serious drinking problem. A general
assignment investigator is charged with a reassessment of this manager. Part
of his investigation includes a personal check of the neighborhood, in which
he confirms that the manager is known as a local lush and in which one

neighbor points out the manager's trash barrel area that's littered with vodka bottles. A reexamination of Joelle's investigation reveals no reference to a neighborhood check. Joelle is asked about the check by her supervisor. She replies she didn't think that a neighborhood check was important, that neighborhood checks had never really uncovered anything important in the past, and that she had thought it would be a waste of time.

In this case, Joelle's work is substandard. Now the company has an executive who's a problem and the Security Department failed in its responsibility to screen out these kinds of potential problems. Irrespective of Joelle's opinion, the job description clearly spells out what the duties of the background investigator are. It's there in black and white. There's nothing vague about expectations here. Joelle failed to perform according to management's expectations and she's culpable.

If Joelle had indeed made the neighborhood check and missed securing the information, it would be an entirely different story.

JOB DESCRIPTIONS ARE CURRENT

If job descriptions are living, viable underpinnings of organizational performance and success (and they are), then they must be tended to and cared for—watered and fed if you please—so that they reflect the present and current organization:

- If a security clerical is now responsible for a new word processor and computer, is that reflected in the job description?
- If credit fraud investigators now inquire directly into credit files by use of computerized cathode-ray tubes (CRTs), is that included in their job descriptions?
- If the company has absorbed a smaller firm in the next state and the Loss Prevention Auditor is now required to visit that new site on a monthly basis, is that travel and out-of-state work referred to in the job description?

The only thing that is constant is change. Modern and progressive security departments are always operating on their tip-toes, that is, alert and sensitive to what's happening and what needs attention, including keeping job descriptions current.

Don't be misled by my emphasis on job descriptions. The importance and emphasis here deal with understanding, agreement, and excellence in performance. One could mistake this emphasis and compare it with the absurdities of organized labor's job descriptions in which a worker is limited strictly to one job category, so that a carpenter can't unscrew a burned-out light bulb and replace it with a new one, even if he or she is in the dark, because it's the electrician's job. In our industry we can change assignments overnight, or sooner, to meet the protection needs of our environment. The background investigator can and is temporarily assigned to surveillance of the parking lot, if the needs of the organization are met by that adjustment in assignments.

COMPOSITION OF THE JOB DESCRIPTION

Examination of most job descriptions reveal that they are composed of three basic elements: (1) functions, (2) responsibility and authority, and (3) relationships. This seems to be too restricting; it fails to depict the greatest possible dimension of the position. Probably the best job description would include the following:

- Objective of the position
- Dimension of the position
- Nature and scope of the position
    - Position in the organization
    - Mission and environment
    - Specific functions of the position
    - Subordinates' functions
    - Primary challenge of the position
    - Authority vested in the position
    - Relationships
    - Requisites
- Principal responsibilities

SAMPLE JOB DESCRIPTION

Let's apply the previous outline for a job description to an imaginary Captain of Security in an industrial complex.

JOB DESCRIPTION

Captain

Objective of the Position
To ensure the physical plant protection program of the Security Department is effective, functional, and properly managed.

Dimension of the Position
In personnel: Directly supervises five (5) sergeants and indirectly supervises twenty-eight (28) security officers.

Nature & Scope of the Position
Position in the organization: Reports to Assistant Director of Security, Physical Security Division. Directly supervises five (5) sergeants.
Mission and environment: Protection of company property, employees and their property, twenty-four (24) hours a day, 365 days a year, in a structured regimen, with emergency response capabilities.
Specific functions of the position: Selects, trains, schedules, and supervises the sergeants.

Reviews all security officer generated or related control documents, forms, logs, and reports.

- Coordinates corrective and/or maintenance follow-up activities identified by the security officers and their supervisors
- Analyzes physical protection strategies, assignments, and posts to ensure work is cost effective and necessary and recommends appropriate modifications and revisions when appropriate
- Develops training and communication programs for security officers to ensure staff is both knowledgeable and productive
- Guides, assists, monitors, and counsels the sergeants to ensure they're motivated, creative, and effective leaders of their subordinates

Subordinates' functions: Sergeants ensure the necessary security controls are in place and functioning at each facility through proper scheduling and inspection activity.

Primary challenge of the position: The primary challenge is ensuring that sufficient planning and training have adequately prepared the security staff to effectively respond to and deal with the unusual/emergency/crisis event at any hour at any facility, including but not limited to a major conflagration, bombing, earthquake, cyclone, or other natural disaster.

Authority vested in the position: Captain has the authority to deny access to the facility, deny removal of property, and conversely, if circumstances warrant, may allow both, contrary to procedure, if in his or her judgment the action is appropriate. The Captain may order evacuation of a facility, make arrests, and call for public protective service assistance as a remedial strategy but may not invite or solicit law enforcement investigative assistance.

Relationships: By virtue of high visibility of the Captain's role and broad range of responsibilities, he or she will invariably come in contact with any member of the total employee population, vendors, resources, job, applicants, business visitors and other guests, and local fire and police personnel. All such contracts will necessarily evolve around security-related problems, questions, or other security activities.

Requisites: Knowledge of:

- Alarm hardware and operations, including its logic
- Fire prevention suppression strategies
- Patrol procedures
- Company policies and procedures
- State-of-the-art in physical security devices and hardware
- Security training techniques and leadership skills

Experience: A minimum of three years' experience as a sergeant in this company, or a minimum of five years' experience as an industrial security supervisor whose duties and responsibilities included security and safety (including fire) training, evaluating performance, scheduling of subordinates, handling disciplinary problems, conducting facility surveys or inspections, and preparing written recommendations.

<u>Education:</u> Minimum of two years of college with at least one quarter of the credits in Security Administration/Management, Criminal Justice or Criminal Administration, or Industrial Safety, or any combination thereof.
<u>Principal Responsibilities</u>

1. Ensure that the company's four (4) facilities and facility occupants are adequately protected against harm or loss, twenty-four (24) hours a day, 365 days a year
2. Ensure that the entire physical plant protection program is effectively and efficiently supervised by the sergeants
3. Ensure that the sergeants are adequately trained and exercise good leadership skills in dealing with their subordinates
4. Ensure that each sergeant is sufficiently trained in and knowledgeable of appropriate response strategies to any emergency that could seriously threaten life on or the property of ABC, Inc.

SUMMARY

There exists an important relationship between an organization's performance and the various job descriptions that cover the assignments of that organization. Those job descriptions must accurately and completely describe the duties, provide for the matching of the candidate to the job, be understood by the employee, be the source of training for each job, be a key source in measuring performance, and reflect the current activities and responsibilities of each job.

REVIEW QUESTIONS

1. Why is a broad definition of a task undesirable?
2. How does a good job description fill the gap between an employee's performance and management's expectations?
3. Cite an example of a training program that could come directly from a job description.
4. Why is it important for job descriptions to be current?
5. What does "dimension of position" mean?

9

Training

Without question the primary contributor to poor job performance is inadequate training. Although the value and absolute necessity of sound training are extolled by all, training dollars seldom materialize. Other demands on the organization seem to push training activities down the list of priorities, and training—real, formalized training—is always going to happen tomorrow. No other single organizational function gets as much lip service as training.

SHORTCOMINGS OF TYPICAL "TRAINING"

Further complicating the dilemma of training is the fact that training means different things to different people; the function itself is misunderstood. The following story might serve as a typical example.

Harry X receives a phone call from a representative of the Personnel Department at Company B, where he was interviewed several days earlier. Harry X accepts the job offer. He is pleased and promptly calls his friends and relatives to tell them about his good fortune. He is to report to work on the following Monday.

When Monday morning comes, Harry X is up early. He has been anticipating this day, and he dresses to look his very best. He heads for work filled with excitement. As the Company B building comes into view, he starts to feel some nervousness and anxiety. The tension increases as he enters the Human Resources offices and is greeted by a somewhat impassive personnel employee who coldly directs him to complete more forms.

Harry is then herded into a "Training Room" with a number of other new and equally nervous employees, where they meet a "Training Officer" who either acts bored or is so enthusiastic that the new employees are skeptical. Each new employee is given a company booklet that is recited to them page by page as if no one can read. The booklet describes benefits, whom to call or what to do if one is ill, retirement programs, the history of the company, and major company rules.

This concludes phase one of Harry's "training." Of course, it is not training; it is orientation. Harry and his peers learned little and will retain less for three reasons: (1) they were not prepared for the presentation, (2) they were given too much information in too short a period of time, and (3) they cannot relate the material to their work.

Harry's state of mind at this point is becoming negative. What he is hearing goes in one ear and out the other. He wants to get to the job he was hired for. He wants to see the area he will be working in, and he wants to meet his supervisor and the people he will work with. However, these personnel and "training" people (training historically falls within the Human Resources pyramid) will not let him go.

Phase two of training is usually a tour of the facility. There is a welcoming address by the Vice President and a luncheon in the company cafeteria. By now Harry has made friends with another new employee, and they privately concur (with elbow nudges) in their negative reaction to every company representative to whom they have been exposed so far.

Finally Harry is directed to his new department and introduced to his supervisor, who, because he was not involved in the selection of Harry, eyes him coolly and suspiciously. Harry is disappointed, hurt, disgusted in part, and close to anger. Typically, the supervisor is very busy. He does make time for the new man up to a point: He calls in one of Harry's peers and charges him with showing Harry around. Thus concludes the first day of training.

The following day, Harry starts on-the-job training on the lobby desk with Frank. It is a good place to start Harry because Frank needs help; he is very busy because of the badge conversion. Frank is annoyed because he knows an inexperienced employee will only be a hindrance. He had asked for an experienced assistant. He makes it a point to let Harry know how he feels.

Harry stands by helplessly not knowing what to do or how to respond to questions and attempting to avoid criticism. Midway through the confusing and distressing day there is a lull. Frank finally decides to accept Harry and begins to confide in him. He tells Harry everything he does not like about the company, about the department, and about supervisors. He also passes on everything he learned (and he learned the same way Harry is now learning). He even advises Harry which company procedures (as Frank interprets them) are to be followed and which are to be ignored. The second day of training ends.

On the third day, Harry is assigned to the receiving docks to work with another officer because "the lobby desk is too busy."

New employee training resembles Harry's experience in far too many cases.

There are many conspicuous problems and lessons in the foregoing. Elaboration is unnecessary, with one exception: A very important and powerful lesson to be learned is that first impressions made on the employee on his or her first day in a new job have great impact. The new employee is disoriented, somewhat intimidated, nervous, self-conscious, and subconsciously crying out for a friend. The manager who recognizes and is sensitive to this can treat the newcomer in such a way as to quickly establish respect and loyalty that otherwise may not be developed.

TRAINING DEFINED

As stated earlier, the training function means different things to different people; it is widely misunderstood. Certainly there is a question of definition, and a typical dictionary definition (*Webster's New Collegiate Dictionary*) tells us little when it describes training in this manner:

> Training (*noun*): the act, process, or method of one that trains; the state of being trained; (*adjective*): that trains; used in or for training; as, a training ship for sailors.

Even aside from its obvious circularity, what does this dictionary explanation really explain? Is it any wonder there is confusion? A more valuable and useful definition might be the following:

> Training is an educational, informative, skill-development process that brings about anticipated performance through a change in comprehension and behavior.

Basically there are three things that management wants new employees to know. It is important for them to understand:

1. What management wants them to do
2. Why management wants them to do it
3. How management wants it done

There are two basic strategies to training: on-the-job training (OJT) and formal classroom training.

ON-THE-JOB TRAINING

OJT can be a totally unstructured, unplanned, ill-advised teaming-up of the new employee with whomever is available (as happened to Harry) or it can be a meaningful and informative process that adequately prepares the novice to perform satisfactorily in a relatively short period of time. The difference lies in properly structuring the experience and the careful selection of the trainer.

Structuring the OJT Experience

Structuring OJT means identifying what the new employee should know, determining how much time it will take to expose him or her to that information, and ensuring that the trainer indeed follows the plan detailing what is to be covered. Unquestionably the best way to do this is to develop a checklist, logically prioritized, that guides both the trainer and trainee through the program. To ensure compliance, the checklist should have the material to be covered spelled out, for example:

> #5 Review of facility occupant fire life safety instructions
> 90 minutes. Date Reviewed: _____ Trainer: _____ Initials of Trainee: _____

This checklist is turned in each day to the new hire's supervisor who can see what progress was made and what remains. At the end of that OJT training period, which may take anywhere from 16 to 40 hours, the supervisor signs off and dates the checklist, signifying that this initial phase of the training has been completed. That checklist is then made a part of the employee's training file.

The On-the-Job Trainer

A popular term used in the public sector for OJT trainers is field training officers (FTOs). In the private sector we can use that same title, and I will do so for the balance of this particular topic. FTO assignments must be coveted and sought after because of the prestige attached to that classification. Only the best security employees should be allowed to train their colleagues and they should receive a bonus or incentive pay. FTOs could be a rank between the line security officer and first supervisorial rank. If the FTO is a uniformed employee, a special uniform designation, such as a gold embroidered star on the sleeve just above the cuff, could visibly identify this employee as someone who is charged with training new employees. This adds dignity to the trainer as well as to the process. These FTOs must also be trained for their special duties as a trainer.[1]

FORMAL OR STRUCTURED TRAINING

Depending on the level or degree of complexity of any given security position, classroom instruction may be mandatory. Classroom settings could include lectures by experts or leaders in the field or professional trainers,

---

[1]Craighead, Geoff. *High-Rise Security and Fire Life Safety.* (Newton, MA: Butterworth-Heinemann, 1996), p. 224.

role-playing with video playback for assessment and analysis, training films, computerized interactive training programs to test judgment, and so forth. As in the documentation of OJT training, the curriculum of the training program and who taught what, when, and for how long must be properly documented and placed in the employee's training file.

Formal training should include the testing of trainees' understanding and comprehension of materials presented with required minimum scores. If such minimum scores are not attained, there must be more training and/or review with retesting and satisfactory scores. If a security trainee cannot pass the tests, even after all of the trainer's professional efforts, that trainee may have to be reclassified or downgraded to a less-sophisticated assignment. Test results are to be kept in the employee's training file and subject to inspection in the event of some subsequent event or problem, such as a lawsuit that alleges that security employees are inadequately trained.

POP FORMULA: POLICY, OBJECTIVE, PROCEDURE

Interestingly enough, that *what, why,* and *how* of training correlate to policy, objectives, and procedures. From this correlation, I have developed the POP formula as the basic building block for job training.

The area of the Why/Objective in Figure 9.1 deserves special attention. Too frequently the training process overlooks the necessity of informing employees why this should be done, why that should not be done, and so forth. When employees are informed as to the whys, their performance will improve. This point cannot be overstressed.

Incidentally, those who are familiar with the *who, what, where, how, why,* and *when* investigative formula may wonder what has happened to the *who, when,* and *where.* The *who* (the employee who is being trained) is obviously implied, and the *when* and *where,* in this context, are included in the *how.*

Now let us translate the POP formula into training for a specific job, such as Shoplifting Detective.

Reexamining the suggested definition, it will be seen that there are three aspects of training: education, information, and skill development. The

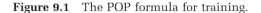

What Management Wants done	POLICY	Education	Employee knows what is expected.
Why Management Wants it done	OBJECTIVE	Information	Employee understands why he or she is doing this job.
How Management Wants it done	PROCEDURES	Training	Employee knows how it is to be done.

Figure 9.1   The POP formula for training.

example in Figure 9.2 makes it apparent that, of the three tiers of the formula, the How or Procedure tier addresses itself to *skill development,* whereas the other two tiers, Policy and Objective, are *educational* and *informative* in nature. It is not enough for the detective to know that management's policy is to arrest and prosecute every shoplifter. He or she must also understand the objectives that make this policy reasonable and necessary and must thoroughly grasp the various procedures essential for the detective's own execution of responsibilities. The proper combination of education, information, and skill development round out and give substance and definition to training.

	COMPANY PROGRAM	EMPLOYEE FUNCTION
POLICY (What Management Wants Done)	Arrest and prosecute every shoplifter.	Has been hired by the company to specifically detect and apprehend shoplifters.
OBJECTIVE (Why Management Wants It Done)	Reduce shoplifting losses Deter others by example of arrests. Punish or discourage offenders.	• Helps to reduce losses caused by shoplifting. • Deters others from shoplifting. • Helps to punish offenders through the criminal justice system.
PROCEDURE (How Management Wants It Done)	Lawful gathering of the necessary evidence to justify arrest and support prosecution of shoplifters.	• Sees customer approach merchandise. • Sees customer select merchandise. • Sees secretion of merchandise. • Sees that no payment is made. • Sees removal of merchandise from store. • Approaches customer and says, "Excuse me," etc. • Carries out arrest with justification. • Makes written report of incident, etc.

Figure 9.2   The POP formula for Shoplifting Detective training.

Detailed Expansion of Procedure

Although each tier of the training formula is important and interrelates with the others, the Procedure tier will receive, by far, the most attention. Consider another job classification, that of Lobby Desk Officer (Figure 9.3). Management's policy of controlling access and unauthorized removal of equipment, materials, or supplies and its twin objectives of preventing trespassing and theft are quickly grasped. What remains, for the new employee, is the question of how to carry out this assignment—how to do the How. Once on this track, the skill development process of training is well on its way.

Consider, for example, just one of the procedural steps:

Confirms visitors by telephone, issues visitor badge, and awaits escort.

How should this be done? The following might be one acceptable procedure:

	COMPANY PROGRAM	EMPLOYEE FUNCTION
POLICY (**What Management Wants Done**)	Control entry and egress of all persons to the facility.	Ensures that no person shall enter the facility without an authorized badge. Ensures that no equipment, materials or supplies may leave the facility without authorization.
OBJECTIVE (**Why Management Wants It Done**)	Prevent losses from theft. Prevent trespassing. Safeguard persons and company assets.	• Helps to reduce losses from theft. • Helps to prevent unauthorized access to the facility for malicious purposes (bombing, vandalism, theft of information, etc.) • Helps to make facility safer for personnel.
PROCEDURE (**How Management Wants It Done**)	Implementing access control program (employee and visitor badging, sign-in registers, package inspection, etc.).	• Permits entry after exhibition of authorized badge. • Refers lost or forgotten badge cases to personnel. • Prior to 6:30 AM and after 6:30 PM requires signature on registry before permitting access to facility. • Confirms visitors by telephone, issues visitor badge, and awaits escort. • Inspects all containers not displaying "Security Parcel OK" slip, etc.

Figure 9.3   The POP formula for Lobby Desk Officer training.

1.   Request visitor to complete Visitor Card, form S647.
2.   Use company directory to call employee whom visitor states he or she wishes to see.
3.   If employee wishes to see visitor, request that employee come to desk to escort visitor.
4.   Issue yellow visitor badge to visitor and record badge number on visitor's completed Visitor Card.
5.   Place Visitor Card in Visitor Aboard Box.
6.   Invite visitor, by name as indicated on Visitor Card (e.g., Mr. Jones), to have a seat until the escort arrives.

The detailed expansion of procedures, or the "How-to-Do-the-How," will be the primary thrust of the training efforts. It is, nevertheless, only a part of the whole—a large part, granted, but still a part.

TRAINING AS ONGOING RESPONSIBILITY

Up to this point we have been discussing individualized and specific job description training. As critical as this type of training is, it is only part of the entire training picture. The training function within the security organization should be continuous and ongoing. Ideally, training should be under the direction of a Training Officer (as opposed to an FTO) whose sole responsibility is security training.

The last person who should be placed in the Security Training Officer function would be a security officer. To ensure total training objectivity, an experienced trainer, a professional trainer, or a bright college graduate with an academic background in personnel, communications, or teaching should be hired and charged with the responsibility of coordinating and administering the training program in the Security Department. Such a person approaches the job without preconceived notions, without bias, and without an "expert's" point of view. Rather, he or she goes about assignment after assignment with wide-eyed, unabashed curiosity and amazement (which tends to be contagious), learning as he or she goes and seeing many things that the experienced security officer does not see. Such people make outstanding Training Officers.

Note that this opinion differs from my recommendation in Chapter 3 on the conduct of training sessions on security for the general employee. In such sessions, only the security employee can speak with authority about the security function.

TYPES OF SECURITY TRAINING PROGRAMS

Following is a list of types of training programs that security management could provide the department's employees.

In-Service General Seminars

General seminars are usually most effective if conducted by employee classification; for example, all patrol and uniformed personnel or all fraud investigators. So-called general programs are a potpourri of subjects that are important and meaningful to the group. One side effect of these sessions, which could be from 1 to 3 days in duration, is the motivational aspect, which should be capitalized on in the agenda. Following is a typical agenda:

9:00–9:30	Welcome and Introduction	*Security Director*
9:30–10:15	Organizational Overview (transparencies and handouts)	*Security Manager*
10:15–10:30	Break	
10:30–12:30	Interpersonal Communications (from outside the department)	*Manager, Public Relations*
12:30–1:15	Lunch	
1:15–2:00	Do's and Don'ts in Handling Company Employees	*Training Officer*
2:00–3:30	Report Writing (work sheets and handouts)	*Chief Investigator*

3:30–3:45	Break	
3:45–4:30	Training Manual Update (revised pages)	*Security Manager*
4:30–5:00	Open Question-and-Answer Period	*Staff*
5:00–5:45	Motivational Film	*Training Officer*

This outline illustrates how flexible a general seminar can be, depending on the objective. In this agenda, for example, the real or primary objective of the session might have been to introduce and explain a major organizational change for the Security Department. This objective was achieved in the morning session. Because people had to come from far and near, the balance of the day was then devoted to training.

Interrogation Workshop

Interrogation workshops are a half- to full-day session of principles and techniques of interrogation with role-playing and, ideally, video playback of role-playing.

Testifying in Court Seminar

Testifying seminars are a half- to full-day program that includes preparation of evidence, dress, demeanor on the witness stand, voice, where to look, "traps," stress, and attitude.

Report Writing Workshop

A report writing workshop can vary from a 90-minute review to a full day on the principles to be followed in reducing events to paper.

Supervisory Training

Supervisory training ranges from 2-hour topic sessions to 3-day seminars. Topic session could be "How to Handle Disciplinary Problems," or "Management Styles, X, Y, or?"

MEETING ORGANIZATIONAL NEEDS

The types of training programs are limited only by organizational needs. Much material is available at local universities and community colleges, and security personnel should be encouraged to further their education at such institutions. Specific organizational needs, however, usually must be met through "in-house" education.

Organizational needs come down to people needs. The agenda of the general seminar discussed previously was in response to needs. Security management had a need to communicate the reasons for and details of a major reorganization. Security management also recognized the daily operating problems connected with poor interpersonal communication skills among security people and between nonsecurity people and security. Therefore a second need was addressed in the program. The remainder of the agenda was the result of a survey (made in advance by the Training Officer) of the employees' stated needs. Thus training objectives are identified and materials are designed to achieve those objectives. Too many training programs are the masterwork creations of training personnel or management, but they miss the mark of satisfying what employees want and need.

SECURITY MANUAL

A Security Manual or Handbook is an absolute essential, not only as an operational tool but also as a training guide, and it must be updated on a regular basis. Each page should reflect the month and year the material was originally written/created or updated. The subject matter should include pertinent company policies; departmental policies; job descriptions; emergency phone numbers; and a great many procedural instructions for specific incidents, such as a telephone bomb threat or a facility blackout. In some organizations the manual is deemed sacred and consequently most employees are not allowed to touch it—a foolish attitude. The manual should be put in the hands of all regular proprietary security personnel.

SUMMARY

Regrettably, oftentimes new employee training is little more than general orientation. The newcomer is usually unprepared for the presentation and is given too much information too fast, in a manner unrelated to the work that he or she will actually be doing. The typical orientation program, in which the employee is lumped with many others from various departments for a day and then thrown immediately into an assignment for OJT, is actually negative training. The employee learns the wrong way—or learns the wrong things—and develops undesirable attitudes.

Effective training is an educational, informative, and skill-development process. The basic building block for training can be summed up in the POP formula:

Policy   What management wants
Objective   Why management wants it
Procedure   How management wants it done

Although the importance of why something must be done cannot be overstressed, primary attention in training will be on the procedural, or skill-development, phase—learning "how to do the how."

Training should be an ongoing process, ideally in the hands of a professional Training Officer selected for qualities other than security experience. Types of training programs may include general seminars or seminars based on specifically identified organizational needs.

The Security Manual should embody the essentials of security responsibilities and should be in the hands of every employee.

REVIEW QUESTIONS

1. What is a useful definition of training?

2. What are the two basic ways to train a new employee?

3. What are the three basic things that management wants employees to know? How does the POP formula relate to these?

4. List four possible topics for security training seminars.

5. What should the contents of a Security Manual include?

10

Discipline

As a rule, the very word *discipline* evokes an emotional reaction on the part of employees at all levels of the organizational pyramid. Most supervisors and managers would rather do anything but discipline, and it is human nature to resist and resent punishment. This negativism surrounding a critically important organizational process is unnecessary and can easily be replaced with a positive approach, called "constructive discipline."

Before discussing constructive discipline, it is instructive to consider a number of dictionary definitions of the word *discipline:*

1. Training that corrects, molds, or perfects
2. Punishment
3. Control gained by obedience or training
4. Orderly conduct
5. A system of rules governing conduct or practice
6. To punish or penalize for the sake of discipline
7. To train or develop by instruction and exercise
8. To bring a group under control
9. To impose order upon

The majority of these explanations emphasize punishment or control, both of which are aspects of discipline. Only the first and seventh in this list call attention to the key aspect of constructive discipline. Training that develops disciplined conduct.

The word *discipline* is derived from the Latin *discipulus* ("learning"). The word *disciple* also comes from the same root; the early Christian disciples were considered "students" of Christ. The origin of the word suggests this important concept: Positive and constructive discipline is training that corrects, molds, or strengthens an employee in the interests of achieving departmental and company goals. Punishment, the factor that is feared and disliked by all, is secondary. Any punishment connected with discipline should always be a means to an end, and that end should be organizational, not personal.

Thus the effective disciplinary process, which condemns the wrongful act but not the employee, says "You're okay, but what you did is not okay." By focusing on conduct and performance rather than personalities, the whole process takes on a constructive dimension that is easy to handle and acceptable to all. Comprehension and subsequent application of this positive concept have helped many managers cope with their disciplinary problems.

It is also important that discipline be swift. The long-range effect of coming to grips with a problem immediately is better than putting off what probably will have to be faced later—irrespective of the nature of the problem, be it simple tardiness or a careless oversight. What could easily be corrected now may be far more difficult to correct later, because the real essence and secret of constructive discipline is its preventive nature. To train, mold, and correct in a timely fashion reduces the need for more difficult training, molding, and correction later.

THE SUPERVISOR'S ROLE IN DISCIPLINE

Discipline is a responsibility that rests squarely on the supervisor's shoulders. It cannot be passed on to a higher supervisor and should never be passed on to Personnel or the Human Resources Department. Some weak supervisors shirk their disciplinary responsibility out of fear that enforcing the regulations will hurt their relations with subordinates. Actually, most people prefer to work in a well-ordered environment. They really do not expect or necessarily want the supervisor to be too lenient all the time, because those who fail to exercise needed discipline and who will not say "no" or "don't" to those who deserve it can make the workload more difficult for everyone else and create an unleveled playing field.

The supervisor who is fair and consistent in the treatment of employees will gain rather than lose respect through being firm and expecting conformity to the rules. Once the proper atmosphere is created through constructive discipline, a request from the supervisor is considered an order. There is no need to be abrupt or overly forceful to get the job done, because employees will respect the supervisor who respects them.

Some make the mistake of believing that discipline is only directed at the inefficient worker. All employees require constructive discipline. There are times when disciplinary action is essential with an outstanding employee, usually because he or she and others have come to think that he or she is so good that he or she is indispensable. The supervisor should never lose respect or control of the organization by being afraid to lose a good employee.

The supervisor who understands the employees' psychological needs will generate less reactive hostility, and consequently experience less resistance, than the supervisor who approaches the employee with insensitivity and harsh tactics. An important key is to recognize the individual differences among employees, handle them on that basis to win their loyalty and support, and then motivate them to greater personal success. The benefit will be a significant reduction in disciplinary problems.

All disciplinary actions commence with an interview and discussion. If handled with sensitivity (which includes understanding the employee's psychological needs and treating him or her as an important individual), the interview can accomplish its basic purpose and at the same time actually serve to improve the personal relationship between the employee and supervisor. The employee frequently expects the worst. With many supervisors the employee leaves the interview feeling misunderstood, mistreated, hostile, guilty, or dejected. If the supervisor remembers that the basic purpose of discipline is correction and training, not punishment, he or she will take a positive approach in the interview. The approach will leave the employee with renewed confidence in himself or herself and in the supervisor and greater faith in and respect for the supervisor's good judgment and fairness.

DISCIPLINARY PROBLEMS ARISING FROM MISUNDERSTOOD ASSIGNMENTS

The following sign hangs in a number of supervisors' and managers' offices:

I KNOW YOU BELIEVE YOU UNDERSTOOD WHAT YOU THINK I SAID, BUT I AM NOT SURE YOU REALIZE THAT WHAT YOU HEARD IS NOT WHAT I MEANT.

The irony here is that the statement is an absolute indictment against the supervisor. When the subordinate has failed to do a task as assigned and the superior proudly directs the subordinate to read the sign, the supervisor obviously fails to recognize his or her responsibility to make each assignment clearly understood. The failure really rests with the supervisor, not the subordinate. Many disciplinary cases are the result of assignment failures. Most assignment failures have nothing to do with the employee's level of competence but rather with a misunderstanding of what was expected.

How many times has a supervisor stopped an employee, given instructions on what he or she wanted done, and then asked, "Do you understand?" The employee nods knowingly, but as soon as the supervisor walks away, the employee turns to a peer and asks, "Do you know what the supervisor wants?" The supervisor's first error is in asking the employee if he or she understands. Most employees will say yes rather than admit that they failed to grasp the instructions.

Other assignment errors include the following:

- Instructions may not have been given in a logical order or sequence.
- The person giving the instructions may have spoken indistinctly or failed to use clear language.
- Instructions may have been too complicated for one simple explanation.

There are occasions when an assignment is indeed understood and yet still not followed because of the manner in which the assignment was given. The ideal way to give an assignment is by a request rather than a demand. Asking an employee to do something makes the employee part of the picture and gives him or her more opportunity to make suggestions and to feel a responsibility to perform the assignment. Requests create a spirit of willingness to do the job.

Following are 10 suggestions to follow in giving assignments:

1. Know the assignment yourself.
2. Do not assign work above the employee's ability.
3. Explain the purpose of the assignment so that the employee understands why he or she is being asked to do it.
4. Request or suggest — do not demand. For example:
   a. "Would it be possible?"
   b. "Suppose we try it this way?"
   c. "Will you take care of . . .?"
5. Give brief, exact instructions with all of the necessary details but not too much to confuse.
6. Demonstrate if possible.
7. Do not assume the employee understands. Have him or her reiterate the instructions.
8. Do not watch every move; let the employee feel responsible.
9. Let the employee know you are there if he or she needs assistance.
10. Be certain these points have been covered:
    a. Who is to do it.
    b. What is to be done.
    c. Where it is to be done.
    d. When it is to be started and finished.
    e. How it is to be done.
    f. Why it is to be done.

Most employees want to do a good job. If care is taken in giving assignments, there will be fewer failures and fewer disciplinary problems resulting from failures.

BASIC RULES OF THE DISCIPLINARY PROCESS

There are six fundamental rules in the disciplinary process that have universal applicability.

Rule #1. Put rules in writing and make certain employees understand them. There should be no assumed rules. If a rule is worth having, it is worth writing down. Employees are entitled to know what the rules are if compliance is expected.

Many institutional rules are peculiar to the organization and therefore not of common knowledge, particularly to someone new to the organization. For example, take the situation of a security officer who forgot his or her badge and being new to the business borrows a badge from another new officer who is going off duty. Experienced personnel would appreciate the logic behind prohibiting an officer from wearing another officer's badge, but a newcomer might not understand. If the employee is to be held accountable he or she should know the ground rules. Many firms provide new employees with a copy of the rules and then have them sign a statement to that effect, which becomes part of their personnel file. This documents the fact that the employee knows and understands the rules. Other companies post rules in conspicuous areas such as employee locker rooms. I suggest doing both.

Not only is it morally wrong to take punitive action against an employee who was honestly ignorant of a given rule but it is an administrative or legal wrong that can be remedied by the courts, especially if the punitive action is termination. The company may be legally bound to reinstate a wrongfully discharged employee, with full wages for all time lost due to the discharge. Many companies have paid months of back wages under such circumstances.

In short, there must be no surprises in terms of company rules.

Rule #2. Discipline in the privacy of an office. To the employee, being corrected for deficiencies in conduct or performance is a sensitive and frequently embarrassing experience. To be corrected in the presence of others is considered degrading, and the end result of that approach is seething resentment and angry embarrassment—emotions that are counterproductive to the true disciplinary goal. In addition, the privacy afforded in an enclosed office permits the participants to hear each other clearly. It is extremely important for the supervisor to hear what the employee has to say and for the employee to hear what the supervisor is saying.

Rule #3. Be objective and consistent. As stated at the outset of this chapter, effective discipline condemns the act not the person. That approach is obviously objective; the issues are not, or at least should not be, personalities. The supervisor who refers to an employee as "dummy," who makes such statements as "Can't you get it through your thick skull . . . ," or who succumbs to personal likes and dislikes loses objectivity and consequently loses credibility and respect. Thus the supervisor is no longer practicing truly constructive discipline but returns to the negative approach of punishing people who fail to meet standards.

Inconsistency is equally deadly. If the policy of the department is to terminate officers who sleep on the job, then all officers so caught must be terminated. To fire one employee but not another breeds contempt for the management of the organization. Conversely, if the same rule is consistently enforced and acted on, genuine respect for the rules and the management follows.

Rule #4. Educate, do not humiliate. The concept here is to help not hurt an employee who has failed to meet standards of conduct or performance. If the disciplinary action truly corrects, trains, or molds the individual to meet standards, the employee comes away from the experience with better insight into himself or herself and what the company expects. The employee comes away educated. If he or she is berated and humiliated, the employee comes away angry and resentful and certainly destined to fail again, sometimes by design. Both the employee and the department suffer as a consequence.

Rule #5. Keep a file on all employee infractions. This is not to suggest that a negative dossier be maintained on each employee. Rather, documented incidents of past failures are a necessary and useful reference for repeated incidents. Compare, for example, the two following situations:

Supervisor: John, I've talked to you before about your uniform, and you're out of uniform again with those red socks.

John: You've never mentioned my socks before . . . when was that? (Supervisor recalls the incident only vaguely, and has no documentation of it.)

Supervisor: John, I've talked to you before about your uniform, and you're out of uniform again with those red socks. In fact, last February 15 we talked about different colored socks, and again on March 30 I talked to you about your shirt cuffs being turned up. Because this is the third time, I'm going to place a formalized written reprimand in your personnel jacket. You must understand that we insist on every officer dressing according to the uniform code. A uniform improperly worn lacks good taste and is a poor reflection on the organization as a whole. (The facts are obviously clear and available, and John cannot challenge those facts.)

The "file" this rule refers to is an informal record, maintained by the immediate supervisor for his or her personal reference. Dates of incidents may or may not end up as formal documentation in the Human Resources records depending on the employee.

Not only does the employee find it difficult to argue with these supervisorial records but so does any administrative hearing board that may someday sit in judgment over the company's more drastic disciplinary action against the employee.

Rule #6. Exercise discipline promptly. Consider again the situation of John and his uniform violation of wearing red socks when he is supposed to wear black. This time, the supervisor has delayed the corrective action.

Supervisor: John, I've talked to you before about your uniform, and last week you were out of uniform again by wearing red socks.

John: I don't recall wearing red socks last week. What day was that?

Supervisor: Well, I recall your wearing red socks, and it happened to be last Friday.

John: If I was wearing red socks they were a dark red and no one would ever know the difference.

Supervisor: They weren't dark red, they were bright red, and dark or bright doesn't make any difference. They were obviously and conspicuously red and not an authorized part of your uniform.

John: Did you see them yourself?

Supervisor: I did.

John: Well, then, why didn't you talk to me about them then if they were so bad?

Good question, John!

It should be apparent that with the passage of time (and distance) from the infraction, whatever magnitude it may have, the issue becomes vague and almost argumentative. If corrective action is appropriate, then it must be handled now or on as timely a basis as possible. It is like catching a child with a hand in the cookie jar. If prompt action follows the detection, the youngster can relate the consequences of the action to the act. If the child must wait until father gets home after work, it is harder for the child to make sense of the scolding or punishment. In addition, depending on the level of sophistication of the youngster (or adult), he or she will rationalize the incident to minimize its importance, and subsequent corrective action can appear unreasonable.

The same concept of the need for prompt action is most evident in dealing with such drastic behavior as theft. If you observe an employee steal and immediately take that employee into custody and commence the interrogation, the interrogator has all the advantages and will experience little in the way of resistance. If that employee is allowed to leave the site, however, and is not interrogated until the following morning, resistance and obstacles will surface, although the same act occurred. The difference is timing. Delays raise questions of credibility.

PROGRESSIVE DISCIPLINE

So-called progressive discipline is another methodology or strategy in addressing disciplinary problems. In the workplace, the purpose is to correct or improve performance or behavior. By it's very title, the process is progressive in nature, beginning with the least severe action necessary to correct the behavior and increasing in severity if the behavior is not corrected. In addition to being progressive, the degree of discipline must be related to the seriousness of the offense or failure as well as to the employee's past history.

The progressive steps may be as follows:

Oral counseling

Oral warning

Written warning

Written reprimand in lieu of suspension

Suspension without pay

Termination

Not all of the previously mentioned steps are required, but every step taken must be documented in detail and maintained in the employee's file. If a suspension is deemed appropriate, the offending employee should be given every opportunity to present his or her side of the incident before implementation of such a drastic action; that is, the employee should be allowed the opportunity for due process.

If company policy does not allow for suspensions without pay, that step may be substituted with two- or three-step written Final Warnings, typically 30 days apart.

Obviously, the basic rules of the disciplinary process already considered apply to progressive discipline too.

SELF-DISCIPLINE

No manager or supervisor can ever hope to discipline others effectively if he or she cannot discipline himself or herself. Disciplining oneself can be accomplished by controlling vanity, likes and dislikes, and negative thoughts and by always exercising humility. Self-discipline will lay a solid groundwork for working with other people and their failures and problems and for setting a climate in which self-discipline becomes contagious.

Self-Discipline and Vanity

The supervisor who misuses authority will evoke resentment instead of earning respect. Barking out commands may seem the quickest way to get the job done, but that technique is a vain self-indulgence that a manager of people cannot afford. Using power in this way is not leadership. Everyone knows the extent of the manager's power; it need not be displayed. Self-control over ego and vanity is sensed by subordinates, and in their own behavior they will respond in kind to that example of personal discipline.

Self-Discipline and Temper

Loss of temper may make a manager feel better for a while, but it will not improve leadership performance or reputation. It's simply a form of immature self-indulgence. If by chance and circumstance one loses control and does "fly off the handle," then be prepared to apologize to everyone who witnessed such a performance, and apologize with sincerity.

Self-Discipline and Arguments

Most arguments are useless. Discussions, not arguments, produce agreement and cooperation.

Self-Discipline and Personal Likes and Dislikes

Nothing creates a better atmosphere than friendly recognition of subordinates on an equal basis. Nothing creates trouble faster than the failure to control personal likes or dislikes or developing personal favorites (including outstanding employees) or exhibiting personal prejudices and dislikes. Real self-discipline is required of those in leadership positions with all personnel, irrespective of race, creed, gender, age, level of competence, or state of physical fitness or health. Objectivity and fairness are the watchwords.

Self-Discipline and Work Habits

Subordinates cannot be expected to discipline themselves in terms of good work habits if the example set by management is one of poor work habits. The manager must discipline himself or herself to be punctual, timely with assignments, thorough, orderly, and accurate knowing that subordinates notice far more than one might suspect. Supervisors truly live in glass houses on the job.

Self-Discipline and Humility

The effective manager should never hesitate to acknowledge his or her errors. The manager is not going to be right 100% of the time, and the rest of the organization knows it. He or she should not be embarrassed to say "I made a mistake" or "I don't know." Although it requires self-discipline, the manager should not be hesitant to ask others, including subordinates, for their opinions knowing that they may have some ideas better than his or hers.

SUMMARY

Discipline is training that corrects, molds, and strengthens an employee at all levels in the organization, in the interest of achieving departmental and company goals. Constructive discipline is positive, focusing on corrective action rather than on personalities; it focuses on the wrongful act, not the employee. Progressive discipline provides the offending employee with ample opportunity to improve.

In the security organization, discipline is primarily the responsibility of the supervisor. Effective discipline begins with effective communication and full understanding of what is required. Its purpose is corrective training, not punishment.

The basic rules of the disciplinary process are (1) put rules in writing, (2) discipline in privacy, (3) be objective and consistent, (4) do not humiliate the employee, (5) keep a record of infractions and disciplinary action, and (6) exercise discipline promptly.

Effective discipline will find its model in the Security Manager's own self-discipline and restraint.

REVIEW QUESTIONS

1. Define constructive discipline.
2. Give several possible reasons for misunderstood assignments.
3. Discuss the six basic rules of the disciplinary process.
4. Why is it a good idea to keep a file of employee infractions?

11

Motivation and Morale

The question of how to motivate employees to do more and better work and how to keep them happy and interested in their work remains a constant challenge to management, a project for researchers, and a thesis subject for academicians. What motivates one person may not motivate another. Motivators that are effective in one industry may be out of the question in another. For example, you cannot motivate a security officer to write more citations to win a free trip to Hawaii, but that type of motivation is used in real estate and other types of sales companies.

There is even disagreement over whether that free trip to Hawaii is in fact a motivator. Some management theorists argue that it is an inducement or a carrot on the end of a stick that keeps employees producing at levels predetermined by management. Others say, "Call it what you will, it gets the job done, and when the employee gets to Hawaii, his or her morale will be way up there." An opposing view holds that if you take away the carrot, fundamentally good people will produce at the same level and poor performers will still be poor performers (they never won the Hawaiian trip anyway). The latter position suggests that perhaps motivation is internalized as opposed to externalized; that is, motivation comes from within the person and not from without. If that is the case, is it really possible to motivate another?

"THEORY X" AND "THEORY Y"

Before we attempt to deal with that question and others about motivation, morale, and human behavior on the job, we should have some understanding and insight into classical studies. Although earlier studies originated some decades back, they are nonetheless valid today. For example, Douglas McGregor's Theory X and Theory Y comprise a number of pervasive assumptions about human nature and behavior. Three of these assumptions, which McGregor collects under what he calls *Theory X*, still have far too much acceptance in our society today[1]:

---

[1]Davis, Keith. *Human Relations at Work*, 3rd ed. (New York: McGraw-Hill, 1967).

1.   The average human being has an inherent dislike of work and will avoid it if he can.
2.   Because of their dislike of work, most people must be coerced, controlled, directed, and threatened with punishment to get them to put forth adequate effort toward the attainment of organizational objectives.
3.   The average human being prefers to be directed, wishes to avoid responsibility, has relatively little ambition, and wants security above all.

In contrast to the autocratic approach to employees that would be implied under Theory X, the set of assumptions under McGregor's Theory Y encourages managers to be supportive of their employees:

1.   The average human being does not inherently dislike work. The expenditure of physical and mental effort in work is as natural as play or rest.
2.   External control and the threat of punishment are not the only means of bringing about effective organizational effort. Man will exercise self-direction and self-control in seeking to obtain goals to which he has committed himself.
3.   Part of the rewards of achievement are found in the ego satisfaction and self-fulfilling aspects of the individual commitment.
4.   The average individual, under the proper conditions, learns not only to accept but to seek responsibility.
5.   The capacity to exercise a relatively high degree of imagination, ingenuity, and creativity in seeking to solve an organizational problem is quite widely distributed throughout the population.
6.   Under the conditions that exist in today's industrial and economic life, the intellectual potential of the average person is only partially tapped.

Theory X is *not* an unpopular theory today. Those who put credence in its three assumptions would have very little interest, if any, in motivation.

On the other hand, the assumptions of Theory Y, certainly a positive and enlightened approach, suggest areas that might indeed motivate employees. However, before we examine those suggested areas, let us look at another classical work, which deals with organizational behavior instead of human behavior. The three theories of organizational behavior are the Autocratic Theory, the Custodial Theory, and the Supportive Theory.[2]

---

[2]Davis, Keith. *Human Relations at Work*, 3rd ed. (New York: McGraw-Hill, 1967).

ORGANIZATIONAL BEHAVIOR

The Autocratic Theory

The Autocratic Theory has its roots deep in history, dating back to the Industrial Revolution of the mid-eighteenth century. The theory is based on absolute power. It tends to be threatening, relying on negative motivation backed by power. The managerial posture is one of formal and official authority.

In practice this theory means that management knows best, and it is the employees' obligation to follow orders without question. ("Yours is not to question why. Yours is but to do or die.") Employees need to be persuaded and prodded into performance, not led. Management does the thinking and employees do what they are told. Management has absolute control over the employee. The autocratic approach is a useful way to get work done and therefore has some merit. Although just a step above the slave-master work relationship, it was the dominant and prevailing theory until very recent times. The autocratic approach did build transcontinental railroads, run giant steel mills, and in general produced the dynamic industrial economy of the early part of the twentieth century.

But even if the autocratic approach gets results, they are only moderate results and are attained at high human costs. Moreover, the Autocratic Theory does nothing to develop human potential in an organization.

The Custodial Theory

The Custodial Theory depends on company wealth to provide economic benefits for the employee. These come in the form of pensions, insurance, medical benefits, salary increases, and so forth. The managerial posture or orientation is toward tangible benefits. The employee relies on the company for security instead of on the boss, as in the Autocratic Theory. The aim is to make the employee happy, contented, and adjusted to the work environment.

This approach does not motivate employees to produce anywhere near their capacity nor are they motivated to develop their full capabilities. Consequently, employees fail to feel genuinely fulfilled or challenged on the job. Thus they must look elsewhere, such as to the bowling team or any other outside activity that holds their interest.

The Supportive Theory

The Supportive Theory depends on management leadership to create a climate in which an employee may grow and achieve those things of which he or she is capable—to the employe's benefit as well as the company's.

When management creates this type of supportive work climate, employees will take on responsibility, strive to contribute to the organization, and work at improving their own skills and performance. The employees in this climate tend to think in terms of "we" rather than "they," and organizational objectives become "our" objectives. Ideally, under this approach, the employee needs little supervision. The primary need is for the employee to tell the supervisor what kind of support he or she needs from that supervisor to do a better job.

WORK MOTIVATION THEORY

McGregor's Theory Y assumptions and the Supportive Theory of organizational behavior are the basis of an enlightened approach to motivation. With those as a backdrop, let us now consider Frederick Herzberg's Work Motivation Theory, a meaningful and outstanding work developed four decades ago.[3]

Dr. Herzberg's position is essentially that motivation—genuine work motivation—comes from the work itself, not from those factors such as salary and job security that surround the work. He breaks down the job into two basic categories: (1) the job surroundings, or hygiene factors, and (2) the job itself and its motivators.

The Job Surroundings	**The Job Itself**
Hygiene or "Maintenance Factors"	*Motivators*
• Pay	• Responsibility
• Status	• Achievement
• Policy and administration	• Recognition
• Interpersonal relationships	• Advancement
• Benefits	• Growth
• Supervision	
• Working conditions	
• Job security	

According to Dr. Herzberg, hygiene factors do not lead to work satisfaction or happiness; rather, they lead to *dissatisfaction* more often than not, whereas the work motivators are the primary cause of *satisfaction*. Further, hygiene factors are *expected;* that is to say, good pay and periodic increases are expected and so are benefits, good supervision, and good working conditions. All are *expected once they have been given.* Certainly if there had been no dental plan, for example, and the company introduced a dental plan, everyone would be pleased. Included in their conversations would be

---

[3] Herzberg, Frederick. One More Time: How Do You Motivate Employees? *Harvard Business Review*, January-February, 1968.

remarks like, "It's about time. So-and-so's had a dental plan for years now." Next year they will expect some new benefit—perhaps eye care. Employees are not motivated to produce more for any extended period of time nor do they find satisfaction in their daily work as a result of factors that surround the work.

Real motivation, then, comes from the work itself and those motivating factors that are intrinsic to the job. Let us analyze how such factors fit into the security environment.

Responsibility as a Motivator

Genuine responsibility is perhaps the most important motivator, and in the security environment, unlike many other types of work environments, real responsibility can be a significant factor in an employee's work. Responsibility in this context includes such things as problem solving, decision making, and accountability.

Why is security unlike many other types of work environments? The answer is that relatively few departments or jobs within departments deal with unusual, erratic, or criminal human behavior; few deal with accidents or other emergency conditions; and fewer still *plan* to deal with such conditions. Thus the security employee who is indeed given the opportunity to solve problems revolving around behavior or emergency situations, *before or after the fact*, really has responsibility. Those security employees who are permitted or are obliged to make decisions as to what to do or not to do when criminal or unusual human behavior occurs or when catastrophe strikes really have responsibility.

If such responsibility is built into the security job, then, one might assume that all security people, by virtue of their chosen vocation, are motivated. Unfortunately, this is not the case, because many security people are given a "sense" of responsibility, which is quite different from *real* responsibility. When the chips are down, the real decisions come from above; the problems are solved by someone higher up, and no real accountability exists. For example, an officer is placed on a surveillance position with binoculars and is told, "Harry we have information that a thief is going to penetrate our facility sometime tonight. You are responsible for this fence line and this side of the facility. We've got to catch this guy tonight, and I'm counting on you."

Does Harry have real responsibility in this assignment? At this point it sounds as if he does, but let the supervisor complete his instructions to Harry: "If you spot the guy climbing over, cutting through, or slipping under your section of the line, immediately contact Sgt. Green on your radio and he'll get there quick and take over."

Harry has no real responsibility here; Sgt. Green has. If you want to *motivate* Harry, then give him the responsibility to capture the thief. Give him a back-up man, a peer who will respond to the radio call that penetration is being made, or match him up with a partner and charge the two with the responsibility of apprehending anyone who penetrates their assigned area. That is responsibility. They will decide when and how to move in on the thief. That problem is theirs and theirs only, and whether they apprehend or lose the thief, they are totally accountable.

Similarly, giving a security supervisor the responsibility to plan for a specific segment of an upcoming special event (say the traffic flow and parking connected with the visit of foreign dignitaries) is, in and of itself, an exciting challenge and a motivator. However, if the supervisor's manager changes the plans, not because they are wrong but because the manager prefers his or her way to the subordinate's (and this is common), the so-called responsibility turns out to be only a facade. It becomes a *demotivator*, inspiring indifference and breeding suspicion of future assignments.

Most security personnel crave responsibility and have the capacity to assume more than most administrators are willing to allow. Give them as much responsibility as possible and let their work motivate them to peaks of achievement.

Achievement as a Motivator

Group and collective success is certainly important to the employee who is a member of the group. However, the employee, from a personal work motivation point of view, must have the opportunity to be singularly successful, even if it is a small success or achievement. The investigator who "breaks" a case or the store detective who catches a shoplifter experiences the full joy of achievement. *He* or *she* did it! Each achievement tends to drive the employee on to another.

More frequently than not, achievement comes through problem solving. Thus the supervisor or administrator who recognizes achievement as a motivator will provide subordinates with the opportunity to solve a problem, to come up with the answer, or to catch the thief for the motivational benefits that success brings. Opportunities, as such, are almost limitless. As an example, ask an employee if he or she could design a better case history form for detainees or an improved filing and index system for security records—any assignment within the limits of the employee's capabilities that will provide a chance for him or her to truly accomplish something, to be able to say proudly, "I did that," or "That's mine!"

Recognition of Achievement as a Motivator

Rare is the person who is not motivated by praise, flattery, or any other complimentary form of recognition. To say "Well done" goes a long way. Not to say "Well done" when it is due goes a long way, too, but the wrong way. It is a demotivator.

Growth as a Motivator

Growth is the consequence of expanding one's horizons, increasing insight brought about by an ever-widening variety of experiences; gathering in new ideas; concepts and information; and coping with new situations and problems. All of these factors increase the individual's personal and professional growth.

Thus it behooves security management to provide a work climate that not only allows for growth but also encourages it. If there is a local security seminar, send as many people as possible. If there are local security associations, encourage appropriate members of the department to join and be active. As new assignments and problems surface, do not always call on the same already proven members of the staff to handle them. Assign someone who has not had that kind of experience so that he or she will have the benefit of the new challenge and subsequent growth. Rotate your people around the organization rather than developing specialists in narrow areas. Rotation provides for growth. Encourage non-college graduates to return to school on a part-time basis.

Care for, water, and feed your people as a gardener tends a garden, and you can actually see them "grow" before your eyes. That growth motivates them to be achievers who seek more responsibility.

Advancement as a Motivator

Opportunities to move up in the department (or in another department of the company) must be clearly visible and, in the eyes of the individual, personally attainable. If vertical movement (real or imaginary) is not apparent, then the persons who seek responsibility—the achievers, the ones who have grown and are growing—will be moved by their inner motivation to seek advancement elsewhere. Ideally, advancements should be occurring throughout the organization frequently, from interdepartmental promotions to advancements to supervisory posts in other departments to managerial positions in Security Departments of corporate sister companies. Such movement is motivational in and of itself.

More production, more creative contributions to the organization, more loyalty, and more dedication to excellence in performance have a better chance of actually happening in a work environment that embraces McGregor's Theory Y, the Supportive Theory of organizational development, and Herzberg's Work Motivation Theory. The department and the organization can only profit when they recognize the value of human dignity and the creative and productive potential of their employees and then give them room to work and to breathe.

DEMOTIVATORS

Naturally there is a very close relationship between motivation and morale. Highly motivated people enjoy morale, and vice versa. Dr. Mortimer R. Feinberg, Professor of Psychology at the Baruch School of Business and Public Administration, has identified a number of factors that can have dramatic negative impact on employees. He calls these factors the "Ten Deadly Demotivators." Every security supervisor, manager, and administrator should be familiar with them[4]:

1.   *Never belittle a subordinate.* Do not subject any employee to the ultimate put-down by calling him or her stupid. The employee might apply the term to himself or herself for some careless mistake, but the manager should not. Generally speaking, you can call an employee almost anything else—lazy, sloppy, slipshod—and he or she will accept the criticism well enough. However, calling an employee stupid will not only deflate the ego but will undermine the initiative. How can a stupid man or woman be ambitious or enthusiastic?

2.   *Never criticize a subordinate in front of others.* A reprimand delivered in the privacy of your office will be accepted. The same criticism delivered in front of the employee's coworkers will breed quick resentment. You have mortified the employee in front of his or her friends—that is unforgivable. Like most of Feinberg's Ten Deadly Demotivators, this rule is or should be familiar to all managers. When it is forgotten in a moment of anger or haste, the damage can be permanent.

3.   *Never fail to give your subordinates your full attention, at least occasionally.* On the positive side, making each employee feel that you care about him or her personally is a strong motivator. Have each employee in your office occasionally, and give him or her your undivided attention. Have your secretary hold your calls. If you allow interruptions, lose the train of thought, and have to say, "Now then, Fred, what is it you were saying about your family?" you will be telling Fred that you do not really care.

4.   *Never give your subordinates the impression that you are primarily concerned with your own interests.* Although your personal goals may very well be your primary concern, it is a mistake to allow your employees to think that you are "using" them for your own selfish ends. For example, if you have a subordinate work late to finish a project that will make you look good to *your* superiors, make a point of sharing the credit for getting the job done. You will still look good—not only to higher management but also to your subordinate.

---

[4] Feinberg, Mortimer R. *Effective Psychology for Managers.* (Englewood Cliffs, NJ: Prentice-Hall, 1966), pp. 127–131.

5.   *Never play favorites.* This is another cardinal rule of supervision, but—human nature being what it is—it is one of the most frequently broken. The moment you start playing favorites, especially when the person in question has been playing up to you to gain favored status, you will antagonize the rest of the staff. Dr. Feinberg cites an example that illustrates this point well.

A supervisor regarded as autocratic was accused of playing favorites. He would not let any of the secretaries in his office get away with anything except for one. He never chastised or criticized this particular secretary, even though she was notorious for spending a lot of time making personal telephone calls. His reason was that she often stayed at the office late to get work done. (Naturally, this was because she wasted so much time during the day.) The rest of the secretarial staff knew that the supervisor was being manipulated, and they resented it. Consequently, the secretaries became demotivated.[5]

6.   *Never fail to help your subordinates grow—when they are deserving.* When employees feel that a supervisor is on their side and will go to bat for them if necessary—in the matter of obtaining raises that are deserved, for example—they will be more loyal and more strongly motivated. Support your employees in their attempts to grow, even if it means that you might lose a good employee to another department. If you stand in the way, you will probably lose the employee anyway. Once an employee believes you are not on his or her side, he or she will be demotivated.

7.   *Never be insensitive to small things.* Avoid loose or rash statements—you may regret them later. In one company a department manager, on being told that one worker was unhappy and might quit, responded "Let him—we won't miss a beat" and accompanied the statement with a contemptuous snap of the fingers. The comment was repeated and became known to the other employees, who began using it as a mocking refrain. The statement said quite clearly, "The employee doesn't matter." In another example given by Dr. Feinberg, a supervisor known for his terrible temper roared to an employee one day, "I don't care how long you've been with this firm. Seniority means nothing in my department." This particular company had been nonunion for the 75 years of its existence, but, exploiting this rash comment, the union finally won a foothold. Its slogan was, "Seniority means nothing."

By the same token, consideration in small things, from remembering to inquire about an employee's wife's illness to congratulating him on his son's graduation, will increase loyalty and desire to work for you.

8.   *Never "show up" employees.* This rule is closely related to the first two demotivators. Just as you should not humiliate employees by calling them stupid or criticizing them in front of others, do not show off at their expense

---

[5] Feinberg, Mortimer R. *Effective Psychology for Managers.* (Englewood Cliffs, NJ: Prentice-Hall, 1966), p. 129.

by demonstrating how you can do a particular job better and faster than they can. The manager should be able to perform many tasks better than subordinates—that is why he or she is a manager. However, it is important to any employee to take some pride in his or her work. If you take away that pride and self-respect, you will discourage and demotivate. Training the employee to do a better job is one thing; embarrassing him or her is another.

9. *Never lower your personal standards.* Care and consideration of employees should not extend to the point of accepting or tolerating inept performance. This will only demotivate the real achievers in the organization. The reasons are summed up in an analysis Dr. Feinberg quotes from the Research Institute of America:

> The mediocrity of colleagues can muzzle the initiative of the dynamic doer who has high standards for his own performance . . . especially when the "mediocres" are permitted to stand on the sidelines and throw darts at new ideas. Management often tolerates a certain percentage of people whom they have given up on . . . men who will never pull their own weight. But if these people are permitted to remain in key positions, just the simple fact of their presence can cost the company the loss of an endless chain of worthwhile people who don't have to work against such odds. And, incidentally, whether they remain on the payroll or leave for greener fields, you've lost a man if he has decided it doesn't pay to knock himself out.[6]

10. *Never vacillate in making a decision.* Effective management is characterized by the willingness and ability to make prompt, wise decisions. Every decision involves an element of risk—the chance that you could be making a mistake. If your employees see that you lack confidence in your own decisions, because you are afraid to take the risks involved in being a manager, they will be demotivated. Employees draw strength from visible evidence of strong supervision and management. Their initiative can be undermined by evidence of weak or vacillating management.

SUMMARY

Among classical theories of human behavior in the work environment, McGregor's Theory X assumptions emphasize negative aspects of employee behavior; his Theory Y suggests that employees do not inherently dislike work and will actually seek responsibility and better performance if encouraged to do so. This latter theory provides a more enlightened, modern approach to motivation.

---

[6]Feinberg, Mortimer R. *Effective Psychology for Managers.* (Englewood Cliffs, NJ: Prentice-Hall, 1966), p. 131.

Similarly, the Supportive Theory of work motivation creates a more effective climate for the development of human potential.

Herzberg's Work Motivation Theory stresses the importance of motivators *in the job itself*, as opposed to such hygiene factors as pay, benefits, working conditions, and so forth.

In the security function, effective job motivators include giving the employee genuine responsibility, providing opportunity for individual achievement and self-satisfaction, recognizing performance, allowing for and encouraging growth, and creating the opportunity for advancement.

Belittling or "showing up" the employee, public criticism, inattention, favoritism, denial of opportunity, insensitivity, lowering standards of performance, or vacillation in decision making are all demotivators, which the effective Security Manager will avoid.

REVIEW QUESTIONS

1. Briefly describe the Theory X and Theory Y assumptions about human behavior.

2. Briefly describe the Autocratic Theory, the Custodial Theory, and the Supportive Theory of organizational behavior.

3. According to Herzberg's Work Motivation Theory, what are the motivators that come from the work itself? Why do the job surroundings or hygiene factors not lead to work satisfaction?

4. What are some of the ways in which security management can encourage growth among security employees?

5. Name five of the Ten Deadly Demotivators?

12

Promotions

Surprisingly, many employees accept mediocrity in management practices as the rule instead of the exception. The selection of new people for the department, the quality of training, departmental disciplinary standards, motivation efforts, and the presence or absence of a structured communication capability have limited impact on the individual security employee and consequently meet with limited emotional reaction from him or her.

This is undoubtedly attributable to the fact that people attracted to the security/law enforcement career field tend to be conservative, "rugged individualists" with a high degree of self-discipline. They tend to equate what happens around them with what it means to them personally. They take note of the following: An undiscriminating process for the selection of new employees enhances the existing employee's chances for advancement; an ineffective training program provides the really ambitious security employee, who is willing to train himself or herself, with an advantage over the less ambitious; strict or erratic disciplinary standards will punish those who are poorly qualified and poorly trained, not those who are well qualified. Rationalization? Probably. The point is that security people are exceptionally tolerant of management practices; they survive the most difficult job conditions with a minimum of complaint—except in the area of promotions.

Employees identify very closely with promotions—"There, but for him, go I." It is a truism that most employees have an inflated estimation of their ability and worth. Most feel they are underused, underpaid, and could quite easily do their supervisor's job and even do it better. Hence the vertical movement of a peer within the organization is an emotionally charged event that is scrutinized with intensity and, unfortunately, too often with suspicion.

Obviously, then, management's objective in the promotion process is to identify and promote the best-qualified candidate, with resultant general acceptance and approval of the promotion. That is an important goal and a formidable challenge.

IDENTIFYING PROMOTIONAL CANDIDATES

There is as much excitement among security management personnel in their role in the promotion process as there is among the ranks. The appointment of a new supervisor or promotion of a supervisor to a position of greater responsibility in most cases has a personal effect on existing managers and supervisors. Naturally, they want the best and most effective person moved up.

In identifying candidates, there is a tendency to get mired down in qualities desired or "qualifications" that should not be at issue. Such factors as one's ability to articulate, popularity, the "halo effect" of some recent incident, and length of service should be considered at some later point but should not be the initial qualifying considerations.

There are three basic qualification factors to be considered in selecting candidates for supervisory or managerial responsibility:

1. The candidate's educational achievements
2. The employee's track record in job performance
3. The anticipated or expected performance in the higher level job

Other factors are peripheral in nature.

The Candidate's Educational Achievements

The successful pursuit and attainment of a college education is a clear indicator the individual was willing to make the necessary sacrifices to grow, was motivated enough to endure through the rigors demanded in higher education, and demonstrated sufficient self-discipline to reach the desired goal. Surely those are critical personal characteristics that are desirable in leadership positions. Numerous factors must be considered and weighed in this area, such as the major focus (degree in secondary education or fine arts versus security administration); 2-year, bachelor's, or graduate degree; college courses pursued in the traditional span of time, for example, four consecutive years or spread out over a number of years on a part-time basis (typically indicative of a tenacious "no surrender" type of person); and the earned grade point average (GPA).

In the unlikely event that no one in the pool of candidates for the promotion has any college education, then only high school graduates should be considered, and such factors as extracurricular activities (serving in student government, athletics, debating team, and school club activities), school honors earned, and GPA should be weighed.

The Candidate's Track Record

Employees whose service and job performance are rated as "above average" or "above acceptable standards" would constitute the first group of candidates. A rating of "average" performance or "meets acceptable standards" should, as a rule, be disqualifying. This is because the highly desirable quality of being an "achiever" is reflected in regular performance evaluations of above average. Average workers are doers. Above average workers are achievers; they obviously go above and beyond what is expected. By most employee performance evaluation standards, they "frequently exceed requirements of the job," always through their own initiative. (Incidentally, employees rated as "outstanding" performers are defined as those who "consistently exceed job requirements" as opposed to "frequently.") Thus the achievement-oriented employee meets the first of the two criteria.

Anticipated Performance in the Higher Level Job

The tentative candidates (the achievers) must now be analyzed, one at a time, as to how they might measure up to or perform against standards of the higher position in question. If the open position requires scheduling employees, for example, those assessing a candidate must look back on prior performance for evidence of some demonstrated behavior or action indicating that the candidate could indeed schedule subordinates (which would include schedule revisions, emergency scheduling, appropriate degree of flexibility, etc.). It could be that the candidate has actually done some scheduling at the request of his or her supervisor. Indeed, any supervisor or manager worth his or her salt would have consistently delegated, in some measure, supervisorial duties to deserving employees to test their ability to perform in this higher arena. In that case, management could properly anticipate or expect good performance in that area if the candidate is promoted.

More often than not, those attempting to qualify candidates for promotion tend to look for disqualifiers in this anticipatory phase. They look for duties that, because of past performance, the tentative candidate could be expected not to perform competently in the higher assignment.

Disqualifiers may be identified by management or by the candidate. For example, otherwise qualified candidates may disqualify themselves because they do not want to travel or move or do not want shift changes. Some may state frankly that they cannot discipline or evaluate others. Employee self-disqualification makes management's decision easier.

It is important to note that disqualifiers, as such, should be understood to apply for the present situation only. Any number of things can happen to change circumstances between promotional opportunities. Management should never assume that an earlier disqualifier still stands.

The most difficult task is the projection that the candidate is not able or qualified to perform the higher level job. If, for any reason, that disqualification is subject to question or is not the unanimous decision of security management, then the candidate should not be disqualified. He or she should move on to the actual competition with the other qualified candidates.

What has not been stated, but should be evident, is that the promotional opportunity is common knowledge; it is not a secret. Thus when the announcement does come, it is no surprise. Most people do not like surprises in the work environment and react negatively to them. In the process of identifying candidates for the promotion, a healthy and open climate about promotions should be established.

SELECTION OF THE RIGHT CANDIDATE

The best selection process comes in the form of a Promotion Board. The Board, preferably three in number, should always have as members the successful candidate's immediate superior, a person who will be a peer of the successful candidate, and someone from the next higher rank above the successful candidate's superior. If the promotion is for a sergeant's position, for example, the Board would include one sergeant, the lieutenant for whom the new sergeant will work, and the lieutenant's captain. The Board's chairperson, as such, would be the lieutenant because the promotion will affect him or her most directly.

The Board members, except the tie-breaking chairman, should be considered as equals; thus the captain's will does not prevail because of rank. The lieutenant, on the other hand, assumes leadership in this case. Leadership includes responsibility because, as stated previously, the selectee will be his or her immediate subordinate and a very important subordinate at that.

A frequent problem in promotions is the exclusion of the promoted person's new superior from the decision. If the lieutenant is not involved in the selection of the new sergeant, he or she may disagree with (if not resent) the decision, with the result that the lieutenant may not work at making the new sergeant successful. (It does require effort from the superior to make a newly promoted employee successful.) Subordinates, especially those moving for the first time into new and unfamiliar responsibilities, must have direction and leadership from their boss, or they may fail. The truth is that some secret pleasure is taken in such failures. In our example, it is a way for the overlooked lieutenant to strike back at management for not including him or her in the selection of his or her people; it is a way of saying, "I told you so," that is, "Management ignored my opinion or didn't seek it."

On the other hand, if the person who is responsible for the new pro-motee is involved in and responsible for the selection, the person is bound to do all that he or she can to make that selection a successful one.

Not more than 10 days should pass from the time the appropriate supervisors are asked for possible candidates, through the screening and identifying of those to appear before the Board, to the day of the actual Board interview. Delays and silence about who has been selected to appear and who is to receive the promotion are counterproductive. They breed suspicion.

THE BOARD INTERVIEW

Nothing can be done to ease the anxiety of the candidate on the appointed day, and perhaps that small amount of stress is acceptable as long as it is not purposefully designed into the process. This interview is an important event in an employee's career and life; he or she will come spruced up as he or she has rarely appeared before—and more nervous than ever before.

Because some degree of anxiety is normal, the Board should seek to enable the candidate to relax as much as possible after he or she has been ushered into the room used for this event. Rather than a very formal civil service type arrangement (single chair poised in front of a table behind which sits the "oral" board), the Board members should be arranged in an informal setting of chairs and/or sofa without a table or desk between them and the candidate—similar to a living room or den arrangement.

The same questions, asked the same way, should be put to each of the candidates and their responses should be duly noted for subsequent com-parison. General questions should be asked first: "Why do you want this promotion?" "Do you feel you are the best candidate for this job and if so, why?" "What special qualities and qualifications do you feel you bring to this job?" Then come the specific and situational job-related questions. The situational question would require a problem-solving answer. Example: "What would you do if you discovered all the telephone lines that carry the alarm systems, including fire system, went down on your watch at the main facility and you were already short one officer?" Each candidate would explain what she or he would do and that answer would be duly noted. Always include a situational question involving the handling of a disciplinary problem. Some answers probably would make sense and some wouldn't.

The combination of the candidate's educational background, and what-ever value you attach to that, and the candidate's performance history, and its value, coupled with the answers to the questions will identify the best candidate. Thus the decision to promote will be, more often than not, rela-tively easy. The best candidate typically rises to the top!

FOLLOWING THE SELECTION

When a promotion follows the selection process described, the attitude of those candidates interviewed who did not get the promotion is usually one of full acceptance of the decision and appreciation for the opportunity to compete. The attitude of the organization is one of full acceptance of the promotee because he or she is the best of the candidates and selection was in no way viewed as political. The attitude of management is one of pleasure and confidence that the best candidate was identified in a totally objective fashion and the newest member of the management team is properly qualified.

Other promotion processes have somewhat less to offer than the Board approach.

PROMOTION FROM "WITHIN"

Certainly the policy of promoting from within the Security Department should always be followed except when it would not serve the best interests of the organization. When would the best interests of the organization not be served under this policy? That situation would arise when an unqualified employee (using the same qualifying criteria outlined earlier in this chapter) is moved up simply to satisfy the "promote from within" policy. This type of promotion will destroy, or at least damage, the person promoted. It will automatically affect departmental performance, and, also of great importance, it will challenge the credibility of the promotional process itself.

If management determines that there is no qualified applicant for a particular post, usually in the higher echelons of the department, then those employees in the rank from which the promotion should come must be advised they fail to qualify for the position and the organization is going to look outside for the necessary talent.

Some employees will initially react against that decision and will ask for specifics as to their deficiencies. They are entitled to such information, which management should be able to provide in very specific terms if the candidates were assessed honestly and the disqualifiers were identified. To share the decision openly and to sit down and talk about it with the employees overshadows the initial resentment and paves the way for the future arrival of the selected "outsider."

If the decision is made to go elsewhere for talent and the organization is not advised of that decision, the predictable result will be resistance to the new arrival, as well as broad resentment not only for the new person but for top security management as well.

VERTICAL PROMOTION OUTSIDE THE DEPARTMENT

There are still many in all levels of management who view promotions as organizationally disruptive. They are secure in the status quo. However, the "disruptiveness" of vertical movement breathes life, excitement, and motivation into the organization. For that reason, promotions—not only upward within the Security Department but throughout the company as well—should be explored and encouraged. The advantage not only of creating promotional opportunities within the organization but of having good security people in responsible positions throughout the company, such as in Human Resources or Auditing, should be obvious.

To purposefully hold people back because it serves the immediate purpose of the security organization is morally wrong. The company as a whole will benefit when there is opportunity for vertical movement both within the Security Department and outside of it to other areas of the organization.

ADVANTAGES OF MULTIPLE LAYERS

Perhaps the best example of the organizational advantages of multiple layers of rank is in the military service. Instead of just three layers of the enlisted ranks—private, corporal, and sergeant—military organizations have many layers with, at last count, six graded army sergeant ranks alone. That is true, too, in the officer ranks of the military. The obvious advantage is increased opportunity for vertical movement. The more ranks, the more chances one has to move up. The fewer ranks, the less chance—not only in terms of layers to go up through but in frequency of openings. Obviously, the greater the number of ranks, the more frequency there is in movement. In the 1990s the trend toward flatter organizational pyramids flies in the face of this vertical mobility, but the concept is valid nonetheless.

The organizational levels in one large retail department store chain are far from typical, but its use of multiple layers may be of value as an illustration. Starting at the lower levels and proceeding upward are the following ranks: Fitting Room Checker, Fitting Room Inspector, Lead Fitting Room Inspector, Security Agent, Special Agent, Resident Special Agent, Senior Special Agent, Special Agent-in-Charge, (Divisional) Chief Special Agent, Security Manager, and Security Director.

Obviously the small Security Department cannot have as many levels of rank, but within the limitations of size the opportunity for progressive movement should still exist. Truncated structures limit movement and contribute to stagnation and frustration among the ranks. Rather than few layers with big pay jumps, it is best to have more layers with smaller pay differences and more frequent advances.

Today, in our fast-moving society, people need to feel they too are on the move, and multiple layers help to satisfy that need.

"TEMPORARY" PROMOTIONS

An excellent way to measure an employee's potential for higher levels of responsibility is to appoint him or her temporarily to such posts during natural absences of the regular supervisors or managers—vacation, sickness, leaves of absence, and so forth. The subordinate's performance while filling in is a measurable indicator of his or her capacity to assume greater responsibility.

Another way to test prospective leaders is to create temporary leadership assignments for special events or projects, appointing one as "team leader" or "project leader" for the duration of the event or project. They not only can be evaluated but they also can gain the otherwise unavailable experience that comes with increased responsibility. People have been known to excel or to fail under such conditions, and that knowledge can be invaluable to management in future promotion considerations.

"RETREATING"

No matter how carefully an organization approaches the promotional process, mistakes in selection are sometimes made. The question is, "What do you do when a person is promoted to a position beyond his or her ability?" The "Peter Principle" (rising to one's level of incompetence) is a well-known management problem because of its common occurrence.

There are but three courses of action available to management on discovery that an employee has been promoted beyond his or her level of competence:

1. Permit the employee to continue performing in an incompetent fashion (which is, regrettably, the most common course of action).
2. Terminate the incompetent employee (which is often unfair—after all, it's a reflection of a poor promotion policy).
3. Allow and arrange for a "retreat" back to the former rank.

Option number one, although frequently exercised, is unacceptable to a progressive and enlightened management for three reasons: (1) it is counterproductive to the organization, (2) it affects the morale of the incompetent employee's subordinates in a very negative way, and (3) a point often overlooked, the person who has achieved the level beyond his or her ability knows it as well as anyone else, and that knowledge places him or her in a dilemma. The person knows that he or she is in trouble but does not want to admit it. The person struggles. Unhappiness sets in. Some actually become physically ill because of the dilemma. It is a rare individual who can come forward and admit he or she is in trouble. The tragedy is that most will not admit it.

Option number two is another popular solution. The tragedy here is that management is culpable, too. The person promoted beyond his or her ability was certainly competent at the lower rank. In fact, his or her skill level and performance evaluation were above average. The person was a good worker. The person is not inherently an ineffective employee — he or she is simply ineffective in his or her new responsibility. To terminate this employee is in part to hide management's mistake in promoting the wrong person.

Option number three, if it can be accomplished, serves the best interests of all concerned. Policies prohibiting voluntary demotions are unrealistic and inhumane. Certainly the person who is willing to retreat to his or her former rank should be given that opportunity, even though his or her ego is going to be bruised for a time. The total honesty in retreat situations is apparent to all observers. The salvaging and protection of an employee's tenure with the firm is important to the misplaced individual and others in the organization also respond to this humane policy.

Retreat should never be a structured or formalized consideration in the promotion process because by all rights it should be the tragic exception in organizational life. To say to a candidate, "Well, if you prove incompetent, Harry, you can always go back to the old job," would discredit the selection ability of the Board (or management), would demean the importance of striving for competence by overcoming obstacles, would turn promotions into a gamble instead of a challenge, and would be an insult to the real achiever's confidence and intelligence.

Retreating is the emergency valve that should be available for those rare instances in which the promotional process fails to hit the mark.

SUMMARY

Because vertical movement in the organization is an emotionally charged event, management's objective in promotion is always to identify and select the best-qualified candidate.

Primary qualification factors in promotions are the employee's record of performance in his or her present job and projected performance in the advanced position. Current job performance should be above average to be considered for promotion.

A Promotion Board provides the selection process most likely to be fair and objective. In all cases, the supervisor for whom the candidate will be working should be a member of the Promotion Board.

The opportunity for vertical movement elsewhere within the company should not be opposed by security management. Such movement serves both the company and the security organization.

The most effective promotion process is a flexible one. It will not make promotion automatic but will promote only the qualified candidate, it will accept the necessity to go outside the department in some circumstances to find a qualified employee, and it will also allow for the possibility of retreat when an employee proves out of his or her depth in a higher level position.

REVIEW QUESTIONS

1.   What is management's objective in the promotion process?

2.   What are the three basic qualification factors to be considered in selecting candidates for supervisory responsibility?

3.   What problems can occur if the promoted person's new superior is not involved in the selection decision?

4.   Discuss the advantages of having multiple ranks of employees.

5.   Discuss the relative merits of the three possible courses of action when an employee has been promoted to a position beyond his or her ability.

13

Communication

Of all the qualities, talents, and skills required of a manager, the art of effective communication must rank first. In fact, all other managerial factors are crystallized by the communication process to form the "whole" administrator and leader. Stated another way, the manager who is a strong communicator is a strong manager, and the manager who is a weak communicator is a weak manager.

Consider this: This manager's task is to get others to do the job when the manager wants it done, how the manager wants it done, where the manager wants it done and (if he or she is a good manager) to make them understand why he or she wants it done. Obviously, to translate desire into the completed task, the manager must communicate the desire and the employees must understand. If a job is done poorly, not done at all, or done incorrectly, it is usually because the employees did not understand. An employee's failure to understand could be because the employee wasn't listening or the manager failed somehow to communicate clearly or both.

The previous example reflects only one type of communication: verbal-down. Other types of communication to be considered include verbal-up, written-down, written-horizontal, written-up, verbal-horizontal, and action. These types of communication may take place in an "open" or a "closed" climate of communication.

TYPES OF COMMUNICATION

Verbal-Down

Traditionally, security organizations generally operate under the closed climate of communication. This is probably due to the quasimilitary nature of most security forces. It is easy to visualize the Captain on the bridge of a Navy vessel shouting directions into a tube that terminates deep down in the engine room and everyone complying with the orders. This type of communication might be called "stovepipe" communication (verbal-down only). Stovepipe communication may also occur when the Captain of the Guards passes word down to the officer to lock Gate 36 at 2:00 A.M. As a rule the gate will be locked as required. However effective this method of communication seems, there is an obvious flaw that haunts managers (or Captains): Sometimes the gate will be found unlocked. The security officer at the bottom end of the stovepipe hears the orders, but there he or she stands silently without the right key!

Ideally, then, management should strive for the development of an open climate of communication.

Verbal-Up

Some readers may feel that the previous example, in which the officer at the bottom end of the stovepipe hears the order and knows he or she does not have the key but remains silent, is unreal. All the officer has to do is tell the closest superior on the stovepipe, probably the sergeant, that he or she does not have the key. This is not likely to happen, however, because the officer knows that if the sergeant is told that the officer does not have the key, the officer will be reprimanded for forgetting it or be embarrassed or abused in some other manner. To protect himself or herself, the officer remains silent, knowing that the job will not be done. Rather than feeling at liberty to openly communicate to the supervisor (verbal-up) to get the job done, the officer voluntarily chooses to undercut the effectiveness of the organization because of the closed climate of communication.

In most cases the organization does not set out to purposefully design a closed climate of communication. It is created at the top (at the Security Director or Security Manager level) by insensitivity to the importance of communication, including verbal-up; they simply don't want to hear it!

Written-Down

There is a classic exercise or game that dramatically points out the unreliability of spoken communications. A group of people is seated around a room. Instructions or a short narrative are whispered to the first person. In turn, that person repeats in a whisper what he or she heard to the next person and so on. It is hilarious to hear the last person in that room speak out loud what he or she was told—but the reality that this game illustrates can be tragic as well, because, in any organization, many failures are attributable to the misunderstanding of directions.

There are many factors in the breakdown of verbal communications:

- People tend to hear what they want to hear.
- Generalizations are narrowed to specifics.
- Different words mean different things to different people.
- The spoken emphasis on a word or phrase can be interpreted differently by the listener, so that he or she assumes a different meaning than the speaker intended.

There is less chance for error in understanding the written word. There is greater acceptance of and reliance on the written word, especially in organizational life. How often does one hear, "I want to see it in writing"?

Logically, then, everything that can be reduced to writing should be. General orders, post orders, patrol orders, inspection instructions, rules and regulations that are to be enforced, rules and regulations governing the Security Department, investigative procedures, emergency procedures, alarm procedures, and other appropriate material and data should be in writing and available to members of the department.

Should all such written material be distributed to all security personnel? Probably not. All written material will fall into three categories: "Nice to Know," "Should Know," and "Need to Know." Certainly every member of the department should be provided with the "Should Know" and "Need to Know" material.

Written material should always be put into a standardized format. For example, Orders of the Day should always be on the same size and color of paper, in the same print, and with the same distinctive appearance. In this way it is recognizable at a distance as an Order of the Day. The same should be true of all other written material. Standardized formats reduce confusion, make for easier organization, and give a professional touch to the department.

Department Handbook or Manual

The need for a departmental "how to" handbook should be apparent to any Security Manager or Director. Even a small security organization typically faces the problem of relatively high turnover of personnel as well as the need for changing or rotating assignments. As the department grows and specific roles become more specialized, the need for standardized procedures becomes even more essential. One store chain's handbook, or manual, contains an assortment of detailed instructional materials, such as a standardized confession format, investigative steps to follow in tracking an "integrity shopping violation," and the proper procedure to follow in processing restitution from an employee's terminal wages.

The manual need not be fancy or pretentious. Many organizations use a loose-leaf format, making it easy to add or revise pages as needs and policies change. The manual must be dated and each revision must also reflect the date of such revision.

What is important is to develop a departmental handbook that will be a truly functional tool—one that will be used, that provides quick instruction for the new employee or the guard assigned to a new post, that spells out procedures to be followed in any given situation, and that serves as a source of authority to settle disagreements or resolve confusion, which is especially valuable when there is wide geographic dispersal of personnel, such as in a large petroleum distribution network or a chain of shopping centers.

The security manual typically would have the same general appearance and format of the other departments' operating manuals and would be one part of the company library of operating procedures.

Departmental Newsletter

In an organization with a closed climate of communication, there is a reluctance to reduce policies and procedures to writing or, if they are put down on paper, a reluctance to make such material available to the employees.

The written-down type of communication goes beyond policies, procedures, and how to. A departmental newspaper or newsletter is an excellent communication medium. In one security organization, *The Rap Sheet* is an 8- to 12-page monthly newsletter written for the general interest of Security Department employees. A typical issue will carry a general motivational or good management techniques statement from the Director; a "Security Officer of the Month" article, with picture; a listing of promotions and transfers; an "In Response to You" column (sort of a "Dear Abby" column answered by the Security Director); pending or new laws that will have an impact on the organization; interesting arrests and/or investigations; interesting security statistics such as arrests for the year to date against last year's figures; a security question of the month, with the answer to the previous month's question; a security-oriented puzzle; and perhaps a security cartoon. As good as an electronic newsletter may be, the old-fashion multi-page printed news, which can be fold up and taken home to share with the family, is still of real value.

The benefits of this type of communication are innumerable. Employees more closely identify with the organization and feel a part of the department. They appreciate being kept abreast of the latest happenings; they are well informed. They love the recognition afforded them in print. The Director has a vehicle to make known his or her standards and goals. In the eyes of the company and its nonsecurity employees, the polished security publication is another indicator of the professionalism growing in the industry today.

Written-Horizontal

An example of written-horizontal communications is a company-wide security newsletter (or column in the company paper) that provides the security administrator with the opportunity to communicate what is happening in the security world to the company as a whole. Too often, Security Departments are considered mysterious and organizationally noncontributory functions. The good security administrator can bring recognition to his or her department by opening up communication and sharing information with management of the company whenever possible.

As an example, one retail security organization publishes a monthly *Security Newsletter for Management.* The objective of this publication is to make management personnel aware of the security risks and security achievements in the industry. This simple, clean-looking, four-page newsletter opens with a series of condensed incidents of recent occurrence in the retail community at large. One typical incident:

> In a competitor's store in the downtown area, four adults of Latin descent, two men and two women, entered the women's sportswear area. While one of the women engaged the saleswoman in a complicated transaction, her companions removed a total of ten fur-trimmed suede coats from the racks. Techniques used: the woman rolled four coats and crotched them (placed them under her dress and held them between her thighs), and each of the men wrapped three coats around his midsection under a raincoat. All four escaped in a white Ford Bronco bearing out-of-state white license plates with red lettering and numbers. Total loss: $6,700.

That story is followed by others, still concentrating on attacks against competitor stores. These might include incidents of malicious mischief (juveniles setting off sprinkler heads, with resultant water damage), use of stolen credit cards, and so forth.

Following these are incidents within the company, chosen for dramatic impact. Again, the objective is to make management aware of security problems and the Security Department's efforts and successes in these problem areas of the business.

Among the incidents described are stories of recent employee dishonesty cases (names of employees are omitted). Each of these vignettes concludes with information on the disposition of the incident, such as termination of an employee or police department booking. Figure 13.1 illustrates a typical page from the newsletter.

Unit managers not only read each and every word of each publication, but they circulate the newsletter to their staff members and then read it aloud at departmental manager meetings. Discussions follow. The monthly impact remains constant: renewed amazement at the scope of the security problems, amazement over cleverness in tactics, and shock at the constancy of internal theft problems.

The end result is greater security awareness within the organization.

Written-Up

It is critical to recognize the need for employees to communicate upward (and the need is as much for the Director to know what is on the minds of subordinates as it is for every employee to have the opportunity to express himself or herself). *The Rap Sheet* already mentioned was originally designed as a two-way communication tool: written-down and written-up.

```
DISHONEST        Region I
EMPLOYEE
                 A member of the Housekeeping staff was observed leaving
                 store with a bucket and mop on his way to clean the Tire
                 Center. His bucket was checked and under the mop was a
                 Craig Stereo cassette tape deck and a Sony AM/FM radio.
                 Employee was escorted back to store where he subsequently
                 admitted theft and was terminated.

DISHONEST        Region I
EMPLOYEE
HANDOUT          An employee in Jr. World had a friend come into department.
                 The friend selected a top and a pair of pants and went into
                 the fitting room. Once her friend had entered the bank of
                 fitting rooms, the employee stood at the entrance and acted
                 as a lookout. When the accomplice emerged from the fitting
                 room she had only the pair of pants. After a brief conver-
                 sation between the two, the accomplice left the store. The
                 accomplice was later arrested in one of the Mall stores
                 where she worked. The employee was terminated and both
                 were booked by the Culver City Police Department.

ATTEMPTED        West Covina
GRAB & RUN
                 Night Service Manager, Mr. Smith, prevented a "grab and
                 run." Smith observed a car parked outside the store's door
                 in an unauthorized parking space and took down the license
                 plate number. He then waited around to see what the two
                 males in the car were waiting for. He then observed a
                 male grab an armful of Dept. 50 merchandise. Smith then
                 took after the suspect, whereupon the suspect turned around
                 and threw the merchandise at Smith.

                     License Plate Number:

                     Total Recovery:  $473.00

SHOPLIFTER       Fashion Valley

                 A Roving Security Officer observed a F/C, 5'6", 115 lbs.,
                 34 yrs. old, blonde curly hair and glasses, carrying a
                 stuffed handbag clutched tightly to her side. The "custom-
                 er" exited the store and came back shortly with an empty
                 handbag. The R.S.O. followed the "customer" to the Chil-
                 dren's Department where she rolled a child's robe and gown
                 and placed them in her handbag. On her way out, she stopped
                 in Cosmetics and picked up some lotion which she also put
                 in her purse. The "customer" was apprehended as she exited
                 the store.

                 During interrogation she confessed to having made several
                 trips into the          as well as other mall stores. Over
                 $600.00 worth of merchandise was recovered...$500.00 from
                          and the remainder from        and        . She
                 was arrested and booked by the San Diego Police Department
                 for Grand Theft.
```

Figure 13.1 Typical page from *Security Newsletter for Management.*

How was this accomplished? The first issue of *The Rap Sheet* stated that, in an effort to further open communication, questions, suggestions, and complaints were solicited from all security employees, with the promise that every such question, suggestion, or complaint would be answered. The response was impressive.

Not all suggestions are adopted. Not all problems are solved. However, all received a response. All employees have a way, without putting themselves in jeopardy, to have their say, to be heard by the Director, and to hear what he or she has to say in response.

If an open climate of communication is to be established, some such two-way avenue of expression is essential.

Verbal-Horizontal

There are two types of verbal-horizontal communications within the context of the definition of an open climate of communication. The first is intradepartmental (i.e., security personnel only) and the second involves communications with other departments in the company.

"Rap sessions" constitute the intradepartmental type. One such session might give subunits of the Security Department, such as the Fraud Unit, the chance to sit down together without regard to rank and talk about their work—the practices, techniques, problems, failures, and successes—with no specific objective in mind except to communicate. As a rule, something of value will surface in these sessions. This could be anything from a clarification of a misunderstanding between two peers to a more realistic deadline on certain types of cases. The important result is that all participants leave the session with a good feeling about themselves, their unit, and the Security Department as a whole. As individuals, they had a chance to be heard, a chance to think out loud, and a chance to be themselves.

The second type of horizontal verbal communication occurs when the Security Director and any number of staff people go out into the company and meet with various units. These meetings are also "sit down around the table and talk" sessions. A certain "ice-breaker" is to ask attendees for their suggestions on how to handle a given situation or problem; for example, what would be the best way to introduce and distribute new bumper decals for specified parking lots? Here's a guarantee: Almost everyone there will have a suggestion (and they'll all be different—with one perhaps a better strategy than the one already agreed on before the meeting!) The most important skill needed by the security representatives in these kinds of communication settings is *listening* skills! It is also important that there is a friendly climate in which questions are encouraged and that Security speaks openly and honestly to the questions.

The benefits of broader communication within the company are invaluable. Questions such as "What right does Security have to search our briefcases and parcels when we leave the building?" give Security the opportunity to cite the authority and talk about the whys. Perhaps not every person will be satisfied with the reasons, but they will leave such meetings with a better understanding and appreciation for security. This assignment calls for a security representative who is comfortable and at ease in this type of challenging environment. How questions and complaints are handled can leave a very favorable impression on participants in attendance or a very negative impression.

Communication, then, is the very lubricant that makes the managerial machinery run smoothly and efficiently.

Action

It is true that action speaks louder than words. The administrator who wants to establish a climate of open communication had better be prepared both to listen and to respond.

If management is sincere in wanting suggestions from employees about the running of the Security Department, it stands to reason that some of their ideas will have merit. In fact, security executives will find it a constant source of amazement to see how smart and creative so many people are. Some managers feel that "I am the boss, and I should have all the valuable ideas!" This attitude is shortsighted but is unfortunately a not too uncommon managerial disease.

Thus if you ask for ideas, you must adopt some—the ones that are meaningful and contribute to the success of the organization. If you ask for complaints, then you must be prepared to take appropriate corrective action to cure those complaints.

If you reject sound ideas, you will discover over a period of time that the sources of those ideas within the organization have dried up; there will be no more upward communication. If you are critical of questions or are unresponsive or evasive, the questioning will taper away to nothing—no more upward communication. If you disregard the message contained in complaints and fail to react in a positive and corrective way, you will lose the benefit of hearing what is troubling your employees. An example in this connection is the case in which the Director hears from a number of employees that a certain supervisor engages in heavy-handed supervisory techniques and intimidates subordinates. If the Director disregards such information and takes no action, or even promotes the supervisor in question, the credibility of the open climate of communication becomes a joke. If, on the other hand, the Director causes the supervisor to be exposed to a leadership-training program, credibility and his or her communication "program" are maintained and enhanced.

ABOUT LISTENING

Early in this chapter there was reference to an employee's failure to understand, perhaps owing to his or her failure to listen. Listening is a skill that every supervisor and manager must understand because it is a vital element in communication. A story attributed to the Bhagwan Shree Rajneesh goes as follows: Two men were walking along a crowded and busy downtown street. One said, "Listen to the lovely chirping of that cricket." The other man said he couldn't hear it and asked his friend how he could detect that sound amidst the din of people and traffic. The first man removed a coin from his pocket and dropped it, whereupon a dozen people stopped and began to look about on the sidewalk. "We hear," he said, "what we listen for." The man who dropped the coin was a zoologist and had trained himself to listen to the voices of nature. Managers must train themselves to listen to what is being said.

Those in management must train themselves to listen to subordinates as much as they listen to those in higher positions. Both are important. One good self-teaching guide is entitled *Listening, The Forgotten Skill.*[1]

SUMMARY

Communication ranks at the top of the effective manager's skills. Both the organization and its employees will be better served by an open climate of communication (both upward and downward), whether verbal or written.

Better understanding is ensured when communications are in writing wherever possible. Written-down communications might include the essential department handbook as well as departmental newsletters. Avenues should also be provided for written-up communications, in which the employees have the opportunity to express their ideas and feelings to management.

Horizontal communications, both within the department and between Security and other employees and units of the company, are mutually beneficial. An open climate of communication will remain viable and credible only when management listens—and responds.

The manager who is a strong communicator and a good listener is a strong manager. By the same token, the manager who is a weak communicator and poor listener is a weak manager.

REVIEW QUESTIONS

1. What is meant by "stovepipe" communication? Give an example of the shortcomings of this type of communication.

2. Discuss several factors that result in the breakdown of verbal communications.

3. Briefly describe two types of newsletters that might be effective communication tools for the Security Department.

---

[1] Burley-Allen, Madelyn. *Listening, The Forgotten Skill,* 2nd ed. (New York: John Wiley & Sons, 1995).

4. Discuss the ways in which a security manager can establish an open climate of communication in his or her department.

5. Describe two types of "horizontal" communication and their potential benefits.

14

Career (Proprietary) vs. Noncareer (and Contract) Personnel

When this chapter was originally written the term *outsourcing* as a management strategy was either unknown or was uncommonly used. Now in the twenty-first century, outsourcing security is viewed as a viable option and is exercised with some regularity. Over the past decade there has been somewhat of a decline of proprietary security employees, giving way to the growth of contract services. However, there was a major reversal of that trend when the U.S. Department of Transportation went to a proprietary security program for baggage screeners at our nation's airports. Aside from the issue of organizational expenses, the question of utilizing career (proprietary) versus noncareer (and contracted) personnel to discharge the security function within a given organization is clearly still worthy of examination.

Career personnel may be defined as full-time (usually on a 40-hour work week) proprietary employees on a "career path," with apparent intentions and aspirations to grow in the organization, in the security career field, or in another career field within the company (such as personnel services). *Career path* means, in this context, a track leading to continual vertical movement within the greater organizational pyramid.

There are two major categories of noncareer personnel: (1) in-house part-time employees with a short work week (e.g., 20 hours) and (2) employees of another company who perform duties for the organization on a contractual or service fee basis.

At the outset it must be understood that many factors have an impact on the type of personnel to be used in the security function. The most important factor is the character and nature of the function. What could very well be an advantage in one security operation might be a distinct disadvantage in another. However, the following somewhat generalized categorization should provide some insight into the difference between career and noncareer personnel.

The title of this chapter may suggest that an axiomatic choice of one approach over the other will be the ultimate result of the comparison, but that may not the case. Rather, an objective consideration will reveal good points and bad points, advantages and disadvantages, to both career and noncareer personnel, and, in view of that, the decision to have a blend of both might well be the best solution to the security manpower needs of a particular organization.

CAREER PERSONNEL

Advantages of Career Personnel

1. Companies with in-house or "proprietary" security programs tend to attract people seeking career positions and career opportunities. Competition for such openings allows selection of the most qualified individuals. Attractions of career jobs include salary, pension or retirement plans, profit sharing programs, the entire employee "benefit package" (which usually includes medical, hospitalization, dental and life insurance, vacation, and sick leave), and employee privileges unique to the company (such as merchandise discounts in retailing and free or near-free travel for those in the transportation industry).

2. Career personnel develop a loyalty to the department as well as to the company. They identify with the organization and see its welfare as synonymous with their own.

3. Career personnel tend to have greater knowledge of the company, its "ins and outs," and with such insight they function more efficiently and smoothly.

4. Career personnel establish an esprit de corps or comradeship, and the resultant pride reflects in their performance.

5. Career personnel tend to be more ambitious and motivated to work due to apparent opportunities for clear steps up the promotional ladder.

6. There is more stability among career personnel in terms of turnover in an organization, primarily because of seniority and vested interest.

7. There is more communication between the security function and the rest of the company when career people are in place, usually because of mutual company identity and common company interests.

8. Career personnel tend to be better trained because training costs are "hidden," that is, the cost of training is part of salary expense and is not identifiable as an extra expenditure. In the case of contractual service, the time that the contract personnel must spend in on-the-job training with the client company is an added cost.

9. There is a higher degree of technical proficiency among career people because the company is willing to invest the necessary time and money to train them in anticipation of pay-back through long-term service.

Example of the advantage of career personnel: Telephone companies are an excellent example of the many security organizations that utilize career personnel almost exclusively. Telephone company security agents identify closely with their firm, have in-depth knowledge of the telephone communication business, and take pride in their department as well as their employer. They rarely change companies. They know people throughout the company, because in most cases they came from nonsecurity ranks. They are well trained and have a high degree of technical proficiency.

Disadvantages of Career Personnel

1. In terms of costs, career personnel are substantially more expensive than noncareer people. For example, it costs an additional 30% of each full-time career employee's pay to fund the employee benefit package. Other costs, either capital or sundry including everything from equipment and office facilities to uniforms, are unavoidable in a proprietary organization. Appreciable savings in this area can usually be realized in contractual agreements with outside security providers because these costs have already been incurred by the contractor.
2. Career personnel constitute a fixed, limited cadre or pool of manpower resources. Special events, special problems, or emergencies could well sap the organization and have an adverse impact on the daily security requirements.
3. There is a certain amount of inflexibility in the deployment of career people in terms of location and time scheduling, more frequently than not due to company policy. Personnel policy might require 3, 5, or 7 days' notice of a shift change, which obviously limits security management's flexibility in its attempt to provide protection. Career employees often enjoy "portal to portal" pay and travel time allowance for reporting to a location other than their regular place of work, whereas contract services might have personnel already in place at the distant location, with no loss of time or additional expense.
4. Because of the employee-employer relationship between the career employee and the company, certain disciplinary restrictions can be departmentally counterproductive. The inherent obligation of management to its employees, the source of which is traceable to governmental, administrative, and judicial rulings, affords every employee job security—to the point that even those employees who, for one reason or another, perform at a marginal if not substandard level must be retained for lengthy periods of time before their discharge. There is no such employee-employer relationship with noncareer (contract) people in place.
5. Career manpower resources have limited parameters and ceilings of talent, and departmental capabilities are restricted as a result.
6. There is the ever-present problem of those career people who "top-out" at one level or position, and when told or otherwise realizing they will not progress any further, become disenchanted or resentful. Such employees frequently will not leave, and even though there is an

attitude problem, management cannot terminate them because their job performance meets standards, however minimally.

Example of the disadvantage of career personnel: Personnel policies of many organizations require a series of job performance cautions and warnings, alerting the employee that he or she is performing below standards and giving the opportunity to improve. For example, one company requires three such warnings, spaced at least 30 days apart, before the employee can be given notice. Thus the department is obliged to endure approximately 90 days or one fourth of a year of substandard work.

In addition, an individual so terminated may file a legal action against the company on the grounds that the company's entire action against him or her was not based on work performance but on one form or another of prejudice (race, creed, sex, or age). The company must then mount a legal defense (at no small expense) and subsequently may be obliged to reinstate the former employee with full back wages for all time elapsed between termination and the final determination of the issue, which could constitute a full year's wages all at once.

PART-TIME NONCAREER PERSONNEL

Advantages of Part-Time Noncareer Personnel

1. Part-time in-house employees are less costly than career personnel because they are not entitled to the full employee benefit package.
2. Part-time employees, by virtue of the agreement made at the time of hire regarding their schedule, allow for security coverage at difficult or unusual hours that otherwise would require overtime or premium pay to regulars. This allows for broad and flexible coverage.
3. Deployment of part-time people permits security management the unique opportunity to analyze their performance over an extended period of time. If a part-timer proves productive he or she can move into an unfilled career position if he or she desires that opportunity.
4. The use of part-time security employees allows management to tap particularly high-caliber people for security service. Local colleges and universities are an excellent recruiting ground for part-timers. Intelligent and capable college students can make a substantial contribution to the security function in a wide variety of capacities. Part-time schedules usually fit into their school schedules as well as their financial needs, and this employment proves to be a bargain both ways.

Also, more and more women are returning to the labor market, many of whom have raised their children and wish to be productive members of the community but do not want or cannot handle career or otherwise full-time jobs. These people bring maturity and common sense to part-time positions.

Finally, a number of people who have retired early still need to be productive, and they, too, can be a definite asset to the Security Department.

Example of the advantage of part-time noncareer personnel: Providing security coverage for an amusement park that is open 12 hours a day would pose a real problem to the security administrator responsible for such coverage—if, that is, all security personnel were career people. For example, assume that 10 officers are required to open and 10 to close and that the park is open from noon to midnight. With full-time employees only, the first 10 officers go on duty at noon and go off duty at 8:00 P.M. The second shift must go on duty at 4:00 P.M. and work until midnight to serve their full 8-hour shift. Between 4:00 P.M. and 8:00 P.M. there are 80 working hours being expended when only 40 hours are required. One full-time unit is wasted each day.

With effective scheduling of part-time personnel, on the other hand, the coverage could be as follows: five regulars and five part-timers (working a 4-hour schedule) start at noon. At 4:00 P.M. the part-timers go off duty and are replaced with five regulars who will work until midnight. At 8:00 P.M. the original five regulars go off duty, replaced with five part-timers who work until midnight. (Actually the two categories would be mixed and staggered.) The schedule of coverage is economical and efficient.

Without question, utilization of part-time personnel helps alleviate scheduling problems.

Disadvantages of Part-Time Noncareer Personnel

1. Part-time employees have a decidedly limited commitment to the job and to the organization. They do not feel the same degree of responsibility as does a career employee. The limited feeling of responsibility results in more part-time employees failing to report, calling in sick, or offering other excuses for not appearing. Therefore, part-timers are less reliable.
2. The primary interest or attention of part-time personnel is somewhere other than the job—school, family, or another job. Consequently, keen interest and attention are usually lacking. They do not identify with the company, and as a result their conduct on the job is affected adversely.
3. The relationship between the company and the part-timer is essentially mercenary in nature: immediate remuneration for services rendered. That means the primary work motivator of the part-timer is money, not achievement, challenge, growth, or responsibility.
4. There are a limited number of people looking for part-time work. By far most people in the job market want full-time employment.

5. By virtue of their own emergency status in the public sector, off-duty police officers who work part-time in security cannot be counted on by the company when a major disturbance or calamity occurs in the area—those very times when they are needed the most.
6. Another disadvantage of the off-duty police officer as a part-time security employee is his or her tendency to take more chances, because of experience and peace officer status, than would a civilian security officer, particularly in making arrests.

Example of the disadvantage of part-time noncareer personnel: A department store plans coverage of a given store from opening to closing, using a part-time employee in the plan for evening protection. Because of absence of a real commitment, the part-timer fails to show for any number of reasons, leaving the store short of security help. The question of dependability is the biggest disadvantage in the use of this type of employee.

CONTRACTUAL NONCAREER PERSONNEL

Advantages of Contractual Noncareer Personnel

1. There is a considerable cost savings, in terms of the expense of the employee benefit package and other career employee privileges, when contractual personnel from outside the organization are engaged.
2. There is complete freedom to terminate the services of an individual serving the company on a contractual basis. Such termination can be immediate and without cause. That means that if appearance, grooming, attitude, age, demeanor, or performance is for any reason below the standards set by the company, the person can be removed from the job and returned to his or her employer, without repercussions.
3. There is good flexibility in manpower resources in a contractual arrangement. The security force can be increased to meet unexpected demands overnight if need be. This can be achieved by the primary contractor sending more personnel or calling on another contractor for short-term assistance.
4. Use of contracted services reduces miscellaneous nonsecurity expenses such as recruiting and advertising costs, personnel interviewing and administration costs, timekeeping, and payroll administration costs.
5. There is freedom to terminate services of a contractual firm if that firm's services fall below required standards. Contracts, whether written or agreed on verbally, usually allow for a 30-day termination clause, and poor performance justifies execution of this clause.
6. Flexibility of coverage and service in a geographically dispersed operation is a decided advantage of contractual help.

7.   The short-term and/or infrequent needs for personnel with unique or highly specialized skills and technical know-how, such as a polygraph operator, can effectively be met on a contractual basis.

Example of the advantage of contractual noncareer personnel: Consider a case in which the Security Department contracts for the placement of an undercover agent in a warehouse for the purpose of gathering information on possible internal theft. The undercover agent's primary employer is a contract service firm. The agent receives a salary from them as well as a regular paycheck, like every other warehouse employee, from the company that owns the warehouse. For a period of time some useful intelligence is obtained, but after a while the undercover agent becomes personally involved with other warehouse employees and the reports become valueless. Even though the agent wishes to remain employed in the warehouse, services can be terminated forthwith without violating the agent's rights to job security, because the real (and primary) employer is the firm that sent the agent to the warehouse and is still paying the undercover salary (although it may be less than the warehouse salary).

If, on the other hand, the Security Department had hired an applicant directly into the warehouse to serve as an undercover agent, that person would be entitled to some job protection and could not be summarily removed from the job. The use of contractual services has some very definite advantages.

Disadvantages of Contractual Noncareer Personnel

1.   Except for those few firms that pay excellent salaries, most contractual firms attract personnel with minimal poor qualifications. In order for the contract firm to be competitive and make a fair profit, the individual must settle for a lesser wage than would be paid for a comparable job in a noncontractual firm.

2.   There is more turnover in noncareer personnel because they may find what they believe is a career or a better job elsewhere or because their talent can best be used elsewhere by the contract firm. That means, of course, that the highest rate of turnover occurs among the most talented people sent to service the client. There are exceptions in which the client recognizes the talent and ensures that the compensation package is competitive and that the responsibilities connected with the assignment provide professional satisfaction.

3.   There tends to be an absence of pride among contractual service people—pride in themselves, in many cases, as well as pride in their organization—and the absence of pride reflects in performance. Note my use of the word *tends.* There are some quality contract security

firms who really do engender pride amongst their employees, but that's the exception, not the rule.

4. There tends to be resentment on the part of many contract people regarding the fact that they work for a company (client) but are not entitled to the benefits the regular employees receive. As a result, some contract employees seek to be hired by the client company as regular employees. Most client-contractor agreements now include provisions prohibiting such job changing or requiring the payment of a fee by the client if the client wants that employee. (*Note:* These agreements only validate the point that contract people frequently would prefer to iden-tify with the other employees and the client's firm.)

5. Ambition and motivation are questionable in many cases because opportunities for advancement seem limited, or the contract firms have failed to lay out meaningful and comprehensible career paths and make their people aware of such opportunities.

Example of the disadvantage of contractual noncareer personnel: A major shopping center contracted for guard services, awarding the contract to a reputable firm with excellent leadership at the top. Securing this particular contract was an important addition to the list of clients being served, and good people were assigned to this most visible job. As time passed, the contract firm grew and turnover increased. The guards on the site became careless in appearance, inattentive, unreliable, and eventually became a source of embarrassment to the shopping center. Such a condition would not have developed had the service been proprietary, with career people in place. (On the other hand, some shopping centers, to name but one of hundreds of types of clients, have had excellent results with contract services.)

COMBINING CAREER AND NONCAREER PERSONNEL

Clearly, then, there are many factors to be considered in weighing the pros and cons of career and noncareer personnel. In addition to those factors dis-cussed previously, there are others not explored but also most important. Those are reflected best in simple good management practices and supervi-sory skills. Despite their disadvantages, career personnel can excel, depend-ing on good management. Noncareer personnel, contractual or part-time, despite the disadvantages enumerated previously, can excel if given proper supervision and good management.

Early in this chapter, reference was made to the possible utilization of both career and noncareer people—a blend of both. That is precisely the practice in many organizations. In one retail chain, the core of the Security Department comprises well-trained professional career personnel. Comple-menting them is a large cadre of part-time security employees including a large number of college students, many of whom are studying in the criminal justice curriculum. At the time of this writing, supplemental contractual services include some uniformed guards, undercover agents, temporary "agent" assignments, and integrity shoppers. To provide adequate protection with career people exclusively would be nearly impossible. To protect the company with noncareer personnel exclusively would likewise be very difficult indeed!

An appropriate balance or blend of both is recommended. There is a need for both and room for both in the security industry.

SUMMARY

There are advantages and disadvantages to employing full-time career security personnel or noncareer employees drawn from part-time workers or contract security services.

Stability, loyalty, improved "local knowledge," superior pride and motivation, and the opportunity for better communications and training are advantages of career personnel. On the other side of the coin are increased costs, limited numbers, the attendant inflexibility of deployment, and potential problems of discipline and limited skill levels.

Part-timers are less costly, provide desirable flexibility in assignment, and allow management to draw from high-caliber sources such as students and women available only on a part-time basis. However, part-time personnel tend to lack the career employee's commitment to job and company.

Contract services offer the benefits of cost savings, freedom to terminate services at any time, great flexibility both in manpower resources and in coverage of widely dispersed operations, and specialized skills. Commonly cited disadvantages include low-paid personnel, high turnover rates, and a lower level of pride and motivation.

No one type of employee is right for all situations; in fact, many companies can best be served by an appropriate blend of full- and part-time and in-house and contract security personnel.

REVIEW QUESTIONS

1. What is the definition of *career personnel?*

2. What are the two categories of noncareer personnel?

3. List six of the advantages of using career personnel in the Security Department. Contrast these with six disadvantages.

4. Give an example of how utilization of part-time personnel can help solve scheduling problems.

5. Describe the advantages, in terms of flexibility, of using contractual personnel.

6. Discuss the statement, "An appropriate balance or blend of career and noncareer personnel is recommended."

III

OPERATIONAL MANAGEMENT

15

Planning and Budgeting

The budgeting process might best be approached in terms of the following questions:

What is a budget?

Why do we have a budget?

When is a budget prepared?

Who participates in the budgeting process?

How is a budget prepared?

Such a broadly pragmatic approach overrides the more detailed concepts, philosophies, and strategies, such as "zero-based budgeting," about which entire texts have been written. The emphasis here is on fundamentals—an understanding of the basics provides groundwork for sophistication and growth.

The established Security Director, moreover, is already involved in an ongoing budget program in the organization. Even the new manager, whether promoted from within or brought in from outside the company, will inherit budgeting responsibilities in an existing framework. A pragmatic approach to the budgeting process, therefore, is most useful.

WHAT IS A BUDGET?

The management process is the coordination and integration of all resources to accomplish organizational objectives. According to this definition, management is understood in terms of the functions a manager performs—that is, planning, decision making, organizing, directing, and controlling. Each of these functions has an impact, to one degree or another, on the budgeting process. Controlling, for example, is that process aimed at ensuring, through overt, timely action, that events conform to plans. Plans must be based on good judgment and good decision-making estimates about the future. The budget is that plan stated in financial terms. Planning and budgeting go hand-in-hand. You cannot have a budget without a plan, and every plan, if it is viable and is to be executed, must have a budget. A budget, therefore, is each of the following:

- A plan stated in financial terms
- A realistic estimate of the resources required to implement a plan
- An allocation of resources to achieve planned objectives
- An instrument that records work programs in terms of appropriations needed to place them into effect
- A management tool intended to ensure that work programs are carried out as planned

Obviously, the definition of the budget must include plans (or programs, which in and of themselves are plans).

The elements of a budget can be illustrated in a practical security situation. The Security Department decides to provide a rape prevention program for the female employees of the company. The objective of the program is obviously aimed at educating employees on ways to protect themselves against the possibility of rape, ways to increase their safety during movement to and from home, and so on. With the objective established, next comes the planning of how to achieve this educational goal. The plans could include the rental or purchase of a commercially prepared film on rape prevention, preparation of posters announcing the program, scheduling of a security officer's time to conduct the program, rental of equipment to show the film, retaining an outside speaker who is considered an expert on the subject, and distribution of an antirape booklet to the participants following the program.

Once the plan spells out what must happen to achieve the stated objective, it must then be costed-out, or restated in dollars and cents.

Videotape purchase	$695.00
Posters	
artwork	330.00
printing	222.50
Rental of VCR	70.00
Guest speaker fee	700.00
300 booklets @ .98	294.00
Rape Prevention Budget	$2,311.50

To repeat, then, a budget is a plan stated in financial terms, a realistic estimate of the resources required to implement a plan, an allocation of resources to achieve planned objectives, a way in which we record programs in terms of the dollars needed to place such programs into effect, and a tool intended to ensure that the program comes off as planned.

WHY DO WE HAVE A BUDGET?

The budget breathes life into a plan and gives the plan direction. It requires the manager to direct the plan in three dimensions:

1. The operation or project must unfold as planned if the budget is followed exactly. (If we planned on a videotape for the rape prevention program, the tape will in fact be used if the allocated dollars are spent to purchase the tape. Without the budget as a guide, something could easily be substituted for the tape, and thus the plan would not be followed.)
2. The operation or project will take place when planned because budgets are time-phased; that is, plans must be executed in keeping with the budgeted availability of funds. In other words, if the salary budget for a 6-month period amounts to $600,000, that money is not available in one lump sum at the beginning of the 6-month period but rather is rationed out through budget management over the planned period of time.
3. The operation or project will not exceed the planned costs if the budget is managed properly. Without a doubt, the person who proceeds to build a house from the ground up without a budget will spend more money than the person who builds the house within a planned budget.

The three variables—the actual operation or project, the schedule or timing of that project or operation, and the costs—must be kept within the parameters of the budget. The budget provides those parameters: It gives direction. That is why we have budgets. The mark of good management is reflected in how closely the budgets are followed.

WHEN IS A BUDGET PREPARED?

Annual (12-month) budgets may be prepared and finalized more than a year in advance. Biannual (6-months) budgets are usually prepared and finalized mid-period, or 3 months before the new budget period.

The novice in the budgeting process finds this aspect of forecasting, or projecting into the future, the most difficult to come to grips with. This difficulty is probably due to our natural inclination to think in terms of the here and now—not 9 months downstream or late next year. Experienced, effective managers more often than not have a reputation of being able to "think ahead" and having certain predictive skills that enable them to anticipate events that will occur in the future. The average line employee tends to think of work in terms of today, whereas the manager thinks of work in substantially larger blocks of time. Thinking ahead is not necessarily a measure of intelligence but rather represents a conditioning and requisite of managerial responsibilities.

How does one plan for security requirements and cost next year? How does one plan for criminal attacks and emergencies, which may or may not occur and which may be large or small in proportion, at times unknown? The answer is that one dos not plan or budget for the unknown or the unpredictable; one budgets for intelligently anticipated and predictable conditions, based on known conditions in the present and the past. For example, security management in the steel-fabricating industry is planning for the following year. In that year labor contracts will expire; already issues are surfacing that could cause serious conflict between labor and management. Under such conditions, along with a past experience of labor violence, extraordinary security measures should be planned to commence with the expiration of the contract. As stated previously, plans must be based on good judgment and good decision-making estimates about the future.

As a matter of fact, the predictability of security requirements for the future is relatively accurate. Truly major emergencies of the type that would have a serious impact on the budget would be incidents of catastrophic proportion, such as natural disasters, for example, earthquake, flooding, and so forth, or an act of terrorism, such as the totally unexpected destruction of the Twin Towers in New York City on September 11, 2001. Such events, fortunately, are few and far between.

The steel manufacturing security planner, then, can count on increased security needs when the contract expires; the university security planner can count on increased problems in June (when the pressure of final examinations is over); the retail security planner can count on increased needs between Thanksgiving and New Year's Day. All can make decisions about plans and costs in the future.

This is not to say that a Security Department should not have emergency or contingency plans for major catastrophes. Indeed they should have. As a rule, however, such emergency plans are broad and generalized "game plans" that include such things as who will be in command, reporting responsibilities and channels, specific asset protection steps, and life-saving/first-aid setups. Such a plan has broad parameters; it is considered a guide or road map and probably has no budget. If the plan must be implemented, costs receive little attention in view of the magnitude of the problems of property destruction and the loss of human lives. Dollars, in this context, do not count, at least during the early stages of the emergency.

WHO PARTICIPATES IN THE BUDGETING PROCESS?

There are "bottom-up and top-down" and "top-down and bottom-up" approaches to budgeting. The latter is preferable because senior management initiates the process by establishing acceptable expenditure guidelines before the detailed planning by the operating or middle management. For a given upcoming budget year, the general guideline could be that middle management should continue their cost-effectiveness efforts in all operations as they have for the previous 2 years. Following the detailed planning by the individual managers (Security Manager or Director in our case), senior management will evaluate and then set the final budget level, based on financial outlook for the budget period.

Top-Down and Bottom-Up Process

Phase One: Senior Management—Top-Down

1. Establishes operating guidelines for the Security Department.
2. Establishes acceptable expenditure guidelines, that is, given number of dollars.

Phase Two: Security (Middle) Management—Bottom-Up

1. Evaluates the security operation and projects. (*Operation* means a continuing, ongoing function; *project* means a short-term activity; for example, a rape prevention program is a project, not an operation.)
2. Submits courses of action for achieving organizational goals.
3. Costs-out such courses of action.
4. Develops and recommends alternative courses. For example, the initial plan (or course of action) for the rape prevention program came to $2,311.50. Alternatives include:

   (a) Do not offer the program at all.
   (b) Do not buy the tape; rent it instead and save $600.000, bringing the cost to $1,711.50.
   (c) Rent the tape and do not call in a guest speaker; simply have a rap session following the tape, thus reducing the program to $1,011.50.
   (d) In addition to (c) previously listed, eliminate posters and announce the program through supervisors, thus reducing the program another $552.50, and so on.

Phase Three: Senior Management—Top-Down

1. Reviews activities, costs, and alternatives recommended by security management.
2. Makes decisions on the Security Manager's recommendations.
3. Allocates funds on those decisions, thus establishing the Security Department's next budget.

The entire budgeting process follows a logical or sequential pattern that brings about the interaction between senior and middle management. The sequence is as follows:

1. Planning
    *   Setting goals and objectives
2. Budget building or budget development
    *   Evaluating current activities
    *   Identifying new activities
    *   Developing alternatives
    *   Determining costs
3. Evaluation and review of recommendations
    *   Comparing against original guidelines
    *   Making decisions regarding priorities or alternatives
4. Budget establishment
    *   Allocating funds

The top security executive should work closely with key staff members in the bottom-up phase of the process, soliciting input on what the current practices are and what they should be. The executive should be asking such questions as "Why are we doing it? Why are we doing it this way? Do we have to do it? Is there an easier or better way to do it? Can we do it with four people instead of five?" To stimulate the thinking of subordinates in this manner can prove productive in efforts to reduce costs to otherwise effect savings in the function. At the same time, subordinates become involved, at least to some degree, in the budgeting function. Subordinates who participate in budget preparation tend to be more diligent in managing their respective areas of the budget later.

HOW IS A BUDGET PREPARED?

Budget costs are classified under one of three categories: (1) salary expenses, (2) sundry expenses, and (3) capital expenses.

Capital expenses will receive little attention in this text because they are usually handled apart from salary and sundry costs. In short, capital expenditures are for physical improvements, physical additions, or major expenditures for hardware. To pay a person for a day's work is a salary expense, to pay for the forms and papers that make up that person's personnel jacket is a sundry expense, and to pay for the metal filing cabinet that houses those personnel jackets is a capital expense. Capital expenses are generally considered one-time expenses, whereas salary and sundry are recurring expenses.

Salary Expense Budget

Perhaps the simplest approach to computing salary costs is to count up the security employees by classification, average out their weekly salary again by classification, and add it up (Figure 15.1).

Several things should be pointed out with reference to Figure 15.1. First, the computation could reflect anticipated overtime pay if there is a history of overtime requirements during the regular pay periods. If that is indeed the case, then the average amount of paid overtime can be included in the weekly totals or could even be averaged out to a monthly total. Thus a 4- or 5-week month could reflect, for example, $500 in overtime that would be part of the salary calculation for the period. In addition, if there is any significant amount of overtime or holiday pay due employees during the budget period, that too should be included in the calculations. Otherwise, salary expenses will exceed the planned and approved budget.

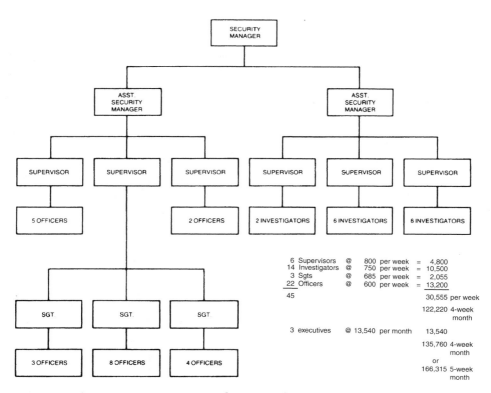

Figure 15.1 Computing salary costs for Security Department.

A standard requirement is that all budget variances in excess of a predetermined amount must be explained by the executive responsible for the budget, the Security Manager or Director. Failure to calculate Labor Day, Veterans Day, Admission Day, Christmas, and New Year's Day in holiday pay owed to personnel (assuming those are paid holidays) could result in a significant "overage." It would be embarrassing to explain that such holidays were overlooked during the preparation of the budget.

First rough then finalized calculations must be transferred to standardized budget forms, controlled by either the company's Controller or Budget Controller (Figure 15.2). Usually one copy (the original) is submitted to the Finance Division and a copy is retained in the department. Figure 15.3 reflects that transfer from the drafting stage to the formal stage. Explanations for lines 1 through 10 in Figure 15.3 are as follows:

Line 1   45 people were used last year and the same number is planned for the coming period. Although the same number of people

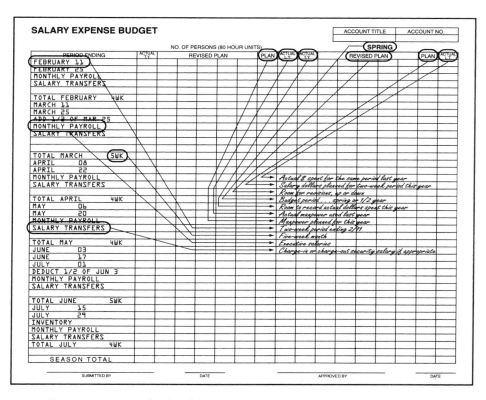

Figure 15.2   Standardized form for calculating salary expense budget.

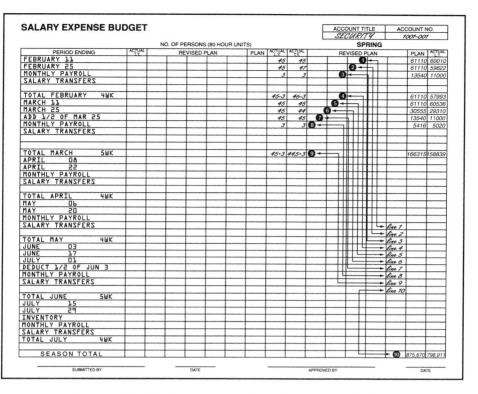

Figure 15.3   Final calculations for salary expense budget.

are being used, the dollar variance represents salary increases due to merit and wage adjustments.

Line 2   Two extra units (people) were used during a 2-week period last year. Because it is only a fluctuation from the norm, we know that it represents overtime.

Line 3   Three security "executives" last year and this year. Again, variance in salary is due to salary increases.

Line 4   Total use of personnel for the month of February, this year against last year, and total salary dollars spent last year against the plan for this year.

Line 5   Same as Line 1.

Line 6   Last year the department was down one person for a 2-week period, perhaps because of a personal leave or because an employee quit. Salary reflects this absence.

Line 7   Budgeting on the "4-5-4" plan is most common in business today. This line represents the fifth week in a 5-week month, and the odd week is so recorded in dollars.

Line 8   Executive salaries in the private sector are normally treated with confidentiality. Obviously the boss's salary would become common knowledge if recorded alone. In this instance his or her salary is folded in with that of the two right-hand people. This is a common practice.

Line 9   Same as Line 4.

Line 10   Actual salary dollars spent for the budget period last year and the planned salary dollars to be spent for the same period this year.

Companywide pay adjustments or so-called cost-of-living increases, regardless of when they take place, force the revision of the budget at the departmental level. Random increases throughout the ranks, on the other hand, normally do not require a budget revision. Revisions, upward or downward, are recorded on a form designed for just that purpose (Figure 15.4).

Sundry Expense Budget

All ongoing nonsalary expenses are considered sundry expenses. Figure 15.5 reflects a Security Department's "supplies" account. Those expenses charged to this particular account are somewhat arbitrary because the division of expenses into given accounts really depends on volume. In a large security organization, it is quite likely that a separate sundry account would be established just for uniform replacement and cleaning. In the same organization the supplies account would reflect only the first four items listed in Figure 15.5.

In addition to volume, another criterion for creating a sundry account would be the distinctive identity of that account; for example, a "travel expense" account, funds allocated specifically for security executives or personnel to travel between facilities and locations where their presence is required.

Sundry security accounts could include the following:

- Supplies
- Uniforms (replacement or upkeep)
- Travel
- Transportation
  - Lease of patrol vehicles
  - Maintenance of vehicles

REQUEST FOR EXPENSE BUDGET REVISION

SECURITY   C. A. MILLER   MAR

Store - or - Multiple Department   Requested by   Rev. Month

Rev. Month	Account #	Payroll Units		$ Amount		Requested $ Incr. $ (Decr.)	Explanation
		Rev.	Orig.	Rev.	Orig.		
MAR	1001-001	46	45	63941	62441	1500	ADDITION OF 1 INVESTIGATOR ON TEMP. ASSIGNMENT TO CLEAR BACKLOG ON SCREENING FOR NEW PLANT
	TOTAL						

Approved   Regional Manager or   Received in Budget Control   Approved
Vice President

INSTRUCTIONS: Store Manager - or - Multiple or Service Building Manager

Send this Request with *your* copy of the Budget Sheet(s) to:

Stores: Regional Store Manager
Multiple and Service Building: Appropriate Vice President

on or before _____
Your copy of the Budget Sheet(s) will be returned when approved/disapproved.

NOTE: If you have no revisions, write "NONE" on this request and return to Budget Control

Figure 15.4   Request form for expense budget revision.

- Insurance of vehicles
- Contract services
  - Central station alarm contracts
  - Employment screening service
  - Polygraph examiner retainer
  - Undercover (intelligence) service
- Professional
  - Organization membership fees

SUNDRY EXPENSE BUDGET								ACCOUNT TITLE	ACCOUNT NO.
								SECURITY SUPPLIES	1000-50

MONTH	ACTUAL T.Y.	DATE	DATE	DATE	DATE	DATE	DATE	PLAN	ACTUAL L.Y.
FEB ☐3								1000	826
MAR ☐3								1000	1151
APR ☐3								650	997
MAY ☐3								950	1084
JUN ☐3								700	1123
JUL ☐3								950	1002
TOTAL								5250	6183

DESCRIPTION OF ITEM	BUDGET AMOUNT IN MONTH IN WHICH CHARGE WILL BE MADE						TOTAL SEASON	
	FEB AUG	MAR SEPT	APR OCT	MAY NOV	JUNE DEC	JULY JAN	BUDGET	LAST YEAR
PRINTING COSTS	200	200	200	200	200	200	1200	1316
COPIER RENTAL	150	150	150	150	150	150	900	900
OFFICE SUPPLIES	50	50	50	50	50	50	300	377
COMPUTER MAINTENANCE POLICY - ALL MACHINES	50	50	50	50	50	50	300	300
RAILROAD SEAL RE-ORDER	350						350	700
UNIFORM REPLACEMENT		300		300		300	900	1111
UNIFORM CLEANING	200	200	200	200	200	200	1200	1391
LOCKS & KEYS		50			50		100	88
TOTAL	1000	1000	650	950	700	950	5250	6183

LIST PRINCIPAL ITEMS INCLUDED IN THIS BUDGET — GROUP SMALL AMOUNTS TOGETHER AND LIST AS MISCELLANEOUS

B - 8040 10/73	SUBMITTED BY	DATE	APPROVED BY	DATE

Figure 15.5 Sundry expense budget for Security supplies.

- Business or professional luncheons and other entertainment costs
- Publication subscriptions

Again, volume and identity (or, perhaps better stated, those expenses that have a common denominator) dictate the number of sundry accounts a given department might have. If uniform-related expenses are not significant in terms of dollar volume, then those expenses can be budgeted under the next most logical account, such as Supplies (see Figure 15.5). If the only travel expense is an annual trip to a convention, then a separate travel account would not be justified. The travel expense could be budgeted under Transportation or Professional.

Because budgets are a management tool, it is reasonable to conclude that one very large budget could be cumbersome and difficult to work with, whereas a number of smaller budget accounts are far more manageable and easier to use. A significant variance in a large "catch-all" sundry account would require the manager to track down all sorts of expenditures to find the cause of that variance. If the same variance is in the Transportation account, the tracking time to discover the explanation is reduced. Thus having a number of manageable sundry accounts is an efficient way to manage money.

As in the salary expense account, sundry expenses should be relatively predictable, based on good planning for the future period as well as experiences of the past. Statements or invoices should never come as a surprise to the account, except for unpredictable emergencies. In those rare cases, the budget should be revised then and there to reflect the increase.

Earlier in this chapter we discussed the three variables in the budget: the operation or project itself, the schedule or timing, and the costs. The timing of costs is most evident in Figure 15.5. So many dollars are budgeted for each month in the upper portion of the form, and then those planned expenses are broken down into specific expenditures, by month, in the lower half of the form. If this particular budget is properly managed, then the railroad seals will be purchased in February not in any other month and similarly with uniform replacements and the purchase of locks and keys.

A word of explanation is in order regarding the "Actual T.Y. (This Year)" column on the sundry as well as the salary expense budgets. As the manager works with the "tools" month by month, he or she records the budget management results in the Actual T.Y. column as the figures become available. Figure 15.6 reflects actual expenses for the first 2 months of the budget period, as entered by the manager. This obviously serves as a red flag that he or she has already exceeded the budget by $210, which should force the manager to look for a comparable savings during the following months so as to come in within the budgeted total amount. Failure to keep a running tab on expenses, sundry or salary, can lull a manager into complacency, and the net results at the end of the budget period can be an unpleasant surprise.

JUSTIFYING THE SECURITY BUDGET

It is clear evidence of poor communications between senior management and security management if the Security Manager or Director must wrestle over the issue of "selling" company management on security. He or she should not be in the position of having to justify the Security Department's existence in the company, nor should the Security Manager have to struggle for his or her fair share of the available budget dollars to be allocated among all departments. The situation in which security management is attempting to justify protection to an uninformed management group is to be avoided; rather, the operating conditions should be an open communications line, an ongoing understanding of the Security Department's objectives and the methods and strategy to achieve those objectives. The

SUNDRY EXPENSE BUDGET

ACCOUNT TITLE	ACCOUNT NO.
SECURITY SUPPLIES	1000-50

MONTH	ACTUAL T.Y.	DATE	DATE	DATE	DATE	DATE	PLAN	ACTUAL L.Y.
FEB 03	1122						1000	826
MAR 03	1088						1000	1151
APR 03							650	997
MAY 03							950	1084
JUN 03							700	1123
JUL 03							950	1002
TOTAL							5250	6183

DESCRIPTION OF ITEM

	BUDGET AMOUNT IN MONTH IN WHICH CHARGE WILL BE MADE						TOTAL SEASON	
	FEB AUG	MAR SEPT	APR OCT	MAY NOV	JUNE DEC	JULY JAN	BUDGET	LAST YEAR
TOTAL								

LIST PRINCIPAL ITEMS INCLUDED IN THIS BUDGET — GROUP SMALL AMOUNTS TOGETHER AND LIST AS MISCELLANEOUS

| B - 8040 10/73 | SUBMITTED BY | DATE | APPROVED BY | DATE |

Figure 15.6   Security supplies budget, showing actual expenses for 2-month period.

objectives should have been established by management and Security, jointly. This is another illustration of the top-down and bottom-up process. Management initially sets operating and expense guidelines, and Security, after doing its homework, comes back with plans, alternatives, and priorities. The entire process, if honest and healthy, is a mutual effort rather than a struggle by one side (Security) for recognition or survival. That honest and healthy process includes, incidentally, the absence of old-fashioned budget padding in anticipation of budget cuts.

Dr. R. Paul McCauley of the University of Louisville, an outstanding scholar of security management, developed a theory in the 1970s called "Security by Objectives" that is exciting in its simplicity and, in my view, still valid.[1] In an abbreviated form, his first four steps in security management's approach to a task are as follows:

---

[1] McCauley, R. Paul. Zero-Based Security, *Security World,* Vol. 14, No. 7, July 1977, pp. 40–41.

What must be done (or what do we have to do)?

How must it be done (or how are we going to do it)?

When must it be done (or when are we going to do it)?

How much will it cost?

Dr. McCauley's theory forms a sound basis for a practical approach to planning and budgeting. It incorporates, in slightly different form, the three variables suggested earlier in this chapter. The first two questions define the operation or projects; the third establishes the schedule or timing; the fourth determines estimated costs. In essence, this is what a budget is all about.

SUMMARY

Planning and budgeting go hand-in-hand; a budget is a plan stated in financial terms. Budgeting requires a realistic estimate of programs and their costs and an allocation of resources to achieve planned objectives.

Because budgets are prepared well in advance, effective budget management requires thinking ahead, anticipating needs based on relatively predictable conditions. The budget then becomes a tool to ensure that plans are carried out. It gives direction to planning by requiring the definition of specific programs, their timing, and their costs.

The top-down and bottom-up approach to budgeting is recommended. In this process senior management establishes goals and guidelines; the Security Manager provides the detailed planning and cost estimates; senior management reviews these recommendations, establishes priorities, and allocates funds. When budgeting reflects this interaction of senior and middle management, the protection program will be "presold," based on a mutual understanding of company goals and departmental objectives.

Budget costs are generally broken down into capital, salary, and sundry expenses. The first category of costs are generally fixed and hence easily determined. The use of detailed records from month to month and year to year makes it possible to arrive at realistic salary and sundry projections. In the area of sundry expenses, such factors as the volume of expenditures in a given category and the distinctive nature of given costs can be used to establish categories. It is generally more efficient to manage a number of smaller sundry accounts than to rely on large catch-all accounts.

REVIEW QUESTIONS

1. What are the five elements in the definition of a budget?

2. What are the three variables in a budget?

3. Briefly outline the steps in the "top-down and bottom-up" approach to budgeting.

4. Give an example of each of the following: a capital expense, a salary expense, a sundry expense.

5. Discuss the approach to setting up a salary expense budget. How should overtime expenses be handled?

6. Give four examples of sundry accounts that might be set up for a Security Department.

16

Program Management

The Security Department of any company provides a protection program that is tailored to the security needs of the company and the presence of known risks. The protection program is comprised of many lesser programs, all somehow interrelated and coordinated to form the entire protective blanket.

Because companies are living, dynamic entities, they constantly change, requiring the security programs to change also. Failure to adjust to the company's constant shifting and movement puts the security efforts out of focus. Take, for example, a firm that changes its policy and commences paying its employees on payday with bank checks instead of cash in pay envelopes. The Security Department's "program" for protecting the large cash payroll and everything surrounding that responsibility, including the arrival of the armored car in the morning, filling of pay envelopes, and disbursement of envelopes, must change.

The need for change in this case may be most evident, but in reality there is a phenomenon of resistance to change. Long after the change is made to payment by check, there is a chance that part of the Payroll Department's program and the Security Department's program will still be in place, functioning inefficiently and at an unnecessary cost. Notice that the Payroll Department is included in this program failure. Program failures are not limited to Security but occur everywhere in organizational life, particularly in large organizations, with the chance increasing in direct relationship to the increased size of the organization.

With change come new risks and hazards that were not necessarily present before the change. The new risk in the previous example might well be the vulnerability of the blank payroll checks to misuse. Thus a new security program is needed.

THE SECURITY INSPECTION PROCESS

Inspection is an important part of the security management process, which ensures that risks are recognized and covered in security programs and that programs are necessary and cost effective. The assessment of what is happening from a security point of view is made through a security inspection program. This may sound familiar, but programs, like people, don't do what you *expect*, they do what you *inspect*. Otherwise, the programs tend to "slip between the cracks." Such an inspection program

1.   Must have full support of senior management to bring about necessary change if it is needed
2.   Must be continuous in nature
3.   May be formal or informal
4.   May be structured or unstructured

Support of Senior Management

If the security inspection, which is a close and critical examination or scrutiny, reveals the need for change, then change must occur. More often than not the change requires money. Using the payroll example, safe storage for the blank payroll checks requires a secured storage room or vault. If management fails to provide the necessary funds to construct, modify, or otherwise secure a storage area and refuses to allow the purchase of an adequate vault, the inspection process is compromised. Such an occurrence is not uncommon: A security inspection will reveal a need, but management decides to incur the risk (gamble that the risk factor is not worthy of the expense) and withholds the required dollars.

In the case of the blank payroll checks, to secure or not to secure is the issue. There is no empirical way of determining the extent of the risk; it is a matter of judgment. Management personnel in the finance division could say that the risk is minimal because the checks must be processed through a check-making machine that imprints the amount as well as affixing the indicia-signature, and the machine is always under lock and key. Security's position could be that an employee intent on defrauding the company by means of the blank checks will bide time until security on the check-making machine becomes lax (and it will). Security may point out that check-making machines are available on the market (as well as underground) and that the indicia-signature is easy to counterfeit.

Because company management and security management do not concur on the level of risk or the probability of loss does not necessarily mean that company management lacks confidence in its security management; on the contrary, company management, which is ultimately responsible for the welfare of the organization, is functioning not ill advisedly or ignorantly but fully advised by protection professionals of the whole spectrum of risks. Company management makes the final decision as to the dollars that they are willing to spend to prevent losses and the chances of loss that they are willing to take by investing those dollars elsewhere in the business. After all, simply being in business is a large risk.

Ideally, Security must have the full support of senior management to bring about change if change is needed. The "if needed" should be the only opposing issue between Security and management. The good security executive more often than not will obtain management's agreement that the change he or she recommends is, in fact, needed.

Continuous Security Inspections

To keep pace with the constant changes in the organization; changes in our society in terms of attitudes, lifestyles, and moral values; and the rapidly advancing technological modifications all around us, the inspection process must be an ongoing, never-ending activity. The larger the organization, the more reasonable that statement sounds; the inspection task never seems to be finished. For smaller organizations, however, down to the one-person operation, the continuous security inspection process may appear less reasonable. However, even the smallest Security Department has a host of internal (Security Department) and external (company) areas to inspect—and inspect in great detail, too. The added advantage in the smaller firm is that the security inspection may also serve the purpose of an internal audit, which is usually conducted in a large company by internal auditors from a subunit within the finance division.

Inspection is one area in which it is fair to say that one's work is never done.

Formal or Informal Security Inspections

A formal inspection is one to which some fanfare is attached; it is usually preceded by an announcement, and the unit under inspection "prepares" for the event, including some extra housekeeping activities that would not otherwise happen at that time. To add to the importance of the occasion, a senior executive may accompany the security executive on the inspection, thereby encouraging total cooperation on the part of the unit management.

For the company that has just upgraded the security function, hired a new security administrator, or initiated a Security Department and program with a new chief, the formal approach to inspections is most desirable, primarily because it tells the company how senior management feels about protection and thus establishes the desirable climate.

Informal security inspections are usually the result of a long and firmly entrenched inspection program, which is understood by all and accepted as part of the organizational life. The inspections have been stripped of all the external trappings of importance, but their functional importance has not been lessened in any manner. They are seriously and quietly executed in a spirit of understanding and cooperation.

Structured or Unstructured Inspections

A structured inspection, as opposed to an unstructured inspection, is one that moves systematically, perhaps even rigidly, from one designated inspection area to the next and from one inspection point to the next. The following could be part of such a structure inspection:

Warehouse Exterior

1. Fencing
   a. Vegetation growth
   b. General conditions
   c. Additions or deletions
   d. Evidence of penetration
2. Gates
   a. Gate schedules
   b. Inventory locks
   c. Lock schedules
   d. Key controls
   e. Gate assignments
   f. Gate traffic logs
      1. Train
      2. Truck
      3. Personnel

Examples of checklists for use in a structured inspection are included as appendixes to this text. They can be used as is, modified individually, or collated into a single modified checklist.

The unstructured inspection, in contrast, would approach the warehouse unit in a more random manner, with less methodical attention to small specifics. The experienced eye of a top security professional would note at a glance, without following a checklist, that weeds and other vegetation against the fence need clearing.

Thus the decision as to which type of inspection format is needed depends a great deal on the expertise of the security executive involved.

Who Conducts the Inspection?

Ideally, the Security Director or Manager should conduct the inspection, along with, in every case possible, the next-ranking person in the organization. For example, in a very small department, with a chief and a uniformed staff of six people including a sergeant, the sergeant should accompany the chief.

Why should the manager conduct the inspection? It would seem that subordinates could easily follow the structured inspection and its checklist.

Certainly any number of security officials, down to supervisors, can conduct inspections. However, the lower in the ranks the function is delegated, the less important the event becomes in the eyes of the management area under inspection. This is one reason why the head of Security should conduct inspections. A second reason is that company management looks to its Security Manager for expertise and wisdom when it comes to protecting the company. His or her involvement in assessing risks and countermeasures assures them of the best assessment.

Why have a second person along on the inspection? There are three reasons. First, the experience is an outstanding training activity. After accompanying the manager on a number of inspections, the second in command—the lieutenant, for example—could move into that function easily and confidently. Second, besides gaining valuable information about the entire process of risk assessment and program evaluation, the lieutenant gains stature in the organization because of his or her relationship with the manager, who invariably holds great respect by virtue of responsibility and position in the company. Finally—and this is particularly true in small security organizations in which the next in command is not necessarily the heir apparent—he or she becomes increasingly "sensitized" to conditions that were never recognized before and conditions that never occurred to him or her. This reason, like the first, is a form of "awareness" training. In the former example, however, the purpose of the training was to prepare the lieutenant to move up to the top; here the purpose is more to increase the level of awareness of a line-type supervisor and improve his or her efficiency on the job.

Another dimension can be added to the inspection process by having appropriate security supervisors quietly make an inspection in advance of the real one, using the structured format as a guideline, and then comparing their results with the manager's. The manager had best be thorough, however, because if he or she overlooks areas that the supervisors found to require change or correction, this failure tends to discredit his or her ability in the eyes of those subordinates.

In a large organization in which the warehouse is to be inspected, the following would probably comprise the inspection party: Security Manager, Assistant Security Manager, Security Supervisor whose area includes the warehouse, and the warehouse superintendent and his or her assistant.

In some situations, particularly in the establishment of new programs or a comprehensive reevaluation of an existing program, it may be necessary or advisable to engage the services of an outside security management consultant to conduct a security survey. In such cases the Security Manager or Director will, of course, work closely with the security management consultant and with company management.

Wise indeed is the security executive who has the foresight and professional confidence to utilize an outside consultant. Other executives in the corporation call on that kind of resource in their efforts to maximize efficiency. Data Processing frequently calls in computer consultants, Human Resources calls in training consultants, and so it goes across the organization. However, I've heard members of our industry say such things as, "If I asked my boss for a budgetary provision for a security consultant he would only laugh and say, 'That's what I hired you for.'" That's fine, as long as that security executive knows everything and always has all the answers to all the problems.

A qualified, professional security management consultant could do, but not be limited to, the following:

1.   Reduce security costs
2.   Recommend alternative approaches, one of which could solve a long-standing problem or budget obstacle
3.   Strengthen Security's position on a given stand or project resisted or rejected by senior management
4.   Obtain concessions from management
5.   Overcome management doubts about the protection program and its expenses
6.   Offer new ideas and insights that can be implemented after the consultant's work is concluded

In the 1960s and 1970s, many Security Managers and Directors were intimidated by consultants and viewed their retention by management as a threat to their personal authority and position with the company. In the mid-1980s there began an understanding of and appreciation for what an outside independent security management consultant can do to enhance a protection program. Today, consultants are accepted as an important resource.

The entire security inspection program, again, has as its objectives (1) the assessment of risks and (2) the assessment of their countermeasures, usually security programs. We will examine both aspects of this assessment.

ASSESSMENT OF RISKS AND COUNTERMEASURES

Risk Assessment

Inspection reveals conditions brought about by any number of things, such as the company's decision to pay by check instead of pay envelopes, that may pose a security risk. The possibility and probability of the risk resulting in a loss and the magnitude of the loss depend on the risk itself (Table 16.1).

For example, every security executive would agree that finding a cigar box used in the Purchasing Department as a repository for a petty cash fund represents a risk. If the fund amounts to $100, the loss could be the entire amount or some lesser figure. That is clear. To "cure" that risk or provide a countermeasure (perhaps in the form of a lockable metal box with the keys in the possession of the accounts payable manager) is a relatively easy and inexpensive thing to do. In the case of the blank payroll checks, on the other hand, the possibility of loss, the probability of loss, the potential of loss, and the cost to cure the risk form a more difficult equation.

It is not within the scope of this text or chapter to delve deeply into the exacting science of risk management; however, the subject is addressed further in Chapters 17 and 18. The key point to be made here is that from the discovery of what appears to be a risk to the decision as to what action to take (i.e., cure it, minimize it, or live with it) there is a close interaction between security management and company management. This interaction takes place in the office of the Security head's superior, where the final decision is made, particularly if the countermeasures involve capital or expense funds.

Table 16.1   Simple Risk Matrix

The Risk	Is It Possible to Have Loss?	Is Loss Probable?	What Would Be Probable Loss?	How Much Would Counter- measure cost?	Cure Risk?
Open petty cash fund	Yes	Yes	$150	$25	Yes
Blank pay- roll checks	Yes	Yes	Many thousands	$1,315	Yes
Unprotected skylights in grain warehouse	Yes	No	Under $3,000	$5,000	No

Selection of Countermeasures

There are four possible cures or countermeasures for every risk:

- Procedural controls
- Hardware (fences, gates, locks, keys, barricades, etc.)

- Electronic systems (facility access controls, alarms, closed-circuit television [CCTV], computer program access controls including passwords, etc.)
- Personnel

In the case of the petty cash fund, the countermeasure was hardware in the form of a lockable metal box. In the case of the payroll checks, hardware (vault or vault-type room) is a countermeasure; other countermeasures include a control procedure such as the accounting for checks by check serial numbers, withdrawing checks from the vault by number (by batch) and the signing for such withdrawal by the appropriate employee, a prompt check reconciliation program after return from the bank, and so forth. The unprotected skylights might require hardware (an inside latch or an outside lock or padlock) and/or electronics (an alarm).

One of the important ongoing responsibilities of the Security Director or Manager will be to evaluate, select, and recommend appropriate deterrents for each significant risk from these four categories of countermeasures.

Procedural Controls

Policy tells us what we must do, whereas a procedure tells us how we are going to do it. Procedural controls are intended to define how any activity is to be carried out in such a way as to prevent or expose any violation of policy (and attendant potential for loss).

For example, a gambling casino's policy is to ensure that the persons charged with making change are accountable for their individual "bank." To make them accountable, which in and of itself contributes to the prevention of theft, they must follow a structured procedure—a procedural control. This procedure might spell out the specific amount of the employee's fund or bank. It would then require that the employee check out his or her bank from the head cashier on reporting for work, count it to ensure the full amount is there, and sign a designated form that he or she did receive the fund in the amount specified. Such a form should also be countersigned by the head cashier and placed in a certain part of the vault, to be removed only when the fund is returned at the end of the shift, at which time the fund is then counted by the head cashier, signed off by him or her, and countersigned by the employee. The procedure might additionally require that the form be filed and retained for 90 days. Each of these steps is designed to establish accountability for valuable assets (in this case, cash) and verification of activity by more than one source.

Because it is often just as easy and involves little or no additional expense to establish a controlled procedure as an uncontrolled one, this type of countermeasure is generally the least expensive. It should be noted that procedural controls in some situations may be automated, as when a computer is programmed to control and monitor the issuance of purchase orders, shipping invoices, bills of lading, receipts, and other paperwork involved in a transaction. In this circumstance the procedural controls have become electronic, moving into a higher category of expense.

Hardware

Many loss risks can be significantly reduced by the relatively simple application of some form of hardware, from a padlock on the company's gasoline pump to a perimeter fence with adequate lighting. Hardware is most common in the average person's defensive strategy in his or her private life. Lockable suitcases, chains and locks to protect bicycles, bars or decorative security screens on residence windows, front door peepholes, night latches, and outdoor lighting constitute hardware. In the business environment, such physical protective measures may become more sophisticated, progressing to security containers (safes, lockable file cabinets, document shredders, and vaults) and other equipment or devices. Hardware is the second least expensive among the four basic countermeasures.

In modern applications, security hardware is often combined with electronics; for example, a truck gate monitored by CCTV that is electronically (and remotely) controlled or a fence whose protection as a physical barrier is supplemented by an intrusion alarm.

Electronics

In addition to CCTV, electronic countermeasures include such devices as automated access control systems and the whole spectrum of alarms. These include intrusion alarms, motion detection alarms, sound or vibration detection alarms, smoke detectors, heat detectors, water-flow alarms, and computer program access controls. Electronic devices constitute the fastest growing category of security countermeasures. Although initially more expensive to purchase and install than procedural controls or basic hardware, they have become a fact of life for almost all businesses, large or small.

Alarms in particular were originally designed to replace the people who were previously deployed and utilized to provide precisely the same kind of "alarm" or warning service. Electronic alarms have proved to be more reliable than people for a number of reasons. They are less costly (when compared to the annual salaries of personnel required to perform the same function); they will not fall asleep; they are always on the job despite deep snow, slippery streets, or a death in the family; and they are honest.

Personnel

Ironically, the utilization of people as a security countermeasure can be the most efficient and effective strategy or, depending on the circumstances, the poorest.

Because of the ongoing expense of personnel (not only for salaries but also full benefit package, supervision, and replacement), every effort should be exercised to cure risks whenever possible by means other than utilizing people. The rule of thumb is to use people only in those areas where procedural controls, hardware, or electronics cannot be employed more efficiently.

Obviously, there are security functions for which people are the best and sometimes the only countermeasure. The greatest attribute of people, one which can never be replaced, is their ability to exercise judgment. In that capability lies a critical factor in the decision to use people. Wherever judgment is essential in carrying out a security function, people should be utilized. A common example might be the job of overseeing employees as they leave work in a production plant by inspecting lunch pails and other containers. Personnel are essential for a variety of other roles that cannot be effected by procedures, hardware, or electronics. Among these functions are guard posts and patrols, inspections, investigations, prevention of criminal attacks, maintenance of order, and crowd control.

Assessment of Countermeasures

The other side of the inspection coin is the examination of existing countermeasures, usually protection programs and activities, originally set into motion to cure the known risks. Whereas the discovery of risks usually comes from conditions that are observable or comprehensible by virtue of what has happened, what is happening, and what could happen, countermeasures are best assessed through an analysis of the countermeasure activity itself. This analysis is usually accomplished by asking questions. The primary and most devastating question is "Why?" Every countermeasure and every security program should be subjected to the following questions:

Why are we doing it?

Must we do it at all?

If we must, is there a better way?

Is there a less expensive way?

In one organization, for example, the new Security Director asked the supervising agent of the main complex what the security officer on the back side of the complex was doing there. The Director was told it was a necessary post because the officer logged all trucks coming through that gate, opened the gate in the morning, locked the gate later in the morning, logged trucks coming from the main entrance that serviced the far side of the complex, and opened the gate late in the afternoon to accommodate employee vehicles. In addition, the security officer controlled traffic when the railroad brought in freight cars and took out the emptied ones. Besides, the Director was told, "We've always had a person on that post. That's why we built a guard [house] and installed a power line and a telephone."

By holding this particular assignment up to the four previous questions, it was discovered that the security officer was a holdover from a former procedure and that the work, such as logging trucks, was a total waste. No one ever checked the logs, and they contained no more information than that gathered at another location. The roving patrol officer could open and close the gates according to schedule, and the railroad's brakeman stopped what little traffic there was when the freight cars were being moved. Thus the company eliminated one officer, as well as the expense of one telephone, and was able to tear down one guardhouse that consumed energy needlessly with its electrical service.

Elimination of functions is obviously the ultimate in reducing costs, but the opportunity for such action proves to be rare. By persistent application of the "Why" test, however, limited opportunities will constantly present themselves. Another outside guard operation was modified, for example, by replacing weekend security officer coverage with an electrically controlled gate, CCTV, and communication phone. The security officers had been poorly utilized during this slow period and were not only unproductive but also unhappy with that assignment because it was boring. These hours were eliminated from the salary budget. The capital expense for the hardware amounted to less than the annual cost of one 40-hour person unit. Thus in 1 year the equipment paid for itself and thereafter effected a cost savings to the company. Now that's what one would call a good return on investment (ROI)!

There is absolutely nothing within Security's spectrum of programs that should be immune from this inspection. The difficulty is not so much in the application of the inspection as it is in getting managers and supervisors at every level in the security pyramid to ask themselves and their respective subordinates: "Why are we doing it? Must we do it at all? If we must, is there a better way? Is there a less expensive way?"

Interestingly enough, whereas managers and supervisors for some reason tend not to question their pyramids (and programs therein), line security people do seem to see better ways. The effective Security Manager will encourage employees to come to him or her with their ideas. Too often they have already suggested improvements that were ignored or rejected by their supervisor; to make the suggestions to the manager might be misconstrued by the line supervisor as insubordination. If an open climate of communication is established, however, as discussed in Chapter 13, there will be a constant flow of new ideas.

Inspecting for Compliance with Procedures

Whereas our discussion of inspections up to this point has focused on finding new risks, primarily brought about by change within the organization, there is another very important dimension to the security inspection process. Inspection provides the additional benefit of determining compliance with already existing countermeasures that are known to be sound. This type of inspection is executed at the line or first-line supervisory level.

We may be satisfied, for example, that the locks on the gates are proper, the control of keys is properly spelled out, and the gates are scheduled to be locked and unlocked at the right time—but are these things happening as they should? As we observed in an earlier chapter, "People do not do what you expect, they do what you inspect."

The Security Director may set up a procedural control that requires the Payroll Department to secure the blank checks behind locked doors at the end of the day, but do they? The Security Director's inspection of payroll does not ensure compliance later. However, inspection by security people will tell him or her whether the Payroll Department is ignoring or forgetting the procedure or in some other way still contributing to the original risk. How Security management responds (or reacts) to such information is absolutely vital, for two reasons:

1. If Security management fails to act on the information that the procedure is not being followed, they permit the risk to exist, which is counterproductive and inexcusable.
2. The line people who make the discovery of noncompliance and consequent risk, and see their management's failure to take prompt corrective action, become discouraged and say "What's the use?" The downside result is that the line employees lose interest and risks increase everywhere.

If Security management is not going to follow-up on inspection deficiencies, then it should not ask line employees to be alert to and report conditions of noncompliance. Furthermore, compliance inspections come to the attention of employees who work in the area being inspected, and if they come to realize nothing is going to happen because of compliance failures, they will laugh at the inspection as nothing more than a meaningless exercise.

If a condition or procedure is worthy of being inspected, it is worthy of a prompt follow-up by management. Many security programs, always aimed at reducing risks, often make nonsecurity people's work more difficult—requiring them to keep certain doors locked, for example. Because it is inconvenient for them to continually lock and unlock the door, they tend to leave it unlocked. Security finds the unlocked condition in its inspection and reports it. Prompt action corrects the offender, improves security by reducing the original risk, and brings a degree of respect to the inspector. If the line employee believes, based on fact or fiction, that his or her inspection report will not be acted on, that employee will ignore the very security risks he or she is there to detect.

STATISTICS IN PROGRAM MANAGEMENT

Statistics constitute another tool in managing security programs. To be an effective and meaningful tool, the statistics must be designed to reflect what a given program is or is not doing—month by month, this year compared to last year by month, and cumulative year to date. If improperly designed, the quantitative figures will either be meaningless or deceptive. Once the statistical format is in place, it too should be inspected on an ongoing basis to ensure that it has not outlived its original purpose and that it accurately reflects current activities and programs.

Not only must the statistical presentation reflect desired and necessary information and currently reflect activities of an in-place program but it must be used, otherwise the value of the statistics is lost.

Figure 16.1 is an important management tool in determining how effective the detection program is in one large security organization located in many cities and divided into districts. Reflected in the chart are the number of dishonest employees (DE) apprehended this month (TM), the number of dishonest employees apprehended this year to date (YTD) against last year to date (LYTD), miscellaneous detection (MIS DET) this month, year to date against last year to date, total detections (TOT DET) this month, and detections made by undercover agents (UC DET) this year to date against last year to date.

In designing this statistical form, security management was concerned not only with totals but specifically with detection activity in every single unit by district and by time (month, year to date, and last year to date). It was also interested in one subclassification or technique; that is, apprehensions of dishonest employees by the use of undercover agents.

The undercover data are an excellent example of designing statistics to serve a purpose. In this case, the statistics do demonstrate the effectiveness of that particular technique when compared to the budget dollars spent for undercover agents. The last two columns alone tell us a great deal, that is, the undercover program has improved on the whole, as reflected by the increase in detections for the same number of budget dollars (not reflected in the chart but known to management). They also reflect a problem in the East District and a lesser problem in the South District. What is the problem? Is it poor security supervision in those districts? Are Human Resources managers in those districts disclosing the identity of the undercover agents, thus defeating the program? Is it improper tabulation of statistical data? Whatever the cause, the statistics have waved a red flag that can lead to discovering and solving the problem.

These statistics also reflect another interesting story behind the sharp increase in apprehensions of dishonest employees. The Security Department pulled together, at an increase in the salary budget, a special detection unit of highly skilled security people to form an elite squad. Their impact on the department's overall effectiveness in detecting internal dishonesty

	DE TM	DE YTD	DE LYTD	MIS DET TM	MIS DET YTD	MIS DET LYTD	TOT DET TM	UC DET YTD	UC DET LYTD
CENTRAL DISTRICT TOTALS	5	40	50	6	10	10	11	4	2
E-1311	0	5	12	1	1	6	5	0	0
E-1312	0	5	10	0	2	0	0	0	0
E-1313	0	6	1	1	2	1	3	0	0
E-1314	0	1	1	0	0	0	0	0	0
E-1315	0	0	0	0	1	0	1	0	0
E-1316	0	0	0	2	5	0	3	0	0
E-1317	0	14	1	2	5	0	3	0	0
E-1318	5	13	4	0	0	0	7	0	0
EAST DISTRICT TOTALS	5	44	29	6	16	7	22	0	0
W-1411	4	26	13	0	0	3	9	4	0
W-1412	0	21	9	0	0	4	8	2	0
W-1413	1	15	5	0	0	2	4	3	1
W-1414	2	2	2	0	0	0	2	0	0
W-1415	0	4	4	0	0	0	3	0	0
W-1416	0	4	7	0	0	0	0	0	0
W-1417	1	5	6	0	0	0	1	2	0
W-1418	1	4	5	0	0	0	1	0	1
W-1419	0	14	12	0	5	0	0	0	9
W-1420	4	8	0	0	0	0	7	2	0
WEST DISTRICT TOTALS	13	103	63	0	5	9	35	13	11
GRAND TOTAL	41	321	213	13	48	39	121	30	23

Figure 16.1   Statistical record of detection activity in different units of a large organization.

is clearly seen in these statistics. Not only can such statistical tools tell the administrator that the programs are working but they also tend to serve as cost justifications.

SUMMARY

As organizations change, so do security needs. The security inspection is the ongoing process that ensures that new risks are recognized and that established deterrents remain necessary and cost effective.

To keep pace with organizational change, inspections must be continuous. The inspection process must have the full support of company management and the active participation of security management. Such inspections may be formal or informal and structured or unstructured. The structured inspection moves systematically from one area of exposure to another, following a detailed checklist.

Risk assessment evaluates the probability and cost of potential loss. From this evaluation comes a decision to adopt deterrents. Countermeasures may involve procedural controls, hardware, electronics, or (the most costly) security personnel.

The inspection process also includes assessment of existing countermeasures. Every security program or practice must be subjected to the basic challenge: Why are we doing this?

Inspection also verifies compliance with protection programs. Are they being carried out as planned? Such verification comes at the supervisory and line employee level as well as from management; the effective manager will be responsive to this input.

Statistics offer another tool for ongoing evaluation of protection programs. Statistical information, too, must be subject to inspection to ensure that it is up-to-date, and it must be used if it is not to be a meaningless exercise.

REVIEW QUESTIONS

1. Define a structured inspection and contrast it with an unstructured inspection.

2. Ideally, who should conduct the inspection? Why?

3. What are the four types of countermeasures? Give an example of each type. How do the costs of each compare?

4. Discuss the possible consequences of security management's failure to follow-up on inspection deficiencies.

5. Discuss the role of statistical tools in program management.

17

*Risk**

Security is more art than science. Few formulas will cover all
organizations, situations and needs, and that's the beauty and
challenge of our profession. We are about probabilities.

—*Richard D. Sem, CPP*[1]

WHAT IS RISK?

Risk is associated with virtually every activity one can think of, but for
the purpose of this text I shall limit the meaning of the word *risk* to the
uncertainty of financial loss, the variations between actual and expected
results, or the probability that a loss has occurred or will occur. In the
insurance industry, *risk* is also used to mean "the thing insured"—for
example, the XYZ Company is the risk. Risk is also the possible occurrence
of an undesirable event.

Risk should not be confused with *perils*, which are the causes of risk
—such things as fire, flood, and earthquake. Nor should risk be confused
with hazard, which is a contributing factor to a peril. Almost anything can
be a hazard—a loaded gun, a bottle of caustic acid, a bunch of oily rags, or
a warehouse used for storing highly flammable products, for example. The
end result of risk is loss or a decrease in value.

Risks are generally classified as "speculative" (the difference between
loss or gain—for example, the risk in gambling) and "pure risk," a loss/
no-loss situation, to which insurance generally applies.

For the purposes of this text, the divisions of risk are limited to
three common categories:

- Personal (having to do with people assets)
- Property (having to do with material assets)
- Liability (having to do with legalities that could affect both of the pre-
  vious, such as errors and omissions, wrongful discharge, workplace

---

*Reprinted from Broder, James. *Risk Analysis and the Security Survey*, 2nd ed. (Boston:
Butterworth-Heinemann, 2000).
[1] Are These Truths Self-Evident? *Security Management*, March 1998.

violence, and sexual harassment, to name a few of the most current legal issues that plague the business community)

WHAT IS RISK ANALYSIS?

Risk analysis is a management tool, the standards for which are determined by whatever management decides it wants to accept in terms of actual loss. To proceed in a logical manner to perform a risk analysis, it is first necessary to accomplish some basic tasks:

- Identify the assets in need of being protected (money, manufactured products, and industrial processes, to name a few).
- Identify the kinds of risks (or perils) that may affect the assets involved (kidnapping, extortion, internal theft, external theft, fire, or earthquake).
- Determine the probability of risk occurrence. Here one must keep in mind that such a determination is not a science but an art—the art of projecting probabilities. Remember this rule: "Nothing is ever 100% secure."
- Determine the impact or effect, in dollar values if possible, if a given loss does occur.

These subjects are discussed in detail in a later section in this chapter, "Risk Exposure Assessment."

WHAT IS A RISK ASSESSMENT ANALYSIS?

A risk assessment analysis is a rational and orderly approach, and a comprehensive solution, to problem identification and probability determination. It is also a method for estimating the expected loss from the occurrence of some adverse event. The key word here is *estimating*, because risk analysis will never be an exact science—we are discussing probabilities. Nevertheless, the answer to most, if not all, questions regarding one's security exposures can be determined by a detailed risk-assessment analysis.

WHAT CAN RISK ANALYSIS DO FOR MANAGEMENT?

Risk analysis provides management with information on which to base decisions. Is it always best to prevent the occurrence of a situation? Is it always possible? Should the policy be to contain the effect a hazardous situation may have? (This is what nuclear power plants prepare for.) Is it sufficient simply to recognize that an adverse potential exists and for now do nothing but be aware of the hazard? (The analogy is being self-insured.) The eventual goal of risk analysis is to strike an economic balance between the impact of risk on the enterprise and the cost of implementing prevention and protective measures.

A properly performed risk analysis has many benefits, a few of which are:

- The analysis will show the current security posture (profile) of the organization.
- It will highlight areas where greater (or lesser) security is needed.
- It will help to assemble some of the facts needed for the development and justification of cost effective countermeasures (safeguards).
- It will serve to increase security awareness by assessing then reporting the strengths and weaknesses of security to all organizational levels from management to operations.

Risk analysis is not a task to be accomplished once and for all; it must be performed periodically if one is to stay abreast of changes in mission, facilities, and equipment. Also, because security measures designed at the inception of a system generally prove to be more effective than those super-imposed later, risk analysis should have a place in the design or building phase of every new facility. Unfortunately, this is seldom the case.

The one major resource required for a risk analysis is trained man-power. For this reason the first analysis will be the most expensive. Subsequent analyses can be based in part on previous work history; the time required to do a survey will decrease to some extent as experience and empirical knowledge are gained.

The time allowed to accomplish the risk analysis should be compatible with its objectives. Large facilities with complex, multishift operations and many files of data will require more time than single-shift, limited-production locations. If meaningful results are to be expected, management must be willing to commit the resources necessary for accomplishing this undertaking. It is best to delay or even abandon the project unless and until the necessary resources are made available to complete it properly.

THE ROLE OF MANAGEMENT IN RISK ANALYSIS

The success of any risk-analysis undertaking will be strongly contingent on the role top management takes in the project. Management must *support* the project and express this support to all levels of the organization. Management must *delineate* the purpose and scope of risk analysis. It must *select* a qualified team and formally *delegate* authority. Finally, management must *review* the team's findings, decide which recommendations need to be implemented, and establish the order of priorities for such implementation.

Personnel who are not directly involved in the analysis process must be prepared to provide information and assistance to those who are conducting it and, in addition, to abide by any procedures and limitations of activity that may result from survey activity. Management should leave no doubt that it intends to rely on the final product and base its security decisions on the findings of the risk-analysis team. The scope of the project should be defined, and the statement of scope should specifically spell out the parameters and depth of the analysis. It is often equally important to state specifically what the analysis is not designed to accomplish or cover; this will eliminate any misunderstandings at the start of the exercise. An example might be the exclusion from a security survey of safety and evaluation procedures in hospital settings.

At this point, it may be well to define and explain two other terms that are sometimes used interchangeably with risk: *threats*—anything that could adversely affect the enterprise or the assets; and *vulnerability*—weaknesses or flaws, such as holes in a fence, or virtually anything that may conceivably be exploited by a threat. Threats are most easily identified and organized by placing each in one of three classifications or categories: natural hazards (such as floods), accidents (chemical spills), or intentional acts (domestic or international terrorism). Vulnerabilities are most easily identified by interviewing long-term employees, supervisors, and managers in the facility; by field observation and inspection; and by document review. In the case of hardware or electronics, tests can be conducted that are designed to highlight vulnerabilities and expose weaknesses or flaws in the design of the system. Examples would be an out-of-date key system or the introduction of a computer virus.

Threat occurrence rates and probabilities are best developed from reports of occurrences or incident reports, whenever this historical data exist. Where the information does not exist, it may be necessary to reconstruct it. This can be accomplished by conducting interviews with knowledgeable persons or by projecting data based on educated guesses, supported by studies in like industries and locations.

RISK EXPOSURE ASSESSMENT

Before any corrective action can be considered, it is necessary to make a thorough assessment of identifiable risk exposure. To accomplish this, it is essential that three factors be identified and evaluated in quantitative terms. The first is to determine the types of loss or risk (perils) that can affect the assets involved. Here examples would be fire, flood, burglary, robbery, or kidnapping. If one of these were to occur (for now we will consider only single, not multiple, occurrences), what effect would the resulting disruption of operations have on the company? For example, if vital documents were destroyed by fire or flood, what would the effect be on the ability of the company to continue in operation? There is a saying common to protection professionals, "One may well survive a burglary, but one good fire can put you out of business forever." If the chief executive officer, on an overseas trip, were to be kidnapped by a terrorist group (or even suffer a serious heart attack), who would make the day-to-day operating decisions in his or her absence? What about unauthorized disclosure of trade secrets or other proprietary data? After all (or as many as possible) of the risk exposure potentials are identified, one must proceed to evaluate those identified threats that, should they occur, would produce losses in quantitative terms —fire, power failure, flood, earthquake, and unethical or dishonest employees, to name a few worthy of consideration.

To do this we proceed to the second factor: *estimate the probability of occurrence.* What are the chances that the identified risks may become actual events? For some risks, estimating probabilities can be fairly easy. This is especially true when we have documented historical data on identifiable problems. For example, how many internal and external theft cases have been investigated over the past year? Other risks are more difficult to predict. Workplace violence, embezzlement, industrial espionage, kidnapping, and civil disorder may never occur or may occur only once. The third factor is *quantifying (prioritizing) loss potential.* This is measuring the impact or severity of the risk, if in fact a loss does occur or the risk becomes an actual event. This exercise is not complete until one develops dollar values for the assets previously identified. This part of the survey is necessary to set the stage for classification evaluation and analysis and for the comparisons necessary to the establishment of countermeasure (safeguard) priorities. Some events or kinds of risk with which business and industry are most commonly concerned are:

- Natural catastrophe (tornado, hurricane, seismic activity)
- Industrial disaster (explosion, chemical spill, structural collapse, fire)
- Civil disturbance (sabotage, labor violence, bomb threats)
- International and domestic terrorism
- Criminality (robbery, burglary, pilferage, embezzlement, fraud, industrial espionage, internal theft, hijacking)
- Conflict of interest (kickbacks, trading on inside information, commercial bribery, other unethical business practices)
- Nuclear accident (Three Mile Island, Detroit Edison's Enrico Fermi #1)

Some of the previously mentioned events (risks) are unlikely to occur. Also, some are less critical to an enterprise or community than others even if they do occur (e.g., fire vs. burglary). Nevertheless, *all* are possibilities and are thus deserving of consideration.

Examples include the nuclear accident at Chernobyl in the Soviet Union in 1986 and the chemical gas disaster ("breach of containment") at the Union Carbide plant in Bophal, India, in 1984. Also, there exists today in the United States chemical and nerve-gas weapons stored in bunkers at military depots near populated areas. Do contingency plans exist to deal with these risks in the event of accidental fire, leak, or explosion? Are disaster drills and exercises conducted periodically to test the effectiveness of the contingency plans, if they exist? There are contingency plans for breach of containment or other industrial accident in nuclear power generating plants in the United States, and they are strictly enforced by the Nuclear Regulatory Commission (NRC), which requires periodic drills to rehearse the plans.

18

*The Security Survey: An Overview**

The Boy Scouts and Darwin had it right: "If you don't prepare, you won't survive!"

> *John Lay, President*, Contingency Management Associates
> Moraga, California

The goal of risk management—to manage risk effectively at the least possible cost—cannot be achieved without reducing, through a total management commitment, the number of incidents that lead to losses.[1] Before any risk can be eliminated (or for that matter, reduced) it must be identified. One proven method of accomplishing this task is the security survey. Charles A. Sennewald, author and security consultant, has defined the security survey as "The primary vehicle used in a security assessment. . . . The survey is the process whereby one gathers data that reflects the who, what, how, where, when and why of the client's existing operation. The survey is the fact-finding process."[2]

WHY ARE SECURITY SURVEYS NEEDED?

The latest reports estimate that the cost of fraud and abuse to American business is in excess of $40 billion per year and rising. The biggest problem, and the one we see most often, is that most corporate managers do not even know if they have a problem. Worse, many do not even *want* to know that they have a problem! Some managers seem to prefer to keep things as they are and to regard any suggestion of a need for increased security as direct or indirect criticism of their abilities to manage their operations. Nevertheless, where fraud exists, most general business security surveys calculate losses

---

* By James Broder, CPP.

[1] The field of risk management encompasses much more than security and safety. These two subjects, however, are the cornerstones of most effective risk-management programs.

[2] Sennewald, Charles A, CPP. *Security Consulting*, 2nd ed. (Boston: Butterworth-Heinemann, 1996).

at 6% of annual revenue; some surveys we have conducted have concluded that losses attributable to theft equaled or exceeded profits. This is especially likely for chain-store operations, where each individual store is regarded as a separate profit center and records of inventory shortages are kept for each location by local managers.

Crime losses far exceed the losses to business caused by fire and industrial accidents. One professional security organization estimates that the annual loss to business from fraud and abuse is twice as great as the total of all business losses due to fire and accident!

Are you really concerned about how crime may affect your business? Take a few minutes and read the 1996 Association of Certified Fraud Examiners *Report To the Nation on Occupational Fraud and Abuse*. Then take a moment to reflect on the following estimates:

- The average organization loses more than 9% a day per employee to fraud and abuse.
- The average organization loses about 6% of its total annual revenue to fraud and abuse committed by its own employees.
- Fraud and abuse cost U.S. organizations more than $400 billion annually.

In the United States alone, estimates of the cost of fraud vary widely. No recent comprehensive studies could be found that empirically measured the economic effects of fraud and abuse. In addition to the direct economic losses to the organization from fraud and abusive behavior, there are indirect costs to be considered: the loss of productivity, legal action, increased unemployment, government intervention, and other hidden costs.

WHO NEEDS SECURITY SURVEYS?

A Stanford Research Institute report, *Business Property Security*, discussing business vulnerability to crime loss states, "Likely victims are growing businesses where expansion occurs faster than control systems are set up and large companies where close control over branches and divisions is not feasible." This fact has been noted by many professional security consultants with whom I have discussed the subject, but every business entity, no matter how large or small, could profit from an objective survey of their security protection. Most surveys show that the majority of business security concern is directed toward external problems, such as theft (burglary and robbery), as the most immediate priority. This situation reflects the development and growth of security in the United States, from a historical perspective: It was once thought that most, if not all, of a company's problems with theft were external in nature.

Up until World War II, before the large-scale expansion of U.S. and Canadian industry and the development of the multinational corporation, many companies in North America were what we now regard as small- to medium-sized industries and businesses. Many retail enterprises were of the "Mom and Pop" variety. Because of close supervision and the personal identification between management and labor that existed, internal theft (that is, by "trusted" employees) was seldom considered, much less planned for. Hence the fire and burglar alarm business developed and proliferated to protect these enterprises from what they considered their internal and external threats, their two "worst enemies."

With the growth of the national and multinational corporations and the almost total demise of the Mom and Pop commercial and variety stores, we witnessed a parallel change in business ethics and standards. These changes also affected society as a whole. As an example, in the turbulent 1960s, a new term was coined: the "Establishment." Crimes against the Establishment were then, and still are, perceived by many to be permissible, in fact not crimes at all. The lack of personal identification with a company by its employees and the dramatic dilution of ethical and moral standards among the general public combined to make internal theft by employees a simple process of rationalization. After all, who *is* General Motors, AT&T, or Safeway? "They" make gigantic profits by "ripping off" the general population (read *us*). "They won't miss one small wrench or screwdriver that I need for my workshop at home." The theft of one small item, multiplied ten thousand times each year in many large companies, adds up to an annual loss that can far exceed the total loss to external theft over the entire period of a firm's corporate existence!

Enlightened students of criminology now understand that the most predominant, certainly the most prevalent, form of business crime is employee theft in its various forms. Asset misappropriation accounts for more than four out of five employee thefts. Bribery and corruption account for about 10% of the offenses. Companies with a hundred or fewer employees are the most vulnerable to fraud and abuse.[3] Businesses reporting a million dollars of revenue per year are particularly hard hit by crime. This is especially true for a retail enterprise that operates on a 2% profit margin, or a grocery store that has a 1% profit line. As serious students of this problem have come to realize, losses due to crime can and do have a dramatic impact on net profits.

Shoplifting, employee theft, and vandalism all cost American business billions of dollars annually. Figure 18.1, based on percentage of a company's net profit, illustrates how much more a company needs to sell to offset losses in stolen merchandise, equipment, and supplies. The theft of one $500 fax machine means the company must sell $25,000 worth of merchandise to

---

[3] Association of Certified Fraud Examiners. *1996 Report to the Nation on Occupational Fraud and Abuse.*

break even, if it is in the 2% net-profit category and $8,333 if it is in the 6% percent category. Worse yet, it is still without one fax machine. For an example of the impact of loss versus net profits, see Figure 18.1.

ATTITUDE OF BUSINESS TOWARD SECURITY

In general, we find that most businesses will take the necessary precautions to protect themselves against the entry of burglars and robbers onto their premises. Most will also give protection to high-value areas, such as computer centers, vaults, precious-metal storage areas, and any location where money is the principal product, such as banks and casinos. Many businesses, however, still do not concern themselves with protection against unauthorized access to their premises—yet 75% to 85% of external theft is directly attributable to this source. A prime example is unrestricted access at many warehouses we have surveyed to the shipping and receiving docks by nonemployee truck drivers.

Likewise, if the cost of security protection is regarded as a capital expense or a yearly expenditure and as reducing the profit line, we can expect the person in charge of that facility to authorize only the minimum and least expensive security protection possible. If, on the other hand, security is required by corporate management or mandated by clients or the various governmental agencies overseeing industries engaged in sensitive government contracts, we find plant managers installing security protection without regard to costs (e.g., nuclear power generating plants).

Actual Loss of:	If Company Operates at Net Profit of:				
	2%	3%	4%	5%	6%
	These additional sales are required to offset an actual loss:				
$ 50	$ 2,500	$ 1,666	$ 1,250	$ 1,000	$ 833
100	5,000	3,333	2,500	2,000	1,666
200	10,000	6,666	5,000	4,000	3,333
250	12,500	8,333	6,250	5,000	4,166
300	15,000	10,000	7,500	6,000	5,000
350	17,500	11,666	8,750	7,000	5,833
400	20,000	13,333	10,000	8,000	6,666
450	22,500	15,000	11,250	9,000	7,500
500	25,000	16,666	12,500	10,000	8,333

Figure 18.1 Loss to sales (profit) ratio.

This latter proposition presupposes another problem. Most plant managers with whom we have worked do not have the foggiest idea what kind of security they need for adequate protection. For sensitive government-contract work, security guidelines are sometimes available. Nevertheless, many are the managers who have fallen prey to the sales pitches of security manpower and hardware salesmen who proposed package deals guaranteed to solve all problems. As a result, we constantly encounter security programs that overemphasize manpower (guards) or hardware (alarms or electronics) when the proper solution to the problem is an effective marriage of the two, coupled with adequate written procedures to deal with the most common occurrences or eventualities encountered in the real, work-a-day world. Life becomes complicated only if we allow it to.

WHAT CAN A SECURITY SURVEY ACCOMPLISH?

One approach to determining whether or not there is a need for a security survey is to find out what services an experienced security expert can provide and then seek information on security (crime)-related losses being incurred by the particular business or company. The security expert can either be in place, that is to say a member of the staff, or an outside consultant, or a combination of both.

Security-related problems might detect any of the problems mentioned in the early chapters of this book. Surveys generally, however, show that most problems encountered in the real world of security are not uncommon ones.

If the company or facility being considered has a security plan, the survey can establish whether the plan is up to date and adequate in every respect. Experience has shown that many security plans were established as the needs of the moment dictated; most were developed without regard to centralization and coordination. On review, many such plans are patched-up, crazy-quilt affairs. More often than not the policies, procedures, and safeguards need to be brought together and consolidated so that the component parts complement, not contradict, one another.

If the facility has no security plan, the survey can establish the need for one and develop proposals for some or all of the security services commonly found in industrial settings. By conducting a comprehensive survey of the entire facility—its operations and procedures—one can identify critical factors affecting the security of the premises or operation. The next step is to analyze the vulnerabilities and recommend cost-effective protection. The survey should also recommend, as the first order of business, the establishment of policies and procedures to, as a minimum:

- Protect against internal and external theft, including embezzlement, fraud, burglary, robbery, industrial espionage, and the theft of trade secrets and proprietary information.

- Develop access-control procedures to protect the facility perimeter as well as computer facilities and executive offices located inside.
- Establish lock and key-control procedures.
- Design, supervise, and review installation of anti-intrusion and detection systems.
- Establish a workplace violence program to help corporate personnel deal with internal and external threats.
- Provide control over the movement and identification of employees, customers, and visitors on company property.
- Review the selection, training, and deployment of security personnel, proprietary or contract.
- Assist in the establishment of emergency and disaster plans and guidelines.
- Identify the internal resources available and needed for the establishment of an effective security program.
- Develop and present instructional seminars for management and operations personnel in all the previously listed areas.

The preceding list is by no means all-inclusive. It does, however, set forth some of the most frequently needed programs and systems recommended for development by security surveys that I have conducted.

WHY THE NEED FOR A SECURITY PROFESSIONAL?

Losses due to all causes continue to represent a problem of major proportions for business and industry. To the extent that the services of security professionals can help in eliminating, preventing, or controlling a company's losses, they are needed. At a security management seminar, Charles A. Sennewald, CPP, once explained, "Crime prevention, the very essence of a security professional's existence, is another spoke in the wheel of total loss control. It is the orderly and predictive identification, abatement, and response to criminal opportunity. It is a managed process which fosters the elimination of the emotional crisis response to criminal losses and promotes the timely identification of exposures to criminality before these exposures mature to a confrontation process." The proper application of protection techniques to minimize loss opportunity promises the capability not only to improve the net profits of business but also to reduce to acceptable levels the frequency of most disruptive acts, the consequences of which often exceed the fruits of the crime.

HOW DO YOU SELL SECURITY?

As mentioned earlier in this chapter, some managers, for a variety of reasons, are reluctant even to discuss the subject of security. In the aftermath of an unsuccessful attempt to burglarize a bank vault, a bank operations manager learned that the anti-intrusion system was 10-years old and somewhat anti-quated. "Why didn't the alarm company keep me advised of the necessity to upgrade my system as the state of the art improved?" he asked. The answer he received was, "The alarm system functioned adequately for 10 years with no problem. Would you or the bank have authorized an expenditure of $5,000 to upgrade the alarm system before you had this attempted burglary?" The bank representative reluctantly admitted that he would not have. This case is typical of what we call the "knee-jerk reaction" to security. One security consultant with whom I am acquainted describes it as locking the barn after the horse has been stolen. We all know that the only thing this protects is what the horse thief left behind.

Nevertheless, it is not uncommon to find that management's attention is obtained only after a serious problem, one pointing to the lack of adequate protection, is brought to attention. The first reaction is often one of overkill; the response pendulum swings from complacency to paranoia, when the facts indicate that a proper response should be somewhere in between. Given this situation, an unscrupulous alarm salesman will prescribe an electronics system worthy of consideration by the manager of the bullion vault at Fort Knox. The true professional will, as the first order of business, try to bring the situation into true prospective by calming the fears of the clients.

There are some things that a Security Director or consultant can do to convince top corporate management that security is worth spending some money to obtain. Some methods that have proven successful are listed in the following:

1. Establish a meaningful dialogue with the decision makers in the management hierarchy. First, try to ascertain their feelings about security. What do they really want a security program to accomplish for them, if in fact they want anything? Do not be surprised to learn that some management personnel regard security as a necessary evil and thus worthy of little attention (i.e., money or resources). Marshal the facts. Research the history of security losses experienced by the company and use this information to develop trend projections.
2. When collecting data to support your position, deal in principles, not personalities. Use the technique of nonattribution for all unpublished sources of information. With published sources, such as interoffice memos, excerpt the pertinent data if possible. Avoid internecine power struggles at all costs. Maintain a position of objective neutrality.
3. Be as professional about security as you can. The better you are at your job, the greater attention you will command from your clients. There are many avenues you can explore to develop the information you need, such as developing contacts with other security professionals who share similar problems. Don't reinvent the wheel: Attend security seminars, purchase relevant books, study, and do research.

4. In making a proposal to management, hit the highlights and make your proposal as brief as possible. Save the details for later. In any proposal that will cost money, make certain you have developed the cost figures as accurately as possible. If the figures are estimated, label them as such and err on the high side.

5. It is a wise man or woman who knows his or her own limitations. If you need outside help (and who doesn't from time to time?), do not be reluctant to admit it. Such areas as electronics, computers, and sophisticated anti-intrusion alarm systems are usually beyond the capabilities of the security generalist. Do some studying. Know where to go to get the help you need.

6. Suggest that management hire an outside consultant. Competent security professionals have nothing to fear from a "second opinion." Often, the "expert from afar" has greater persuasiveness over management than do members of their own staff. More often than not the consultant will reinforce your position by reaching the same conclusions you did and making the same or similar recommendations.

7. Present your position at the right time. Recognize that management's priorities are first and foremost the generation of profit. To capture management's attention, wait for the right circumstances. It is difficult to predict when this may occur; therefore, have your facts developed and be ready at a moment's notice to make your presentation. It will be too late to do the research when you are called before the board of directors without notice to explain how the breakdown in security that just happened could have occurred, and what you propose to do to solve the problem for the future.

8. Develop a program of public relations. Security represents inconvenience, even under the best of circumstances. Once you have management thinking favorably about your proposal, you will need to sell it to everyone in the organization for it to be successfully implemented. Most employees enjoy working in a safe and secure environment. Use this technique to convince employees that the program was designed as much for their safety and security as for the protection of the assets of the corporation.

For a comprehensive treatment of the role professional security consultants can play and how they can help the security professionals properly define their security exposures, refer to Charles A. Sennewald's 1996 text *Security Consulting*, second edition, published by Butterworth-Heinemann. Do your homework in a thorough manner, and you cannot help but impress management with your capabilities as a security professional. Remember, be patient. Few have been able to sell 100% of their security programs to management the first time out of the starting blocks.

19

Office Administration

In an efficient and well-managed organization, general security office administration has six distinctive functions, each of which plays an important role in the success of the total back-office effort (Figure 19.1). Irrespective of the number of employees available for office duties, the functions are constant. People may change, but functions do not. Like the placement of stones in a pyramid, each office administration function is unique, critical to the whole, and conspicuous. The functions are as follows:

1. Office supervision/management
2. Secretarial
3. Reception
4. Clerical
5. Records (data retention and retrieval)
6. Mail

The functions obviously suggest the type of employee required to discharge each function—but that does not preclude the possibility of joining two or more functions together under the responsibility of one employee or, conversely, of having two or more employees assigned to the same function. The interrelationship between functions is most important in the daily office effectiveness and orderly workflow. Figure 19.2 illustrates possible compacting configurations, depending on the size of the organization.

The problem with combining functions is that they tend to lose identity; the employee tends to focus or set priorities on personal preference or workload demands. As a consequence, less desirable tasks such as filing become backlogged. An understanding of the risks of combining functions is necessary to provide adequate training and supervision for employees who are handling multiple functions.

DESCRIPTION OF FUNCTIONS

Supervision/Office Management

In addition to the traditional and necessary supervisory responsibilities, such as performance evaluations, training, discipline, and scheduling, the supervisor of the overall office activities would be responsible for the following:

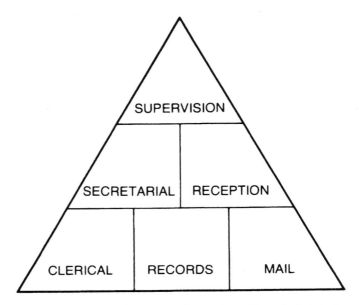

Figure 19.1   The six functions of security office administration.

- Monitoring the daily workflow to ensure that everything is following plan
- Coordinating activity between the various functions
- Assigning tasks and special projects
- Projecting supply needs, then ordering and controlling supplies
- Arranging for maintenance and servicing of office equipment
- Personally overseeing special projects, including doing such projects himself or herself
- Ensuring security of records and files
- Arranging for replacement of absent office personnel, reassigning their functions to others, or filling in temporarily himself or herself
- Inspecting work to ensure standards are maintained

Secretarial

The secretarial function primarily services departmental management. In a large organization, there may be an executive secretary (personally serving the Security Director or Manager) as well as an office manager. Secretarial service usually includes the following functions:

- Coordinating appointments
- Preparing managerial correspondence

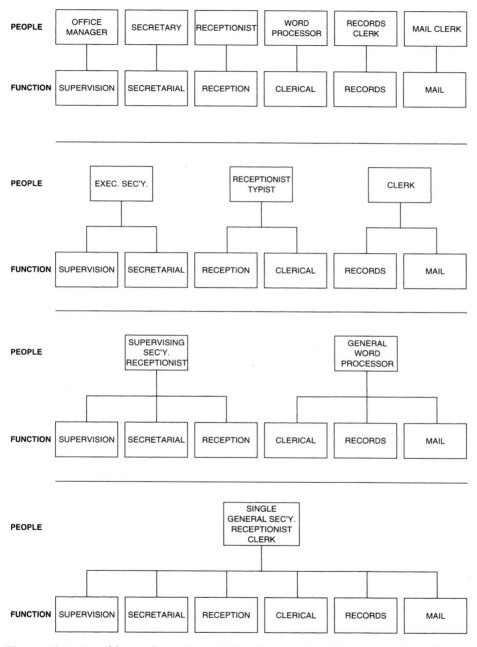

Figure 19.2 Possible configurations of functions and employees in office administration.

- Assembling and presenting those documents requiring executive signature, such as invoices, expense and travel vouchers, and so forth
- Gathering data as requested for budgetary submissions or explanations
- Screening calls to management and rerouting if appropriate
- Gathering files, reports, and statistics as requested for specific managerial needs
- Arranging for travel accommodations for management and/or other security employees
- Acting as a communication link between the organization and management when management is not in the office

Reception

The employee who serves as a receptionist, whether a man or a woman and whether in uniform or in regular office attire, should be well groomed, perhaps even exceptionally so because of the function's high visibility and the impression that the person makes on the public. If the function is more that of a telephone receptionist, telephone answering training (offered by local phone companies) should be required before assignment to the phone board or desk.

People rarely come to or call the Security Department with good news. Meeting a cold, somber, or aloof receptionist or hearing an unfriendly voice on the phone only compounds the problems, or it tends to discourage future contacts, even if future contacts would be beneficial to the department. Persons assigned to the receptionist function should be pleasant and courteous in person and have a "smile" in their voices.

Receptionist duties may include the following:

- Knowing the names and responsibilities of all personnel in an investigative, supervisory, or managerial position
- Knowing the current status of such personnel throughout the day, that is, at lunch, in a meeting, in court, and so forth
- If the caller is vague as to the party he or she wants, determining the nature of the call and routing it accordingly
- Taking messages for those not in and ensuring that messages get to the proper party in a timely manner or routing the caller to the absent person's voice mail
- "Matching up" visitors or callers with the appropriate party
- Having guests sign visitor ledger and obtain visitor badge, if required
- Accomplishing sundry light tasks during slow periods, such as matching trailer security seal numbers against manifests, logging data, and so forth

Clerical

The clerical function is normally filled by an employee who has a range of office skills including proficiency in the use of the personal computer and word processing. This person is the office "generalist," and as the chart in Figure 19.2 suggests, this is a fundamental office function. A sampling of clerical activities includes the following:

- Transcribing recorded field reports into formal documents
- "Packaging" files or assembling the contents of a given file into the standard format
- Logging incoming data on appropriate forms or charts for subsequent compilation
- Converting compiled statistical data into charts or forms for duplication and distribution
- Processing, sorting, and distributing forms and documents as required
- Inputting and retrieving computer data
- Preparing an index card for each name processed through Security, with appropriate source reference if a manual system is used, or making entries into the appropriate flat file database, if computerized
- Preparing memoranda, notices, instructions, orders, and training materials for duplication and distribution
- Acting as relief for secretary, receptionist, records clerk, and mail clerk

Records

Records and the records maintenance program may appear to be relegated to a low status, but in actuality the whole record function is the lifeblood of a security organization. The records of a Security Department, whether paper or electronic documents, really constitute the detailed diary or historical recordings of all security-related events up to the present. So that the reader may better appreciate the scope and importance of this function, the following list represents a sampling of the types of records that may be found in a security records section:

- Company arrest records of all nonemployees
- Company arrest records of employees
- Employee security terminations for violation of policy, rules, or regulations
- Open investigation files
- Reports on all burglaries against the company
- Reports on all arson attacks against the company
- Reports on all vandalism or malicious mischief

- Reports on all bomb threats
- Reports on all obscene phone calls
- Reports on all major thefts
- Reports on all suspicious circumstances
- Reports on all intrusion, waterflow, fire, or other security-monitored alarms
- Reports on all daily patrol activities
- Reports on all fraud, counterfeit, or impostor incidents
- Security intelligence files (undercover reports, information received)
- Security attendance files
- Construction, blueprints, and so forth on company properties
- Files on truck schedules and security seal numbers
- Document files (usually exception or "authorized OK" forms)
- Files of training materials
- Memo reference files
- Correspondence files
- Equipment and resource files
- Contractor and supplier files
- Special events files
- Emergency procedure files
- Fidelity bonding file
- Master indices (master database)
- Accident/injury reports
- Files on former security personnel

The foregoing list in no way constitutes a necessarily complete records configuration nor does it suggest that every security organization requires all such categories. It does illustrate the wide spectrum of possible categories that a Security Department may be required to retain.

Record Filing Systems

There's no question that the computer is the state-of-the-art security management tool not only in accessing control programs but also in capturing, storing, and retrieving important security data. However, the manual system is still a viable form of record retention in our industry and an in-depth analysis of how that system works can still serve as a logical foundation or format for computerized programs.

To bring order to the records is, of course, the challenge. *Order* means that any given record or file can be located promptly and pulled on demand. Delays or the excuse that "we can't find it" reflect, to some degree, disorder. Order means the material is filed in a systematic way and the system is logical and disciplined.

There is no one correct filing system. The design of the system must serve the particular needs of the given organization. The simpler the system, the better. As an example, the entire list on the previous pages could be filed in a basic alphabetic arrangement, in which all burglary files would naturally be filed in the *B* section. An alternative would be to file burglaries under the *C* section for "Crimes" or "Criminal Investigations." For the sake of this presentation, I use the straight basic alphabetic system.

The alphabetic (alpha) system provides the rough or first division of materials. It cannot stand by itself in every case, so a secondary alphabetic or numeric system is necessary. This can best be illustrated by the alpha-alpha system; in filing arrested shoplifters, for example, *S* for "Shoplifters" is the first alpha, and the names of each shoplifter (Abrams, Brown, Cole, Davidson, etc.) form the second alpha.

In the alpha-numeric system, on the other hand, burglaries would be filed under *B* (the alpha) and an individual case number (B-1, B-2, B-3, etc.) assigned to each, the number constituting the numeric control. Depending on the volume of activity, the system can be "annualized" for increased control and ready statistical information, as illustrated in Figure 19.3.

The difference between the alpha-alpha and alpha-numeric method is that the former readily identifies and stores names of people and the latter identifies and stores incidents in which people are not always known, arrested, or identified. If the burglar is caught and known, the master index file (usually a 3×5 index card filed alphabetically or entered into the flat file database) of the suspect's name refers to the appropriate file, as shown in Figure 19.4.

Code for   Year in which   36th burglary case
burglary cases   burglary occurred   of 2003

Figure 19.3   Sample of annualized alpha-numeric filing system.

DOE, John Howard
BURGLARY SUSPECT
SEE B-03-36

Figure 19.4   Master index file card of suspect's name.

Control Ledger

The key to this system is discipline in the controls. A control ledger must be maintained for all alpha-numeric systems. Usually the ledger is maintained in front of the controlled section and the next file number is assigned to each case as it occurs. What typically happens is as follows: The investigator is either dispatched to the scene of a reported or suspected burglary, or a security employee comes across the scene of such a crime and calls into the security headquarters for a file number. The records clerk pulls (if manual) or calls up (if electronic) the control ledger for burglaries and gives the next unused number to the investigator, noting the assignment on the ledger by date, location, and investigator's name. That case is then an assigned and pending case. The investigation must be complete, "packaged," signed-off (approved by the appropriate supervisor), and filed. Once in file, the control ledger is checked-off by date and thus accounted for. If the file is then subsequently removed, a note is made on an "Out" card, filed behind the control ledger, as to who removed the file and on what date (Figure 19.5). If the file is not in its proper place, yet the control card shows it's in and no entry is noted on the Out card, someone failed to follow the procedure.

The Out card is required for all alpha-alpha and alpha-numeric records not for simple alpha files, such as correspondence records.

Master Index

An extremely valuable tool in the area of records is the master index file. Not only is it an alphabetical locator reference card but it also can serve as

OUT

FILE #	DATE OUT	TAKEN BY		DATE RETURNED
B-02-41	DEC. 6, 02	JONES	COURT	DEC. 9, 02
B-03-6	MAR. 11, 03	ALTON	SUPPLEMENTAL REPORT	MAR. 12, 03
B-03-6	MAR. 16, 03	ALTON	SUSPECT IN CUSTODY- TO P.D.	

BURGLARY

FILE #	DATE ASSIGNED	INVESTIGATOR	LOCATION	DATE IN
B-03-1	JAN. 1, 03	Case	Greenridge pump house	JAN. 4
B-03-2	JAN. 3, 03	O'Rourke	Crenshaw tire center	JAN. 8
B-03-3	JAN. 22, 03	Christman	Optometrist office	JAN. 24
B-03-4	FEB. 16, 03	Wagner	Montclair	
B-03-5				
B-03-6				

Figure 19.5   Sample control card and "Out" card.

a record in and of itself. Incidental information of a derogatory nature can be noted thereon, from a wide variety of sources, and filed for future reference. As one example, local newspapers provide a wealth of information about individuals in the community involved in antisocial behavior or criminal activity. Such information can be extracted, noted in the index, and filed away. If, at a later time, a person by the same name applies for work with the company, the automatic search of the master index (part of the new employee screening process) will automatically surface that name. An investigation can determine if the applicant is indeed the same person named on the card. Certainly the fact that the names are identical should never be the grounds for action against the person, but it does give direction to the background investigator.

File Control

Security files should never be accessed or pulled and released without supervision of the responsible records clerk or supervisor.

Mail

The humble task of processing mail, both incoming and outgoing, receives a lot of attention, and rightfully so. A great deal of business communications is by necessity reduced to the written word and dispatched by mail, whether e-mail, in-house mail, the U.S. postal system, or private sector services such as Federal Express. Queries, answers, instructions, notifications, and a host of other written message must move expeditiously between given parties. Failure to receive such communications can be costly, cause failures, or at the least be embarrassing. As a consequence, mail failures or undue delays can provoke emotional reactions. Therefore, the mail function should include the following:

- One person, whether full-time, part-time, or combined responsibility, should be clearly charged with mail responsibility; there should be no confusion as to whose assignment it is
- Scheduled daily pick-up from the main company mail distribution center
- Opening and date-stamping of all mail except those envelopes marked confidential
- Knowledge of who's who, past and present, in the security organization and the company as a whole (to expedite misdirected or improperly addressed correspondence)
- The capability to hand-deliver or hand-post special correspondence
- Last, but not least, an appreciation for the importance of the function, that is, this position should have some dignity (this can only be achieved by management)

OFFICE SECURITY

The security office is the repository of a vast amount of information, factual and otherwise (suspicious, not yet verified, and still under investigation). All of this data must be categorized as highly confidential and demands security. There are three aspects of security in connection with this information: one is personnel, the second is physical, and the third is electronic. The people who are hired to work in the office administration area of a Security Department should undergo precisely the same degree of thoroughness in the background investigation as any other security employee. The sensitivity of information contained in the files, even in the kind of company not engaged in national defense or other highly sensitive activities, deserves maximum security, even if only from a company liability point of view. The release of information concerning a janitor's discharge due to writing obscene letters to a secretary in the blueprint office, for example, could bring serious and unnecessary repercussions from a civil lawsuit.

Proper physical security requires that all filing cabinets be equipped with a lock as well as a drop bar that runs vertically down in front of the drawers and is secured in place with a padlock during non-office hours.

In addition, if the office area is in a separate security building, it should be protected by fire and intrusion alarms.

Electronic protection requires the assignment of authorized access codes into computerized files, including, of course, the capability of interrogating the system to determine who accessed which files and when.

THE OFFFICE ENVIRONMENT

The fact that a Security Department is not a profit center, or is considered nonproductive in terms of the industry or business it serves, in no way justifies hand-me-down equipment or furniture. The security office deserves the same quality of work environment as any other department in the organization, and it is the responsibility of the Security Director to insist on that equality. Office personnel need a clean, fresh, open space in which to work, with good equipment, sufficient light, a place to relax, and a general climate that shows that they, too, contribute to the overall success of the firm so that they can take pride in their department and in their work.

SUMMARY

Security office administration includes six key functions. Each is unique and critical. Although it is not always possible that they be performed by different people, it is essential that the specific functions do not lose their identities.

Supervision covers the day-to-day responsibility for the effective functioning of the security office, including planning, provision for supplies and equipment, coordination of work assignments, and inspection.

The secretarial function provides internal secretarial services for departmental management. The clerical role is that of the office "generalist," including data input, filing, processing forms and documents, and so forth. The receptionist, as the department's first contact with outsiders, should project an image of courtesy and cooperation. The handling of mail is also a specific and important responsibility.

Records maintenance is a significant part of the security program. Examples include records of arrest, termination, investigation, crimes of all kinds, reference material, and equipment and resource files. Whatever filing system is used, it must provide accessibility of information with disciplined controls.

Finally, it is important that principles of security be embodied in the hiring of office personnel and in the internal practice of physical and electronic security. The physical environment of the security office should reflect the importance attached to this function by the company.

REVIEW QUESTIONS

1.   What are the six basic functions of security office administration? Give examples of several of the responsibilities that come under each function.

2.   Describe the alpha-alpha and the alpha-numeric systems of filing records.

3.   What is the purpose of the control ledger in an alpha-numeric filing system?

4.   What are the three aspects of security for the office administration area of the Security Department?

20

Written Policies and Procedures

The difference between a policy and a procedure is somewhat vague, but I've been comfortable in defining the two as follows:

> *Policy:* Management's position, statement, purpose, or direction (what management wants)
>
> *Procedure:* The detailed steps management requires its employees to follow to achieve desired results (how management wants it done)

Policies and procedures (or operating practices) more often than not develop slowly, informally, in an unstructured fashion over a given period. This could range from months to years, depending on the nature of the organization. Of course, they evolve from the passing on of instructions — word-of-mouth communication. Sooner or later these policies and procedures are documented in writing.

Experience plays an important role in the formalization of policies and procedures. Consequently, new security organizations typically may have few written policies and procedures; conversely, more established departments have sophisticated and comprehensive written policies and procedures.

HISTORICAL EVOLUTION

Let's examine a case study that should clarify the evolutionary process so common in the formalizing of policies and procedures.

> Ron Mint recognizes the need for a quality guard service in his community. He has an outstanding guard dog that serves as his partner. He approaches a prospective client with the dog. The client, owner and operator of a shopping center, is impressed by this unique team and gives Ron the task of securing the complex at night.

Ron does an outstanding job, resulting in another company asking for his service. Ron hires someone he knows who also has a trained dog. Now he has two clients.

After a while Ron has a staff of 20 security officers, 11 dogs, and a small kennel. As he continues to grow, he passes on his philosophy of "maximum protection with quality personnel that's unequivocally dependable" by informal discussions with his employees. In addition, as each new employee joins the team, Ron, or now one of his supervisors, actually works alongside the novice to show him or her "the ropes" to ensure that the assignment meets the standards of Fort Patrol, as Ron's company is called. Policies and procedures have yet to be written.

After a period of time and a variety of experiences, situations arise, such as an officer who's injured on duty and unable to perform the assignment for the balance of that particular shift. Some decisions regarding what should be done when such a situation arises were good and some were not. Based on those experiences it becomes reasonable to devise a plan for the next similar eventuality. That plan is the procedure to follow, the step-by-step activities various employees will follow to deal successfully with the problem and effect a satisfactory resolution. Post orders is one form of written procedures that is site specific as to what must be performed at a given assignment or post. Hence the substitute who replaces the injured officer has instructions as to what's expected at this location (more about post orders later in this chapter).

As the organization continues to grow, Ron can no longer personally share his philosophy with each and every new officer. Thus it's written down to be read and shared by all. Part of Ron's philosophy finds its way into policies and procedures in the following fashion:

POLICY

To ensure that Fort Patrol provides quality personnel, all applicants for employment will be required to successfully pass the authorized psychological test. Furthermore, the personnel officer will require a background investigation verifying employment for the past 7 years and ensuring that the applicant has not been convicted of any crime, other than a minor traffic violation.

PROCEDURE: PSYCHOLOGICAL TESTING

1. Advise an applicant at the time he or she submits the completed application for employment that candidates are required to take a psychological (paper and pencil) test and that the results are considered in the final employment assessment.
2. If the applicant agrees to take the test, provide him or her with the instruments and a place in a room that is quiet, well lit, and ventilated.
3. When the candidate completes the test, place the document into the preaddressed, prepaid envelope and place in the mail out-box.

PROCEDURE: VERIFICATION OF FORMER EMPLOYERS

1. The Fort Patrol employee responsible for verifying applicant's former employment first must examine the application for discrepancies of dates in the applicant's employment history; for example, is there any time not accounted for? Overlapping dates?
2. The employee must inquire into and require satisfactory explanations for any discrepancies or omissions.
3. If there are no discrepancies or if satisfactory explanations have been offered, then the employee should verify the existence of those former employers listed on the application by
    A. Telephone directory or information
    B. City business license or other governmental licensing bodies
    C. Listings in professional directories such as the American Society for Industrial Security
4. The employee should telephone the Human Resources office of the applicant's former employers or the Security Department, if appropriate, and identify himself or herself and the wish to verify the former employment of a candidate. Ask initially only for dates of employment and job title.
5. If that information is secured, the employee should inquire into the rehireability of the candidate. If yes, so note. If no, inquire as to why.
    A. Document the phone conversation by noting on the application the date and time of the call and the name of the person with whom you spoke.
    B. Employee making the inquiry must sign and date the application.

BENEFITS

The benefits and logic of the written policy and procedure should be self-evident; however, they are worthy of examination in some depth, including such factors as consistency in performance, reduction of decision-making time, enhancement of controls, and provision for objective performance evaluation.

Consistency in Performance

The written procedure contributes to performance consistency because it requires each employee to do a given task or process the same way; thus we can predict the end results. If employees don't have a procedure to follow (and a procedure is like a road map), they'll do things in a way that we can't predict with any degree of certainty.

Reduction of Decision-Making Time

The written procedure has most, if not all, of the necessary decisions built right into it; thus time need not be spent deciding what to do, how to do it, where to do it, and when to do it.

Enhancement of Controls

Certainly an important function in the whole management process is the maintenance of control. The written procedure is a control because it controls behavior (action) before it occurs. Case in point: To ensure against a lawsuit for negligent hiring, certain prehire actions are most important in our society today. A well-written procedure on how to conduct the background investigation of an applicant protects the company because it controls all those necessary prehire steps. If there was no written procedure on how to screen new applicants, I guarantee that there would be as many ways to check the applicant's background (or not to check it) as there are individuals charged with that responsibility. In other words, no control.

Provision for Objective Performance Evaluation

The written procedure is simply another tool that can be used to objectively evaluate an employee's performance. It only makes good sense that if the procedure spells out what to do and an employee does otherwise, that deviation is a discussion point for correcting the performance.

COMPLIANCE

The question of how closely one must adhere to, or comply with, policies or procedures is a problem. A security executive may spend 10 minutes emphasizing the importance of a given policy or standard operating procedure (SOP) and conclude by saying something to the effect of, "On the other hand, we want some flexibility here." What kind of flexibility?

Too often, ranking executives will massage policies and procedures to meet particular circumstances, such as when Security discovers an executive involved in some form of internal theft and the amount stolen is not substantial. The policy of the company is to terminate all employees caught stealing. The procedure for terminating such employees, step-by-step, clearly defines the discharge process. However, a company officer or executive in a position of power may, for a variety of reasons, exert his or her influence and override the policy such that the dishonest executive is not terminated but only warned. A case can be made for such an exception:

1. The executive has been with the company for 25 years and has dedicated a great deal of time and effort to the success of the company (and everyone agrees that's so).
2. The executive is known to spend many hours each week above and beyond the call of duty and deserves consideration.
3. The amount of the "indiscretion" is so small in contrast to the contribution that the executive has made that termination would be too severe.
4. All the other executives have done exactly the same thing—you want to fire everybody?

The list of reasons to not comply with company policies and procedures could go on and on. One more example: He or she didn't do it intentionally!

The question is whether flexibility should be permitted. The answer is: Of course! The dangers inherent in written policies and procedures, particularly procedures, are that they become inflexible and outdated and no longer viable. However, some employees follow them religiously or follow them in malicious obedience; that is, following the rules to the letter knowing full well that the consequences could be counterproductive. On the other hand, unless "flexibility" is managed with great care and caution, it is easy to abuse this capability, and regrettably abuse still tends to be a prerogative of some managers.

To avoid conflicts over compliance with written procedures, some firms operate under "guidelines," which lie somewhere between policies and procedures. Guidelines, by their very name, suggest direction but avoid any hint of absolute compliance. One would have to stray far afield before being guilty of violating any of the guidelines—they're just that loose and flexible.

Of course the looseness or flexibility leaves a lot of latitude for the operating manager—it allows wide variances in interpreting guidelines and, inevitably, permits inconsistencies in handling similar situations. Until a company gets "burned," perhaps in a litigation regarding how a problem was handled, the guidelines are the easiest "rules" for everyone to live with. After all, compliance is a disciplinary problem, and with compliance issues removed from the scene, problems don't exist. Right?

COMBINING POLICIES AND PROCEDURES

Some organizations combine policy (the what) with their SOP (the how). The following is an example taken from the contents of one firm's procedural manual; following that is the actual statement of policy and procedure.

Note the logical division of security activities/categories and how reasonable the codifying system is. Let's look at section 11.06 to see what the policy statement says about interrogations. (Remember: this is an example of the combined policy and procedure.)

11.06 INVESTIGATIVE AND SECURITY INTERVIEWS

Purpose

To define and establish standards for interviewing that will ensure maximum results and fair and consistent treatment and that will protect the company against subsequent civil liability arising therefrom.

Scope

All employees.

Policy

It is the policy of the company to differentiate between investigative and security interviews. With respect to the latter, it is the policy of the company that they be conducted by specifically trained personnel and be handled in the most professional manner possible and then only when there's reasonable evidence—direct or circumstantial—indicating that the employee is culpable.

Definitions

1. Investigative interview: The questioning of an employee seeking information and/or explanations. It is a fact-gathering process without challenges or accusations. The information gathered during such an interview is subsequently evaluated and may or may not lead to a security interview.
2. Security interview: The security interview is an accusatory confrontation and is used only in cases of dishonesty or other extremely serious violations of rules, such as narcotics offenses.

Procedures

1. Employees being interviewed must be advised at the outset that they are not being forcibly detained and need not choose to submit to questioning.
    A. If an employee opts not to be interviewed, such a decision constitutes insubordination and the employee will be terminated. The matter may then be referred to local law enforcement authorities, if circumstances and evidence warrant same.
2. Security interviews must be conducted in the privacy of an enclosed office.
3. If a female employee is the interviewee, a witness is required, preferably another woman.

FREE-STANDING POLICIES

Procedures invariably are related to a policy because they provide the detailed instructions for employees to carry out the intention of a policy. Conversely, there may be policies for which procedures are not required— free-standing policies. The following is an example of a free-standing policy of one firm with respect to applicants.

CRIMINAL HISTORY

1. An applicant will not be refused employment solely based on the fact that he or she has been convicted of a criminal offense unless said applicant deceived the firm about such history and falsified employment application forms or bonding forms.
2. A criminal record may disqualify an individual from being hired or promoted to assignments such as, but not limited to, management, security, personnel, or positions of fiduciary trust.

Such a policy statement obviously stands by itself, and no particular procedure is required to carry it out.

IMPORTANCE OF THE WRITTEN POLICY

In our litigious society, in which major employers are deemed desirable targets for lawsuits, the existence or absence of a written policy could be a significant factor in the final litigation outcome. An example is the aforementioned policy of the hiring of applicants with criminal backgrounds. If by chance an applicant was denied employment for some reason other than the fact that he or she had a criminal arrest and conviction record and if there were no written policy stating that convictions are not a bar to employment, an applicant could conceivably instigate and successfully pursue a cause of action based on criminal conviction discrimination. The written policy, however, would be an important defense in this case.

POLICIES, PROCEDURES, AND THE SECURITY MANUAL

In the security industry, departmental as well as corporate policies and procedures frequently are brought together in a main and central source of reference—the security manual. The following is the table of contents from the manual of a major retailer in the United States. Retail personnel arrest literally thousands of customers and employees each year and have, over the years, evolved into a highly sophisticated and professionally managed organization, as evident from the manual's detail.

LOSS PREVENTION MANUAL

Chapter	1	Loss Prevention Program
	1.00	Purpose
	1.01	Organization

The security manual, then, is the repository of all written policies and SOPs that pertain to the security function. The security manual of course contains other material and information, such as job descriptions for all security classifications, training materials, reports, and forms used by security personnel. However, the contents of the manual are constituted mainly by written policies and procedures. Today, word processing enables procedures and the manual to be more easily created (and revised) in a timely manner and with relative ease.

FORMAT AND MECHANICS

Written policies and procedures deserve a special look, a format that sets such important documents apart from more routine documents. Figure 20.1 is an example of the format I recommend:

1. Each page should reflect the name of the particular procedure.
2. Each procedure and the contents therein should be codified for easy reference. In Figure 20.1 the General Security Committee procedure is Security Procedure 11.01, and bomb threat incidents reported to that committee are 11.01.2.e.
3. That special look in this case is a vertical line margin with company logo on the lower left bottom.
4. Logo identifies the company. This procedure is unquestionably an SSI Corporation procedure.
5. Each procedure should be dated. The presence of the date could suggest it's time to reassess its viability or could reflect its absolute timeliness.
6. A two-page procedure noted.

POST ORDERS

Post orders are the written procedures for security officers assigned to a specific location or function. These orders are typically posted on the wall or placed in a folder for ease of reference. They contain such site- and task-specific information that even a stranger to that post should be able to read the orders and, based on the instructions, perform the security tasks required. The following list is but an example of the kinds of information that may be found in post orders:

*   Telephone numbers to call in the event of an emergency
*   Names and numbers of key personnel
*   Opening and closing procedures for that post
*   Patrol routes and locations of mandatory checks
*   Samples of authorized badges and passes (for pedestrian and vehicles)
*   Samples of forms and documents that are required to be filled-in or completed
*   What the security officer's purpose and mission is for this assignment
*   What to do in the event of . . .

SUMMARY

The difference between policies and procedures is best described as follows: A policy tends to be a guide to what management wants and a procedure specifically prescribes how it is to be accomplished. The development tends

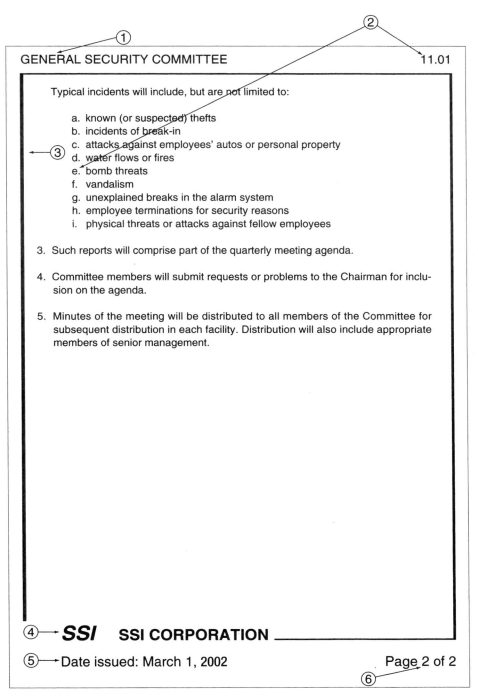

GENERAL SECURITY COMMITTEE   11.01

Typical incidents will include, but are not limited to:

    a. known (or suspected) thefts
    b. incidents of break-in
    c. attacks against employees' autos or personal property
    d. water flows or fires
    e. bomb threats
    f. vandalism
    g. unexplained breaks in the alarm system
    h. employee terminations for security reasons
    i. physical threats or attacks against fellow employees

3. Such reports will comprise part of the quarterly meeting agenda.

4. Committee members will submit requests or problems to the Chairman for inclusion on the agenda.

5. Minutes of the meeting will be distributed to all members of the Committee for subsequent distribution in each facility. Distribution will also include appropriate members of senior management.

SSI   SSI CORPORATION

Date issued: March 1, 2002   Page 2 of 2

Figure 20.1 Format for written policies and procedures.

to be an evolution from the spoken to the written word. Policies and procedures are tools for controlling and measuring performance. There's a degree of flexibility required when following procedures, and not all policies require procedures for implementation. Security policies and procedures tend to be the core of the department's operating manual.

REVIEW QUESTIONS

1. Define the difference between a policy and a procedure.

2. Guidelines are more stringent than a standard operating procedure. True or false? Why?

3. If the policy is to terminate employees for theft and the procedure spells out that process in detail, then every employee caught stealing will automatically be terminated. True or false? Why?

4. For every policy there must be a procedure. True or false? Why?

21

Computers and Effective Security Management*

> As computers evolved, operating systems evolved with them, making computers more economical and easier to use even as the machines grew more and more powerful and complex. In consequence, computers were harnessed for an ever-widening range of applications.
>
> — *The Computerized Society*[1]

Since the day Chuck Sennewald positioned himself in front of a typewriter to write the first edition of *Effective Security Management,* the computerization of society has grown at an ever-increasing rate. Today's Security Manager greatly benefits from tremendous strides that have been made in computer technology. From writing a simple memorandum to preparing an annual budget, from creating a professional-looking presentation and publishing a security manual to analyzing a myriad of incident reports, from designing and monitoring an on-site integrated security system to monitoring alarms and video at an off-premises central station, from communicating with the Security Department to accessing current security information via the network, the computer is an extremely powerful business tool.

The microcomputer, or personal computer (PC), has changed information processing and affected the way that Security Managers work. The role it plays varies, depending on the organization in which a Security Manager is operating. However, there are distinct applications that the microcomputer can have in the administrative, managerial, and supervisorial aspects of the security function. The purpose of this chapter is to explain these applications. Included are details of the development of microcomputers, their operation, benefits, and risks. Due to the complexity of this emerging technology, a glossary to explain certain technical terms is provided.

---

* By Geoff Craighead, CPP.
[1] Taming the Mainframe. *The Computerized Society.* (Alexandria, VA: Time-Life Books, 1987), p. 9.

There are several main types of computers in use today. They are as follows:

1. *Supercomputers,* the fastest class of computers, are used to carry out vast mathematical calculations for extremely complex programs such as weather predictions, earthquake simulations, and so forth.
2. *Mainframes,* large and powerful computers, can accommodate many users simultaneously executing many programs.
3. *Minicomputers,* or midsize computers, are like mainframes in that they are multiuser and multitasking machines.
4. *Microcomputers* are small, powerful microprocessor-based machines usually designed for single users.
5. *Microprocessor-based computers* typically lack a hard drive and are designed to download software, files, and data that are stored on powerful servers that manage network resources.
6. *Stand-alone microprocessors* installed in household appliances, telephones, alarm systems, and automobiles are dedicated to performing a single, specialized function.

The computer that most Security Managers interface with, the microcomputer, or PC, is addressed in this chapter. This material is written for both the computer literate manager and the manager who is learning this new technology.

HISTORICAL OVERVIEW

The manipulation of numerical data has been going on for thousands of years. The ancient Chinese used the abacus, and the Incas of Peru used quipas, or knotted cords.[2]

Computers, or electronic data processing machines, have been around since the mid-1940s. Manipulation of numerical data was the primary function of these earliest calculators. Their significance was the speed with which they could perform numerical calculations and the amount of data that they could process.[3]

How Computers Work

It is helpful to digress here and basically explain how computers work. A computer is a series of "on" and "off" switches that produce a series of electrical pulses. Each switch can be thought of as a single "bit" of infor-

---

[2] Gaur, Albertine. *A History of Writing.* (New York: Cross River Press, 1992), p. 207.
[3] Ibid.

mation. The status of each switch can be written as "on" or "off," or more simply by using the number "1" to represent on and a "0" (zero) for off. These 1s and 0s are used to form binary number groups that can be read by the computer. The binary number system uses a base of two rather than the normal base of 10. "Binary expression is the alphabet of electronic computers, the basis of the translation, storage, and manipulation of all information within a computer."[4]

The first electronic computational machine was the Electronic Numerical Integrator And Calculator (ENIAC). It used vacuum-tube switches and cables that were reconfigured by hand when different functions were to be performed. ENIAC took up a whole room. ENIAC was programmed by computer engineers who manually changed the "off" and "on" status of the thousands of switches that specified instructions. Hundreds of cables established the order in which these instructions were to be performed.

In the early 1960s, technology developed that enabled multiple transistor circuits to be compressed onto a single silicon chip, thereby creating an integrated circuit. Each of these thousands of transistors performed as a single electrical switch, as did each vacuum tube in ENIAC. However, instead of occupying an entire room, transistors, due to their size and low production of heat, could be contained in small desktop containers.

"In November 1971, Intel Corporation introduced the 4004, a 'microprogrammable computer on a chip' in a modest advertisement in Electronic News. . . . It contained as much computing power as ENIAC. . . . But instead of filling an entire room, the 4004 was smaller than a postage stamp. . . . Instead of performing a single fixed function, the microprocessor chip could be programmed to perform many functions."[5] Figure 21.1 shows a microprocessor chip manufactured by Intel Corporation.

Four years later, the first computer that contained a microprocessor appeared. Despite the absence of a keyboard or a monitor, manually inputted software instructed the computer to perform its calculations. The Altair 8800 became the world's first home computer. To operate, electrical switches were set by hand to input data and tiny light bulbs indicated the "computerized" results.

Since the appearance of this home computer, there have been numerous developments in the PC field. Modern technology has made it possible for microprocessor chips to contain millions of transistors. As a result, microprocessors are becoming faster and faster at processing information. The design and intricacy of *hardware*—or the physical equipment that makes up the microcomputer and its peripherals—is expanding and diversifying. This affects the way data is inputted, stored, retrieved, and converted into a usable form. *System software* that controls the microprocessor

---

[4] Gates, Bill. *The Road Ahead.* (New York: Penguin Books, 1996), p. 24.
[5] "The Microprocessor Turns 25," special report by Intel Inside program participants. *The Microprocessor.* (A special advertising section in *Time* magazine, October 7, 1996).

Figure 21.1   An Intel microprocessor chip. Courtesy of the Intel Corporation.

is automatically loaded when the computer is switched on. This has made the microcomputer much easier to use. *Applications software,* which consists of programs other than system software, has enabled a microcomputer to perform a wide variety of business functions. The microcomputer evolved from being a stand-alone unit that communicated only with its user to being part of a worldwide network of computers — the *Internet.* Although both the computing power and capacity of microcomputers and the availability of user-friendly software dramaticallyincreased, the computer's size and the cost of acquiring such power drastically decreased.

MICROCOMPUTER HARDWARE

The physical components that make up a computer system are called *hardware.* The following sections describe these parts. *How Computers Work,* by Ron White; *The Way Things Work,* by David Macaulay; and *Networks,* by

Timothy Ramteke were used as invaluable aids for understanding the inner workings of computer systems.

PCs are manufactured in both desktop and smaller portable models. A portable computer may be a laptop; a slightly smaller notebook; or an even smaller handheld or pocket-size device, including a palmtop computer or personal data assistant (PDA). Computers are also found in cellular or mobile telephones, and pagers or beepers. Figure 21.2 shows (a) a desktop, (b) a notebook, and (c) a hand-held microcomputer from IBM Corporation.

PCs basically consist of the central processing unit (CPU), the memory, and peripherals such as adapters that connect the computer to networks, printers, and other devices.

Central Processing Unit

The CPU—the brain of the computer—is a microprocessor that accepts digital data and carries out instructions. It manipulates this data and stores it in memory before outputting the results. Under the control of the operating system (e.g., DOS, Windows), the CPU manages the other hardware components of a microcomputer.

Memory

The CPU uses instructions permanently held in read-only memory (ROM) chips and carries out a particular function by accessing information temporarily held in random-access memory (RAM) chips. (As RAM increases, a computer can process larger amounts of information in a more efficient manner.)

Data is permanently stored in two locations:

1. The *hard drive,* which is usually located within the computer (data is actually stored on the rotating hard disk that is located within the sealed housing of the hard drive[6])
2. *Portable devices* such as floppy disks, optical disks (such as CD-ROM disks), or cartridges (each containing a magnetic tape, a disk, or a memory chip) that can be inserted into the computer or a device attached to it

The parts of the computer used for reading (i.e., retrieving) and writing (i.e., saving) data are called *disk drives.* Disk drives differ according to the types of disks they handle. For example, the hard drive reads from and writes onto a hard disk, the floppy drive reads from and writes onto a floppy disk, and

---

[6] The terms *hard disk* and *hard drive* are used interchangeably.

(a)

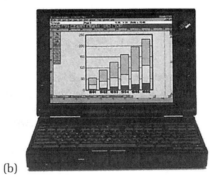

(b)

(c)

Figure 21.2   (a) A desktop, (b) a notebook, and (c) a handheld computer. Courtesy of International Business Machines Corporation. Unauthorized use not permitted.

the CD-ROM drive reads and writes data from a CD-ROM disk. Figure 21.3 shows various portable data storage devices.

Peripherals

Peripherals are devices that are attached to or built into the microcomputer. They include those for inputting information—such as a keyboard; a mouse; a trackball; a joystick; an optical scanner; a digital camera; a video camera; a microphone; and various tablets, pads, and screens that are touch- or light-sensitive. Other peripheral devices are for outputting information—a display screen, a speaker, and a printer. A data communication device called a *modem* is often included. It has both input and output capabilities. It translates digital information into analog signals (audio tones) that can be transmitted over telephone lines and then translated back into digital data. Thus, computers can talk to each other via the telephone system. Today, most modems enable computers to operate as facsimile (fax) machines.

Networks

Microcomputers can be connected together to form a local area network (LAN) or a wide area network (WAN) and may have connections to the Internet. "These interconnections of computers, which are self-governing and

Figure 21.3   Various portable data storage devices. Photograph by Edmund Lau.

[usually] not controlled by another, are called networks. An Internet is a network of networks."[7] ([Usually] is added here because some specialized utility software programs can be used to allow an authorized person to control another person's computer via a network. The authorized person is able to temporarily take over the operation of the computer for a specific reason, such as to diagnose software problems.) Network connections may consist of telephone lines, twisted-pair cables, coaxial cables, or fiber-optic cables (commonly called "fiber"). In addition, wireless[8] networks, satellites, and other appliances can be used.

A LAN connects two or more microcomputers, often called work-stations, to each other and sometimes to a minicomputer, a mainframe, or a common printer. (The term *workstation* is also used to refer to high-performance computers that are more powerful than microcomputers.) The main computer that serves all the other personal computers in the LAN is called the *server*. As their name implies, LANs normally serve a small geographical area. "LANs typically provide networking capabilities within a facility (or a building). However, they can extend to adjacent facilities in a campus environment and can span distances of two or three miles. WANs span much greater distances and [may] even go around the globe."[9]

Often referred to as the "information superhighway," the Internet is a worldwide "loose connection of interconnecting commercial and non-commercial computer networks. The constituent networks are tied together by telecommunication lines and by their shared reliance on standard communication protocols (rules)."[10] The collection of protocols that allows computers to transmit data across the Internet is called Transmission Control Protocol/Internet Protocol (TCP/IP). IP requires that every computer on the Internet have an individual address.

When a stream of data, such as an electronic mail (e-mail) message, is to be transmitted, TCP software breaks it into manageable "packets" of digital information and numbers each packet in order. The IP address of the destination computer is marked on each of these numbered packets and they are dispatched. Packet switchers, or *routers,* are computers on the Internet that read the IP address on each packet and expeditiously direct each to its destination. On arrival of the packets at their final desti-nation, TCP software checks that all the packets are present and then reassembles them into the original e-mail message. *The Internet,* by Kerry Cochrane, provides a fundamental, easy-to-comprehend explanation of how the Internet works.[11]

---

[7] Ramteke, Timothy. *Networks.* (Upper Saddle River, NJ: Prentice-Hall, 1994), pp. 10, 11.

[8] "Wireless networks are becoming more and more popular. Unless good encryption is used, they are inherently insecure. Unfortunately, that has not stopped their use." (Comments by Kelly J. "KJ" Kuchta, CPP, CFE).

[9] Ramteke, Timothy. *Networks.* (Upper Saddle River, NJ: Prentice-Hall, 1994), pp. 10, 11.

[10] Gates, Bill. *The Road Ahead.* (New York: Penguin Books, 1996), pp. 110–112.

[11] Cochrane, Kerry. *The Internet.* (New York: Franklin Watts, 1995), p. 11.

The Internet has its origins in a government network, called the Advanced Research Projects Agency Network (ARPANET), developed in 1969[12] by the U.S. Department of Defense. Designed to be a communications network that could withstand a nuclear holocaust, it evolved into the Internet in 1989[13] when government funding for the ARPANET ceased.

> The word [*Internet*] came to mean both the network itself and the protocols that governed communication across the network—a dual meaning that has been a source of confusion ever since. Even when it became a commercial service, the Internet's first customers were mostly research organizations, computer companies, university scientists, and graduate students, who used it to exchange e-mail.[14]

The Internet has many components, two of the most widely known being e-mail and the World Wide Web (WWW). These are discussed later in this chapter.

An *intranet* is a private Internet within a corporation or organization. Whether a corporate network uses a LAN or a WAN, it can be designed to function with Web documents that can be accessed only by the private network users.

MICROCOMPUTER SOFTWARE

"The essence of software [is] a comprehensive set of rules that tell a machine what to do, that 'instruct' it, step-by-step, how to perform particular tasks."[15] Two main types of microcomputer software are system software and applications software.

System Software

System software consists of the operating system and other special programs that oversee a computer's operations. "An operating system is the fundamental software that tells a computer system's components how to work together and performs other broad functions. It's a platform on which all the software applications—such as accounting or payroll or word processing or electronic mail programs—[operate on]. Without an operating system, a computer is useless."[16]

A number of operating systems have been developed for different types of microprocessors: character-based ones, such as UNIX, Linux, and DOS,

---

[12] Gates, Bill. *The Road Ahead.* (New York: Penguin Books, 1996), pp. 110–112.
[13] Ibid.
[14] Ibid.
[15] Ibid, p. 24.
[16] Ibid, p. 41.

and those based on graphical user interface (GUI), such as Apple's Macintosh and Microsoft's Windows.

GUI-based operating systems use icons, scroll bars, and menus of commands or instructions. Graphical features are easier to learn than the typing of arcane commands that may be difficult to remember. Using GUI, various tasks can be performed more quickly and conveniently.

The operating system resides on a storage device, typically a hard drive contained within the computer. When the computer is turned on, the operating system is automatically loaded into the computer's memory and begins to execute. This process is called, "the bootstrap, or simply, boot—a small amount of code [i.e., software] that's permanently a part of the PC. The bootstrap is aptly named because it lets the PC do something entirely on its own,"[17] prior to the operating system taking charge. This analogy stems from the idiom "to pull oneself up by one's (own) bootstraps."

Utilities, or *utility software*, are programs that also help to maintain the smooth running of a computer. Some utilities display information about a computer's hardware and its memory, consolidate data storage on the hard drive, keep files and directories organized on the hard drive, and manage other devices (such as printers). Others are designed to restrict access to files and recover lost data. Some utilities come installed in a computer or are purchased separately.

Other special programs involved in computer operations translate programs written in programming languages into digital form, or machine language. Every microcomputer uses a specific machine language designed for its CPU to execute.

Applications Software

Applications software enables the microcomputer to perform specific functions such as word processing, database management, spreadsheets, desktop publishing, encryption, computer graphics (including business presentation graphics, computer-aided design (CAD), geographic information systems (GIS), global positioning systems (GPS), and image processing), telecommunications (including electronic mail [e-mail], instant messaging [IM], voice-mail, teleconferencing, the WWW, online services, and intranets), specialized management programs, and artificial intelligence (AI).

WORD PROCESSING

Word processing software converts the computer into an electronic typewriter that can be used to easily create, edit, store, and print text documents such as letters, memoranda, forms, employee performance evaluations (such

---

[17] White, Ron. *How Computers Work,* 2nd ed. (Emeryville, CA: Ziff-Davis Press, 1995), p. 13.

as Appendix A), proposals, reports, security surveys (such as Appendix B), general security checklists, security manuals, books, articles, press releases, and speeches. It is also an invaluable tool for keeping the Security Manager's resume current. A professional-looking document can be easily created and readily updated when necessary.

The length of created documents is limited only by the storage capabilities of the computer, which are enormous. Also, if multiple copies of a working document exist, changes to it should be promptly communicated to all persons who use the document. Specialized software, using network features, can be programmed to automatically route changes to those persons needing to know.

Word processing is a business tool and as such must be wisely used. Considerable time can be wasted endlessly editing and revising a document. A manager must decide whether this extra time is warranted in view of its importance and value. If administrative assistance is available, a manager may use word processing to simply rough out material. The assistant can then format and clean up the document before printing it.

DATABASE MANAGEMENT

A database is an organized collection of information. [The ASIS*Dynamics* member's directory is an example of a database.] A computerized database management system is a computer application that helps you to store, retrieve, sort, analyze, and print information in a database. . . . Two types of database management systems exist: file management systems and relational database management systems. File management systems, sometimes called flat file databases, store data in files without indexing, which means that data is processed sequentially. File management systems lack flexibility in data manipulation.[18]

A flat file database operates in a similar way to a handwritten card file. Each card may contain information such as a person's name, company, address, telephone, e-mail address, and fax number. However, each card can only be accessed separately. There is no relationship between each card. A flat file database can only individually access files.

"[Relational] database management systems enable users to manipulate data in more sophisticated ways by defining relationships between sets of data. The relationship is a common element."[19] For example, specialized incident reporting software can be used to capture, store, and retrieve important data. When an incident or event occurs, entering information in certain user-defined fields can create a record of it. Analytical reports, graphs, or

---

[18] Gates, Bill. *The Road Ahead.* (New York: Penguin Books, 1996), pp. 110–112.
[19] Using *Microsoft Office.* (Indianapolis, IN: Que Corporation, 1994), pp. 577, 578.

charts can be created by sorting data according to a common element such as time of day, day of week, month, year; type of incident; suspect; or other user-defined field. Such information can be invaluable in tracking incidents and analyzing trends, conducting investigations, devising loss prevention strategies, effectively using resources, benchmarking, and budgeting. Another type of useful application is case management. "Case management refers to investigations management, where cases (investigations) are managed in a similar fashion to incidents, preferably in a relational database system. Case management software essentially provides for a 'paperless' and data-driven investigation process."[20] Shepp goes on to say that,

> The power of analysis using the data-driven model provides for a very detailed analysis of trends. For example, in a traditional "paper and pencil" incident or case management model, how long would it take to determine the number of notebook computers missing from a company, from where, on what days of the week and what time of day they went missing, their locations, the total cost of the loss, the average cost of each computer, the brand and age of each computer, and what locations are considered "hot spots"? All of this would take considerable time. However, automating this same analysis would take minutes, with graphs, charts, and narratives provided with reports.

Database management software allows information to be stored, retrieved, sorted, and analyzed far more quickly and easily than information recorded on paper. In addition, these electronic databases take up much less space than paper records. Information that can be managed this way includes names, addresses, telephone and fax numbers, e-mail addresses, birthdays, dates of contacts, meeting times, appointments, time and attendance records, employee background data, staff training records, security reference books and articles, incidents, investigations, key records, asset inventories, equipment inspection, and maintenance records. The last two applications can be enhanced using barcode-labeling software. "The automation provided by barcode technology also integrates guard tour and activity cost tracking into case and incident management."[21]

SPREADSHEETS

An electronic spreadsheet can be used to automatically perform numerical calculations. "First, you set up a template that can perform a series of calculations automatically. Then you enter the data, and the spreadsheet performs the calculations. If you make a mistake entering a number, you can

---

[20] Comments by Dennis Shepp, CPP, when reviewing this section.
[21] Ibid.

go back, change only that number, and tell the spreadsheet to recalculate the result."[22] Spreadsheet programs are usually set up in the form of a table with rows and columns. Each row and column intersects to form a cell in which data may be stored. The data may be a text label, a number, or a formula that combines data from other cells.

"It is interesting to note that until spreadsheet software came onto the market, personal computers were mostly used by hobbyists. The advent of the spreadsheet in the late 1970s caught the attention of businesspersons worldwide. This development was largely responsible for the meteoric rise of computer popularity."[23]

Spreadsheets are of immense value in preparing and tracking budgets, calculating expenses, estimating job costs, and conducting other numerical analyses. Results can be obtained more efficiently and rapidly, and with less chance of error, than if done manually. Data entries can be easily changed to analyze their effect. For example, in preparing a budget for security staff wages and benefits, different wage levels can be specified to determine their impact on cost. Another useful feature of most spreadsheet programs is the ability to graphically display results. Different types of graphs and charts can be used to visually display fluctuations and trends in the relationships between different variables within a spreadsheet.

DESKTOP PUBLISHING

Desktop publishing software can transform the manager's computer into a mini–publishing house. Text and graphic material can be incorporated into a single document. Departmental newsletters, bulletins, posters, manuals, brochures, books, articles, and business cards can be produced without time-consuming collaboration between the person designing the document and those responsible for printing it.

Corrections and revisions can be quickly done on the computer. Images can be scanned into a document or imported from a digital camera. Text and graphics can be easily altered to appear exactly as wanted without messy cutting and pasting. Modern desktop publishing software includes features that flow text around graphic images. Different fonts and clip art can be accessed from within desktop publishing software or imported from other commercially available programs. The Security Department is able to produce professional-looking documents in a timely and cost-effective manner.

---

[22] Kraynak, Joe, Wang, W. E., and Flynn, Jennifer. *The First Book of Personal Computing.* (Carmel, IN: Alpha Books, 1992), p. 99.
[23] Comments by Mike Leonardich.

An excellent reference for information about some of the afore-mentioned applications software programs is *The First Book of Personal Computing* by Joe Kraynak, W. E. Wang, and Jennifer Flynn.

ENCRYPTION SOFTWARE

Encryption software is a highly recommended application that can be used to protect sensitive data from unauthorized use. There are two types of uses of encryption: for communication and for the protection of the data itself when it is being stored.

COMPUTER GRAPHICS

Computer graphics are diagrammatic representations of digital information. This technology is used for a wide variety of applications including business presentation graphics, CAD, GIS, GPS, and image processing.

Business Presentation Graphics

Business presentation graphics software allows for the production of professional-looking materials that can be displayed on black and white or colored paper, overhead transparencies, 35-mm slides, a computer, or a projector screen. This facilitates the design and delivery of an entire presentation.

There are many ways a Security Manager can apply this software. New employee induction sessions can be illustrated with pictorial representations and graphs. Teaching aids such as flow charts and illustrations showing the sequence of events in handling an emergency can be prepared. Executive orientations can be performed using information graphs depicting the Security Department's effectiveness in protecting assets and reducing inventory shrinkage. Security consultants can innovatively present the findings and recommendations of a risk assessment analysis and security survey to their clients.

Computer-Aided Design

CAD software allows the microcomputer to be used for graphic designing and drafting. CAD programs enable the creation of two- and three-dimensional architectural plans or drawings and the visualization of facilities. This software has many uses. For example, the design of security equipment and the layout of a security console can be achieved. A simu-

lated walk-through of a planned building can be used to help design its security systems. Visualization can be used for forensic analysis after an incident or crime has occurred.

Geographic Information Systems and Global Positioning Systems

"A geographic information system (GIS) is a generic term for a family of computer software packages that store, process, and display geographically referenced information. A GIS has the capability of importing data in a variety
of formats and associating the information with geographic coordinates in
two or three dimensions."[24] Computer-aided dispatching of security staff and
patrol vehicles and analyzing crime reports and security incident patterns
by neighborhood are potential uses of GIS.

Similarly, GPS software can be adapted for tracking company vehicles,
containers, and other cargo and, potentially, many other uses.

Image Processing

Image processing software enables the microcomputer to capture, store,
display, and output text and graphic images. Images can be retrieved and
sorted far more easily and use less space than paper.

Such technology is very useful in the digital processing of two- or
three-dimensional images. Inputting the image requires imaging software
and devices such as an optical scanner, a digital camera (or a video camera),
and a video capture card. For example, a person's image can be digitally
inputted into the microcomputer and displayed on the computer screen; the
image will be frozen and stored in the computer's memory, and then the
image can be printed onto a customized polyvinyl chloride (PVC) photo ID
card. The software may allow the cardholder's name, the company's name
or logo, the department name, the card's expiration date, and the cardholder's signature to be displayed on the badge. This process is commonly
known as "video badging" or "photo ID badging." It is much faster and more
convenient than the time-consuming process of taking a photograph, cutting
it to size, and affixing it to the appropriately labeled card. Also, when a
badge is damaged, lost, or stolen, the digital image can be retrieved from the
computer and a new badge easily made. This dispenses with the need for
another photograph to be taken.

Because digital images are a series of small dots—knows as
pixels—they can be altered or their appearance enhanced. This fact
has important ramifications for the Security Manager because it pertains

---

[24] Watts, John M. Jr. *Fire Protection Handbook,* 17th ed. (Quincy, MA: National Fire Protection
Association, 1991), pp. 10–142.

to the admissibility of evidence, including standards for the collection of electronic data.

TELECOMMUNICATIONS

Telecommunications software is used in conjunction with telecommunication networks for transmission between computers of data, ranging from text to graphics to audio to video. Telecommunication networks include LANs, WANs, intranets, and the Internet.

Using e-mail, IM, voice-mail, and teleconferencing, Security Managers can communicate both inside and outside their organizations. Using the WWW and online services, Security Managers can access specialized information and programs outside of their organizations. Using corporate intranets, Security Managers can access and disseminate information within their own organizations.

Electronic Mail

Electronic mail (e-mail) is a process by which digital information can be sent, received, forwarded, and stored using telecommunications networks. Basically, e-mail works in this way: One logs on to a microcomputer (using a user ID and password) and connects, via a telecommunications network, to a file server that controls the e-mail system. Using e-mail software, the file server receives incoming mail and distributes messages addressed to persons using the system. Each user has an electronic mailbox that stores incoming and outgoing messages. Messages in the mailbox can be downloaded to the user's workstation. Each message can be opened, read, replied to, forwarded to another person, deleted, electronically stored, or printed. New messages can be sent to specific persons using their mailbox addresses. By grouping e-mail addresses together, a single message can be simultaneously sent to multiple e-mail users. This makes e-mail a very efficient mechanism for widely distributing information.

Using the Internet, e-mail can be transmitted outside of corporate networks. The Internet has in recent years become "the backbone connecting all the world's different electronic mail systems."[25] On the Internet, an e-mail address is composed of a user ID (usually consisting of part of the user's name), the @ symbol, and the address of the online service, the Internet service provider, or the host computer that provides access to the Internet.

---

[25]Gates, Bill. *The Road Ahead.* (New York: Penguin Books, 1996), p. 112.

Messages can also be sent to bulletin boards. Here, information, including files and programs pertaining to topics of interest, is posted on computer networks for review.

E-mail has transformed business communications. It is convenient, fast, economical, and reliable to use. Memoranda, reports, notices of meetings, minutes of meetings, newsletters, security bulletins, notifications of alarms, and messages with easily attached files can be effortlessly sent at any time to one or many persons. Modern e-mail software can even notify the sender when the intended recipient has accessed an e-mail message. Documents can be conveniently and expeditiously edited with input from workgroups employed at widely dispersed locations. This is accomplished without the expense of traditional mail services. Shared folders that can be accessed by all employees of a firm can be used to store information such as company security policies and procedures. A manager's appointment calendar can be electronically accessed by authorized persons and updated pending approval from the manager. (Similarly, a group of persons can coordinate their schedules using a common electronic calendar.) When a manager is away from the office, most e-mail software can be programmed to so inform those sending incoming messages; also, by using a microcomputer that is part of the telecommunications network (such as a portable computer equipped with a modem) managers can remotely access e-mail.

Like all business tools, e-mail must be used properly. Received or sent messages needed for future reference should be stored using a well-organized folder system. All messages should be written with words that express ideas clearly, concisely, and accurately. All text should be checked for spelling errors. Confidential information should not be transmitted via e-mail; indeed, all e-mail communications should be treated with no expectation of privacy. (Some companies require that e-mail being sent outside of their corporate networks be encrypted for data security.) Care should also be exercised in sending urgent messages via e-mail. It may be some time before the recipient accesses them. E-mail should not be used to send unimportant data. Information that is of no importance to the recipient is both a waste of time and nonproductive.

Instant Messaging

A new form of communication being used in both personal and business settings is called IM. This allows two or more people to have an online (real time) conversation. "A message is typed and the return key is hit. A second later the recipient receives the message, types a reply and hits return. Back and forth it goes. Such instant messaging applications are changing the way people communicate."[26]

---

[26] Comments by Kelly J. "KJ" Kuchta, CPP, CFE.

Voice-Mail

Common telephone answering machines have evolved into computerized voice-mail systems (VMSs). Instead of having a prerecorded greeting and the caller's voice being recorded on an audiocassette tape, VMSs utilize special applications software. A voice message (i.e., an analog signal) is converted to digital data and stored, for example, on a computer's hard drive. Stored messages can then be later retrieved from the computer. Most VMSs can be programmed to automatically send a signal to a person's pager when a voice-mail message has been received. Also, most systems also have the capability of being accessed remotely—that is, from a hotel, an airplane, a residence, a car, or wherever a telephone may be available.

Teleconferencing

Teleconferencing, the sending of live voice and real-time video from one microcomputer to another, has been made possible with the development of high-speed telecommunications networks. This is an important application for Security Managers, particularly for those whose responsibilities encompass widely separated multiple locations.[27]

Videoconferencing enables a person to use a specially equipped microcomputer to conduct a conference with others with similar equipment at another site (or at multiple sites). Such equipment would include a video camera, a video capture card to translate video images to digital data, a computer screen, a microphone, a sound card that makes it possible for the computer to handle audio, speakers, specialized software, and access to a telecommunications network.

"A lot of people are using a product in conjunction with teleconferencing called NetMeeting or Webex. This is basically an application that allows conference call attendees with a computer and Internet access to see a document on the Web during a conference call. The advantage of this is that everyone views the same document. When one person makes a change, everyone sees it. This facilitates online collaboration. Such communication is very useful for geographically diverse organizations to create documents."[28]

---

[27] Although not addressed in this chapter, "there is a growing demand for remote monitoring and playback capability of CCTV cameras. For example, a security director responsible for multiple buildings may be notified of a serious incident that is occurring, or has occurred, at one of the facilities. The ability to use a home or office computer or wireless technology (such as a cellular telephone or PDA), to remotely access the building's CCTV system to view live video or a recording of the incident would be very useful. The means of video transmission will largely determine the quality of the video. Such means may include a local area network (LAN), a wide area network (WAN), the Internet, or wireless methods" (Craighead, Geoff, CPP. *High-Rise Security and Fire Life Safety,* 2nd ed. [Burlington, MA: Butterworth-Heinemann, 2003] p. 157.)

[28] Comments by Kelly J. "KJ" Kuchta, CPP, CFE.

World Wide Web

The World Wide Web (WWW or Web) is a worldwide electronic database containing vast amounts of information. *Random House Personal Computer Dictionary* defines it as, "a system of Internet servers that support specially formatted documents. The documents are formatted in a language called HTML (HyperText Markup Language) that supports links to other documents, as well as graphics, audio, and video files." The Web "began as a set of specifications written by Tim Berbers-Lee of the European Laboratory for Particle Physics (CERN) in 1989. He proposed a series of protocols, or tags, that would allow one document (also called a page) to link to another and make navigating the huge Internet easier for researchers."[29]

A website is a specific location on the Web. Each website has a home page that has its own address, known as its uniform resource locator (URL). When a site is entered, the home page first appears on the computer screen. This page contains information and HyperText links, which are words or pictures that appear on the computer screen (usually in a different color) that each connect to another piece of information. By pointing and clicking with a mouse on such a link, another page that contains more information, and perhaps additional links, is displayed.

For example, the online website of ASIS International is located at URL: http://www.asisonline.org (Figure 21.4 shows the ASIS Online WWW home page.) Typing in this URL in the Netsite box of the Web browser accesses this website. Using the HyperText Transfer Protocol (HTTP), the Web-browsing software retrieves www.asisonline.org[30] information from the host computer. Pointing and clicking on various HyperText links on the ASIS Online home page provides additional information.

Other professional security societies and associations, suppliers of security services and systems, equipment manufacturers, and consultants have websites available to advertise their services, products, and expertise.

Some websites provide bulletin boards that offer a means for networking and for the exchange of information.

There are popular search services that categorize websites and help one to find areas of particular interest. These tools can be particularly useful because searching topics of interest on the Internet can often result in hundreds of suggested references being obtained. Wading through this information can be very time consuming.

---

[29] Bodensiek, Paul. *Intranet Publishing.* (Indianapolis, IN: Que Corporation, 1996), p. 10.

[30] The *org* portion of the address indicates that the host computer site is operated by a private organization. If an Internet address finishes with *net* this indicates a network site, *mil* indicates a military site, *gov* indicates a government site, *edu* indicates an educational site, and *com* indicates a company or commercial site. Countries outside of the United States do not use such nomenclature. Rather, they use two-letter designations, such as *ca* for Canada and *nz* for New Zealand, at the end of their addresses (Cochrane, Kerry. *The Internet.* [New York: Franklin Watts, 1995], pp. 12, 13).

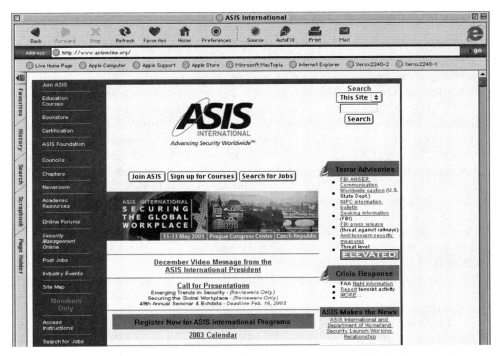

Figure 21.4   The ASIS Online WWW home page. Courtesy of ASIS International.

There are other Internet servers that are not part of the WWW. Many of these operate in a text-based environment. However, the WWW, with its primarily GUI, has become the most widely accepted application of the Internet.

Online Services

Today's Security Manager has a wide variety of commercial online services from which to choose. Using a PC, subscribers to online services can access the Internet, send and receive e-mail, participate in online conferences, and connect to various third-party providers of information. An example of a third-party provider would be one that supplies personnel background information. For a fee, investigation of a work applicant may be performed using databases that provide criminal histories, civil records, driving records, worker's compensation records, credit reports, and verification of education. Such information is obtained in a timely and confidential manner. Other commercial online services, for example, allow subscribers who have overseas interests to review overseas travel advisories and daily intelligence reports.

One of the largest online information services in the world is Lexis-Nexis. It has two parts representing both the legal (Lexis) and the news (Nexis) information services. This information is updated daily and includes articles from newspapers, business magazines, journals, news releases, broadcast transcript, and wire services.

Intranets

The same technology used for the WWW can also be applied to corporate intranets. Private websites can be used by Security Managers to educate and inform company employees about the company's Security Program; security bulletins, policies, procedures, and newsletters can be linked to the home page on the company's intranet. A website that is accessible only to the company's security staff can also be designed. In this way, documents such as emergency contact lists, security manuals, security alerts, scheduling information, newsletters, a video of the Security Director thanking the department for a job well done, and "Recognition of Achievement" awards can be designed exclusively for the Security Department to access.

Excellent references for information about the Internet and intranets are *Special Edition Using the Internet*, by Jerry Honeycutt and Mary Ann Pike; *Intranet Publishing*, by Paul Bodensiek; and *The Security Professional in Cyberspace*, by Ronald Lander and James E. Roughton.

SPECIALIZED MANAGEMENT PROGRAMS

There are many types of specialized software applications designed to perform various management functions. Some of these integrate applications such as word processing, database management, spreadsheets, computer graphics, and telecommunications programs. Others are applications within themselves. Accounting functions, payroll, financial analysis, business planning, insurance, legal, marketing and sales, human resources, security staff scheduling, patrol management, time management calendars, contact management, and project management are but a few of the commercially available programs. Also, the monitoring and controlling of integrated security systems and central station monitoring of remote alarm signals has greatly benefited from the development of specialized programs. Due to space considerations, it is not possible to elaborate on all such software. However, the last two programs are addressed.

Monitoring and Controlling Integrated Security Systems

In monitoring and controlling on-site security and fire life safety systems,

> Industry standards previously relied mostly on panels with many different services being installed side-by-side without any physical connection between displays. Warning lights, buzzers, beeping and visual displays were all designed to attract the attention of the human operator. The operator in turn had to sense the signal(s), interpret its meaning and decide on a course of action (sometimes using an elaborate alarm instruction book), and finally, instigate proper responses. This type of system relied heavily on the ability of the operator to properly respond to each different problem as it occurred. Many factors such as lack of training, varying responses by different operators, or not performing each operation in the proper order could easily lower the effectiveness of the response.[31]

Specialized software has been developed to integrate access control with systems such as intrusion detection, photo ID badging, closed-circuit television (CCTV), and fire life safety. In this context, "access control" refers to a microprocessor-based system in which electronic card readers are connected to locking devices (or in elevator installations, the elevator system itself). Such systems may link together using separate databases that communicate with each other, or by sharing a common relational database. A fully integrated system behaves as though it were a single entity, sharing information and being monitored and controlled using a single-user interface. The user interface of choice is GUI-based rather than text-only. An ever-increasing number of access control systems are being built using an operating system such as Microsoft's Windows NT. NT (New Technologies) has both multitasking and multiuser capabilities and built-in security features. Multitasking means that more than one task can be simultaneously performed. Multiuser means that more than one person can simultaneously operate the system. In very large facilities and multibuilding campuses, multiple persons or multiple command centers may be able to interface with the one integrated system.

A benefit of integrating access control with, for example, photo ID badging, is that it alleviates the need for duplication of data. The information input to a database to produce a photo ID badge is similar to that needed for access control (although the latter will require additional data such as specific privileges). By sharing the same database, duplication is thereby eliminated. "The best benefit, and the one that increases both the security level and the system's usefulness, is that, in a truly integrated system, any access control system CRT screen can display the person's original digital photo. The display can be initiated automatically by the presentation of an

---

[31] Comments by Dan Cossarek.

ID badge at a card reader or by operator manual selection via a keyboard, or [a] mouse. The operator can then visually compare the retrieved digital photo with the face, either directly or remotely via a CCTV image, of the cardholder."[32] Such integration improves system operations by providing a secondary means of identification.

An advantage of a fully integrated system is that the software may be programmed to produce automatic responses when certain events are triggered. For example, when a fire alarm occurs in a facility, the computer system may automatically retrieve a CAD floor plan or digitized photograph of the involved area and display it on a computer screen in front of the system operator; initiate a flashing icon depicting the type of device in alarm and its exact location; activate a CCTV camera in the alarm area to display the scene in a window on the operator's screen (including icons for controlling the camera's pan, tilt, and zoom functions) or full-screen on an adjacent monitor; record the event in real time; and display text informing the operator of specific steps to be taken to address the situation. Simultaneously, a computerized incident report may be automatically downloaded to document the response.

Such examples of integration may simplify and assist operations. Security staff may be more easily trained. Overall, installation and operating costs may be reduced.

Central Station Monitoring

Specialized programs, such as *Monitoring Automation Systems* (MAS) software, is being used in many central stations. This assists operators to monitor alarm signals from remote facilities. The software automatically determines whether a signal received at a central station is scheduled, such as the regular everyday opening or closing of a facility, or unscheduled, such as an unauthorized entry or fire alarm. When scheduled alarms are received they are automatically logged to the account history of each facility being monitored. When unscheduled alarms are received they are automatically distributed in an order of priority to the next available operator.

To help an operator correctly respond to an alarm, appropriate information is displayed on a computer screen. This information may include the name, the address and the telephone numbers of the facility; contact telephone numbers and e-mail addresses of facility representatives, private security, local law enforcement, and the fire department; the alarm history; and required response procedures. The operator must carry out specific

---

[32] Integrating Access Control Systems with Badging, by David Aggleton, CPP, *The Protection of Assets Manual*, editor, Timothy L. Williams, CPP. (Los Angeles: POA Publishing, LLC, 323-663-4887, copyright February 1997), Bulletin, p. 7.

actions before an alarm can be cleared from the screen. Operator responses are automatically documented using the software.

Such specialized software facilitates the systematic and efficient handling of multiple remote alarm signals. This may lead to reduced fees charged to clients for this service. This software can also provide a tool for analyzing alarm activity. Central station managers can use such analyses to advise their clients of alarm trends. Alarm handling activities within a central station can be tracked. This can assist a manager in making better-informed decisions about the operation of the central station.

ARTIFICIAL INTELLIGENCE

Artificial intelligence (AI) is an area of computer science that attempts to program the computer to think like a human being. *Webster's New World Dictionary of Computer Terms* defines AI as,

> A group of technologies that attempt to emulate certain aspects of human behavior, such as reasoning and communication, as well as to mimic biological senses, including seeing and hearing. Specific technologies include expert systems (also called knowledge-based systems), natural language, neural networks, machine translation, and speech recognition. AI is the branch of computer science that is concerned with developing computer systems capable of simulating human reasoning and sensation. It involves using computers and software that, like the human mind, use stored knowledge to make decisions involving judgment or ambiguity.

Expert systems can be used to perform computerized risk analyses and security surveys. They not only guide the decision-making process but also help ensure that appropriate areas are adequately addressed and that thoughts and ideas are logically and clearly communicated.

Another outgrowth of AI is robotics. Robots are computer-controlled machines engineered to perform specific human tasks such as security patrols, specialized fire fighting, and bomb disposal operations.

Table 21.1 is a summary of the kinds of applications software and their potential uses.

Before discussing how to select the right software, it is appropriate to address another extremely valuable computer tool, namely multimedia. Multimedia facilitates the integration of text, graphics, animated images, video, and audio. It has many uses, particularly in the area of education and training. By designing a multimedia presentation with distinct levels of learning, a powerful interactive training tool can be created and stored on a hard drive or a CD-ROM disk. This medium can be used for new employee induction programs and security staff training. When new staff is hired they

Table 21.1 Application Software Programs and Their Potential Uses

Types of Application Software	Uses
Word processing	Creating, editing, storing, and printing documents such as letters, memoranda, forms, employee performance evaluations, proposals, reports, surveys, checklists, manuals, books, articles, press releases, speeches, and resumes
Database management	Storing, retrieving, sorting, analyzing, and printing information such as names, addresses, telephone and fax numbers, e-mail addresses, birthdays, dates of contacts, meeting times, appointments, time and attendance records, employee background data, staff training records, security reference books and articles, incidents, investigations, key records, asset inventories, equipment inspection, and maintenance records
Spreadsheets	Preparing and tracking budgets, calculating expenses, estimating job costs, and conducting other numerical analyses
Desktop publishing	Creating, editing, storing, and printing text and graphical documents such as newsletters, bulletins, posters, manuals, brochures, books, articles, and business cards
Encryption	Protecting sensitive data from unauthorized use
Computer graphics • Business presentation graphics	Designing business presentations and developing teaching and educational aids
• Computer-aided design (CAD)	Designing security systems and conducting a forensic analysis
• Geographic information systems (GIS)	Computer-aided dispatching of security staff and patrol vehicles and analyzing crime report and security incident patterns by neighborhood
• Global positioning systems (GPS)	Security patrols and tracking vehicles, containers, and other cargo
• Image processing	Capturing, storing, displaying, and outputting text and graphic images, including photo ID badging
Telecommunications • E-mail	Sending, receiving, forwarding, and storing digital information

Table 21.1   Application Software Programs and Their Potential Uses *Continued*

Types of Application Software	Uses
• Instant messaging (IM)	Allowing two or more persons to have an online conversation
• Voice-mail	Recording voice messages for on-site or remote access
• Teleconferencing	Conducting audio- and videoconferencing
• World Wide Web (WWW)	Providing a worldwide information network
• Online services	Providing convenient access to the Internet, e-mail, online conferences, and specialized information
• Intranets	Sharing information within a company
Specialized management programs	Accounting, payroll, financial analysis, business planning, insurance, legal, marketing and sales, human resources, security staff scheduling, patrol management, time management calendars, contact management, project management, and monitoring and controlling of security systems
Artificial intelligence (AI)	Performing risk analyses and security surveys and robotics

might be given a multimedia presentation stored on a CD-ROM disk or instructed to access it through the company's intranet.

CHOOSING THE RIGHT SOFTWARE

In choosing applications software, it is vital to select a program that closely meets the needs of the business application it is designed to address. It must be able to work with the computer hardware that it is to run on (i.e., it must be compatible), including the printer and typefaces that the printer supports.

Software should be easy to use (i.e., user-friendly). GUI programs, with their largely point-and-click environments, are preferable to command-driven programs that require multiple commands to be memorized. The inclusion of online help within programs makes software easier to learn and use.

All software should be accompanied by adequate documentation explaining its installation and use, incorporate security features such as passwords to restrict unauthorized use, have adequate customer support by the software vendor, and be affordable. Because earlier versions of a program may have bugs, it is usually best to select the latest version in which such defects or errors will have probably been corrected.

The Software Encyclopedia is an excellent guide for personal, professional, and business users. It provides comprehensive and detailed information on microcomputer software. The 17th edition contains more than 39,100 software titles from 3,760 publishers and distributors.[33]

BENEFITS OF MICROCOMPUTERS

PCs have an ever-expanding range of applications that can be harnessed by a Security Manager. The following benefits to the Security Department can be derived from using computers:

1. Word processing allows text documents to be more easily created, edited, stored, and printed. Previously stored documents can be easily accessed and used to construct new documents. The ease of making changes helps a manager to systematically develop and arrange ideas. High-quality documents can be produced on a manager's computer.
2. Database management software enables organized collections of information to be stored, retrieved, sorted, and analyzed quickly and easily and to use less space than paper. Information can be better managed. Readily retrievable information not only saves time spent searching through files but also helps a manager work more effectively.
3. Spreadsheet programs calculate complex algorithms more efficiently and rapidly and with less chance of error than if done manually. Data entries can be easily changed to analyze their effects. Graphically displayed spreadsheet results enable data to be viewed in different ways. Information can be better understood, enabling a manager to make more informed decisions.
4. Desktop publishing software can transform the manager's desktop into a mini–publishing house. Professional-looking documents can be produced in a timely and cost-effective manner.
5. Encryption software can be used to protect sensitive data from unauthorized use.
6. Business presentation graphics programs allow the production of professional-looking materials that can be displayed on black and white or colored papers, overhead transparencies, 35-mm slides, a computer, or a projector screen. This facilitates the design and delivery of an entire presentation. Such presentations can be used to perform more effective induction sessions for new employees, teach security staff,

---

[33] *The Software Encyclopedia 2002*, 17th ed. (New Providence, NJ: R. R. Bowker, 2002).

educate executives as to the effectiveness of the Security Department, and innovatively present the findings and recommendations of a risk assessment analysis and security survey.

7. CAD software can be used to create two- and three-dimensional architectural plans or drawings and to design security equipment, systems, and consoles. Such design capabilities can save time and help avoid costly mistakes. The visualization of incidents or crime scenes can be invaluable in forensic analysis.

8. GIS can be used for computer-aided dispatching of security staff and patrol vehicles and analyzing crime reports and security incident patterns by neighborhood. GPS can be adapted for tracking company vehicles, containers, and other cargo.

9. Image processing software enables the microcomputer to capture, store, display, and output text and graphic images. Images can be retrieved and sorted far more easily and using less space than paper. Scanning text documents into the computer rather than using keystrokes can save considerable time and effort. Also, photo ID cards can be rapidly and efficiently produced using this technology.

10. E-mail, IM, voice-mail, and teleconferencing facilitate communication both inside and outside of organizations. E-mail has transformed business communications. It is convenient, fast, economical, and reliable to use. (IM further expedites this form of communication.) E-mail gives managers better access to people at all levels of an organization and by its very nature creates an open-door policy. Similarly, voice-mail has greatly assisted audio communications. Videoconferencing is an important application for Security Managers, particularly for those whose responsibilities encompass widely separated multiple locations.

11. The Internet, in particular the WWW, allows Security Managers to access information and programs outside of their organizations. Managers can stay current and gain a greater depth of knowledge about various topics of interest. Bulletin boards also provide a means for networking and for the exchange of information.

12. Online services may be used for accessing the Internet, e-mail, online conferences, and specialized information. Security Managers can increase their productivity and stay on the cutting edge of technological advances.

13. Corporate intranets allow Security Managers to disseminate and access information within their own organizations. Web pages can be used to educate and inform employees about a company's security program. Also, a website designed specifically for a company's Security Department can be used to publish information exclusively for security personnel.

14. Specialized management software can be used for a wide variety of business functions. These programs have benefits that vary according to the specific business application that they are designed to address.

15. Expert systems assist Security Managers in performing computerized risk analyses and security surveys. They not only guide the decision-making process but also help ensure that appropriate areas are adequately addressed and that thoughts and ideas are logically and clearly communicated.

16. Multimedia permits creative, multisensory learning by integrating text, graphics, animated images, video, and audio. It has many uses, particularly in the area of education and training. By designing a multimedia presentation with distinct levels of learning, a powerful interactive training tool can be created.

PCs save time by enabling certain functions to be more efficiently performed. They also facilitate work being performed away from the workplace. Consultants, in particular, can be more responsive and productive.

In organizations where the use of computers is pervasive, Security Managers who are computer literate can better understand how their organization operates. In addition, they can more competently address security issues, particularly as they relate to the use of computers. "No one person can possibly know everything about computer technology. Security [Managers] must understand enough of the details to be able to recognize security concerns, ask the right questions, and contribute effectively to the information systems [i.e., computer-based information processing systems] security program of their organizations."[34]

RISKS OF MICROCOMPUTERS

In effectively managing people, the computer should not be used as a substitute for personal interaction. Face-to-face contact is critically important in successfully managing people and fostering loyalty. The computer must be used wisely.

Exaggerating the authenticity of information generated by a computer can lead to problems. The mere fact that results were computer generated in no way authenticates their reliability. If incorrect data is input it will lead to erroneous results. This is also applicable to the Web. "Casual users and serious researchers place their trust in the accuracy and completeness of data on the network. They're relying upon information of unknown pedigree and dubious quality, since little on the Internet has been refereed or reviewed."[35] The key here is to always consider the source of information. Likewise, in searching for information, one should not falsely assume that if something cannot be found on the Internet then it doesn't exist.

---

[34] Jacobson, Robert V., CPP. *The Protection of Assets Manual*, vol. I, editor, Timothy L. Williams. (Los Angeles: POA Publishing, LLC, 323-663-4887, copyright 1997), pp. 12–17.
[35] Stoll, Clifford. *Silicon Snake Oil: Second Thoughts on the Information Highway* (New York: Doubleday, 1995), p. 125.

As with any business tool, there are threats that can affect the use of microcomputers. These include power surges, power failures, theft, natural disasters, lightning, water leaks, fires, sabotage, explosions, accidents, user errors, and hardware and software problems. Contingency planning should address the issue of accessing electronically stored data if a computer is unavailable. Such planning may be as simple as maintaining backup copies of software programs and sensitive data in a separate, safe location.

Data imported to a microcomputer may be infected with a computer virus. A virus is a program that can copy itself into the computer's operating system or onto other user files. It then can be transmitted from these infected programs or files onto other programs with which they come into contact. Such replication has resulted in a computer's entire memory and files being destroyed. With the advent of networks, there exists the potential for downloaded virus-infected information to contaminate all computers within a network. Therefore, one should be careful about the source of programs and files, particularly those received via e-mail. Commercially available antivirus software can assist in scanning for known computer viruses. It needs to be regularly updated especially when new viruses are produced. The software does have limitations; some viruses can avoid detection.

Misuses of microcomputers in the workplace may involve workers playing electronic games and pursuing personal interests. For companies that allow employees to access the Internet, workers may waste time visiting multiple websites (commonly known as "surfing the Web") and accessing and downloading non–business-related information. Due to the largely unregulated content of the Internet, such information may include pornographic material. The presence of such material in the workplace can lead to issues related to sexual harassment.

Networks are susceptible to unauthorized intrusion by outsiders, such as hackers and crackers.[36] Security Managers should be aware of ways to protect a company's network.

> Firewalls are essentially either software or a combination of software and hardware designed to serve as a gateway between the corporate computer network and any external networks [such as the worldwide Internet]. . . . Putting up a firewall is no different than putting in a physical access control system. The Security Manager must assess the company's risk exposure, determine its needs, and, after understanding the technology, decide on a proper level of protection.[37]

---

[36] *Hacker* is a slang term often used to refer either to a computer enthusiast or, increasingly, to one who tries to gain unauthorized access to computer systems for malicious purposes. *Cracker* is a derogatory term with the latter meaning.

[37] Thompson, Amy. Smoking Out the Facts on Firewalls, *Security Management*, January 1997, pp. 25, 30.

Firewalls can be used both to control and audit or to monitor network traffic. Unlike a physical access control system, firewall software must be constantly updated to add protection against new threats that are growing at a rapid pace as more and more people acquire computers.

The use of illegal or counterfeit software is another problem. Security Managers should ensure that software within their organization is being used in accordance with end-user license agreements. Computer users who knowingly violate license agreements (e.g., illegally copy or "pirate" software) can be held personally liable to both criminal and civil prosecution. "Another risk to corporations is that employees may use the corporate network to sell pirated software, videos, and music. Such activities can expose an organization to lawsuits and the issues involved if law enforcement confiscates IT [Information Technology] equipment used to sell such contraband."[38]

A well-defined computer security policy, well-coordinated technical and physical security measures, and a strong security awareness program minimize computer crime. Good internal controls and checks aid in the detection of computer crime. The principles that govern ordinary investigation[s] apply equally to the investigation of computer crime, but to investigate a computer crime effectively, one must understand how the target computer system works.[39]

This fact alone is a compelling reason why Security Managers should become familiar with computers. A Security Manager, particularly one working in a corporation that is heavily computerized, may be called on to conduct an investigation related to their use.

SUMMARY

Microcomputers have become an essential part of business life in most organizations. Word processing, database management, spreadsheets, desktop publishing, encryption, computer graphics, telecommunications, specialized management programs, and artificial intelligence are important software applications. They can be adapted to the administrative, managerial, and supervisorial aspects of the security function. Security Managers of the future must know how to employ many such applications and manage others who use them. They must also be aware of the benefits and the risks of microcomputers. Managers who do so increase their skill level and opportunity to succeed. They also become of greater value to the organizations they represent.

---

[38] Comments by Kelly J. "KJ" Kuchta, CPP, CFE.
[39] Jacobson, Robert V., CPP. *The Protection of Assets Manual*, vol. I, editor, Timothy L. Williams. (Los Angeles: POA Publishing, LLC, 323-663-4887, 1997), pp. 12–86.

REVIEW QUESTIONS

1. What three basic parts make up microcomputer hardware?

2. What are the two main types of software designed for micro-computers?

3. What are nine software applications designed for microcomputers?

4. What things should you consider when choosing applications software?

5. How can a Security Department benefit from the use of micro-computers?

6. What functions does a firewall perform?

7. What three precautions can minimize computer crime?

ACKNOWLEDGMENTS

Special thanks to David S. Barkley; Dan Cossarek; Sarah Craighead; Edward G. Hallen, CPP; Francis Hamit; Kelly J. "KJ" Kuchta, CPP, CFE; Mike Leonardich; and Roger Linan for reviewing this chapter and making helpful suggestions.

ADDITIONAL READINGS

Better Buys for Business, Inc. *The Business Computer Guide.* (Santa Barbara, CA: What to Buy for Business, Inc., March 1996).

Bodensiek, Paul. *Intranet Publishing.* (Indianapolis, IN: Que Corporation, 1996).

Boone, Mary E. *Leadership and the Computer.* (Rockline, CA: Prima Publishing, 1993).

Bowie, John. Return to Sender: E-Mail Survival Guide, *Hemispheres.* (Nashville, TN: Pace Communications, October 1996).

Cochrane, Kerry. *The Internet.* (New York: Franklin Watts, 1995).

Davis, Williams S. *Fundamental Computer Concepts.* (Reading, MA: Addison-Wesley, 1986).

Gates, Bill. *The Road Ahead*, rev. edition (New York: Penguin Books, 1996).

Geis, George T. *Micromanaging: Transforming Business Leaders with Personal Computers.* (Englewood Cliffs, NJ: Prentice-Hall, 1987).

Honeycutt, Jerry, and Pike, Mary Ann. *Special Edition Using the Internet*, 3rd ed. (Indianapolis, IN: Que Corporation, 1996).

Internet Literacy Consultants. ILC Glossary of Internet Terms (http://www.matisse.net/files/glossary.html, 1994–1996).

Jacobson, Robert V. Information Systems Security—An Overview. *The Protection of Assets Manual*, vol. I, chapter 12, edited by Timothy J. Williams. (Santa Monica, CA: The Merritt Company, 800-638-7597, copyright 1997).

Kaiser, Thomas E. The Computer Caper. *Security Management*, November 1996.

Kephart, Jeffrey O., Sorkin, Gregory B., Chess, David M., and White, Steve R. Fighting Computer Viruses. *Scientific American*, November 1997.

Kraynak, Joe, Wang, W. E., and Flynn, Jennifer. *The First Book of Personal Computing*. (Carmel, IN: Alpha Books, 1992).

Lander, Ronald, and Roughton, James E. The Security Professional in Cyberspace. *Security Management*, January 1996.

Levin, Richard B. *The Computer Virus Handbook*. (Berkeley, CA: Osborne McGraw-Hill, 1990).

Lubar, Steven. *Infoculture: The Smithsonian Book of the Inventions of the Information Age*. (Boston: Houghton Mifflin, 1993).

Macauley, David. *The Way Things Work*. (Boston: Houghton Mifflin, 1988).

Maxwell, Christine, and Grycz, Czeslaw, Jan. *New Rider's Official Internet Yellow Pages*. (Indianapolis, IN: New Riders Publishing, 1994).

McGraw-Hill *Encyclopedia of Personal Computing*, edited by Stan Gibilisco. (New York: McGraw-Hill, 1995).

Mead, Hayden, and Hill, Brad. *The Online E-mail Dictionary*. (New York: Berkley Books, February 1997).

Nowak, Eric, and Ingersoll, Wyllys. Tracking Down Trouble. *Security Management*, January 1997.

Pearson, Robert. Use of GUIs in Subsystems: A Complex, High-Tech Solution That Makes Security Easier. *Security Technology & Design*, January–February 1996.

Pfaffenberger, Bryan. *Webster's New World Dictionary of Computer Terms*, 6th ed. (New York: Simon and Schuster, 1997).

Ramtek, Timothy. *Networks*. (Upper Saddle River, NJ: Prentice-Hall, 1994).

Random House Personal Computer Dictionary, 2nd ed. Margolis, Philip E. (New York: Random House, 1996).

The Software Encyclopedia 2002, 17th ed. (New Providence, NJ: R. R. Bowker, 2002).

Stewart, Michael M., and Shulman, Alan C. *How to Get Started with a Small Business Computer.* (Fort Worth, TX: U.S. Small Business Administration, Management Aids Number 2.027, 1987).

Stoll, Clifford. *Silicon Snake Oil: Second Thoughts on the Information Highway.* (New York: Doubleday, 1995).

Thompson, Amy. Smoking Out the Facts on Firewalls. *Security Management*, January 1997.

Watts, John M. Jr. Microcomputer Applications in Fire Protection. *Fire Protection Handbook*, 17th ed. (Quincy, MA: National Fire Protection Association, 1991).

Webster's New World Dictionary of Computer Terms. (New York: Macmillan General Reference, 1994).

White, Ron. *How Computers Work*, 2nd ed. (Emeryville, CA: Ziff-Davis, 1995).

White, Ron. *How Software Works.* (Emeryville, CA: Ziff-Davis, 1993).

GLOSSARY

Adapter.   A device that enables a computer to work with another device. Adapters may be add-on or add-in circuit boards called expansion boards or cards, or they may be built into the computer's main circuitry.

Address.   An address may refer to the precise storage location of data, the URL of a document on the Web, or the specific address of a computer on the Internet.

Algorithm.   A series of steps that are carried out in a specific order to provide a solution to a problem or to execute a task.

Analog signal.   An electronic signal that represents data as a continuously changing physical measure.

Antivirus software.   A program that scans the hard drive and software programs for known computer viruses.

Applications software.   Programs that perform functions such as word processing, database management, spreadsheets, desktop publishing, computer graphics, telecommunications, and artificial intelligence.

Artificial intelligence (AI).   An area of computer science that attempts to program the computer to think like a human being.

Backbone.   A single protocol that connects different systems.

Backup.   The process of copying or backing up files to a secondary location. In the event that primary files are unavailable, backup files can be used.

Barcode.   Code embodied in infrared or ultraviolet form on an object.

Bit.   Acronym for binary digit. Smallest unit of computer information valued at 1 ("on") or 0 ("off").

Boot.   A process that uses a small amount of software that's permanently a part of a computer to automatically load the operating system into a computer's memory when a computer is turned on.

Bug.   A flaw in computer software that results from mistakes in design or programming, or a fault in hardware that causes a computer to operate incorrectly.

Bulletin board.   An electronic message system whereby messages, files, and programs pertaining to topics of interest are posted on computer networks.

Byte.   A unit of memory that usually holds eight bits of information and represents one character.

CAD.   Acronym for computer-aided design. The use of computers for graphic designing and drafting.

Cartridge.   A self-contained, removable data storage receptacle that contains a magnetic tape, a disk, or a memory chip. (There are also special cartridges for some printers.)

Cathode ray tube.   See *CRT.*

CD-ROM.   Acronym for compact disk-read-only memory (pronounced *see-dee-rom*). An optical disk used to store large amounts of data. A CD-ROM drive or player is needed to read (CD-RW) this data.

Central processing unit.   See *CPU.*

Character.   A symbol such as letter, number, punctuation mark, or a space. It occupies one byte of memory.

Chip.   Another name for an integrated circuit. There are memory chips and the CPU chip (or the microprocessor).

Clip art.   Digital images of objects and pictures that can be inserted into computer documents.

Coaxial cable.   An insulated wire, contained in an insulated tube, that is used for transmission of data over networks.

Code.   A set of symbols that represent data; written instructions for the computer to execute.

Command.   An instruction to the computer or a peripheral device to carry out a particular function.

Computer graphics.   A diagrammatic representation of digital information.

Computer literate.   A degree of competency and understanding of computers.

Computer virus. See *Virus.*

CPU. Acronym for central processing unit. The microprocessor is the brain of the computer.

CRT. Acronym for *cathode ray tube.* The CRT is a picture tube used to display information on a computer screen. Sometimes, the term CRT is used to mean the display screen itself.

Cursor. A usually blinking symbol or small pointer (such as an arrow) that is displayed on the computer screen. It indicates where data may be inputted or graphics altered using a keyboard, mouse, or other device.

Data. A term used to describe items of information.

Database. An orderly collection of information.

Dial-up modem. A modem that uses a telephone line to connect the computer to another computer system.

Digital camera. A camera in which images are stored digitally rather than on film.

Digital data. Information recorded as a series of 1s and 0s.

Directory. An organized arrangement of files on the hard disk and on portable storage devices.

Diskette. See *Floppy disk.*

Disk. A device for storing data. There is the hard disk housed within the computer's hard drive; portable disks such as floppy disks, optical disks, and removable hard disks.

Disk drive. An electromechanical device for reading (i.e., retrieving) data from and writing (i.e., saving) data onto a hard disk and onto portable disks such as floppy disks, optical disks, and cartridges.

Display screen. A screen for displaying computer data.

Document. In computing, a document is a file that contains data.

DOS. Acronym for disk operating system. An operating system usually designed for IBM-compatible personal computers.

Download. The process of copying data from one location to another.

E-mail or electronic mail. A process by which digital information can be sent, received, forwarded, and stored using telecommunications networks.

Encryption. An algorithm for protecting electronic data from unauthorized use (the data must be decrypted before it can be used).

Execute or run. To carry out an instruction or perform a task. Reference is often made to executing a command or running a program.

Expert system. An interactive computerized knowledge-based application. It utilizes a database of knowledge and opinions compiled by a human expert to question and direct a user's decision-making process.

Facsimile (fax) machine. A machine for sending and receiving text and graphics over telephone lines.

Fiber-optic cable or fiber. Thin glass fibers used for high-speed transmission of data over networks.

Field. A specific area where data can be stored.

File. A collection of data. Each file is assigned an identifying name.

File server. The main computer that stores files and serves all the other computers in a network.

Firewall. As defined by *Security Management,* "Firewalls are essentially either software or a combination of software and hardware designed to serve as a gateway between the corporate computer network and any external networks."

Floppy disk or diskette. A disk, enclosed in a plastic envelope, for magnetically storing data.

Font. An assortment of characters of the same typeface, style, and size.

Format. This term refers to the processes of preparing a disk to store information and to defining text using different page size, margins, alignment, spacing, fonts, and so forth.

Gateway. A combination of software and hardware to interconnect networks that have different protocols. The purpose of a gateway is to allow data to be exchanged between networks.

GIS. Acronym for geographic information system. Programs used for storing, processing, and displaying geographically referenced information.

GPS. Acronym for global positioning system. A system that uses satellite tracking to determine the position of an object on the earth.

GUI. Acronym for graphical user interface (pronounced *gooey*). The computer interface, between a person and a program, that uses graphical displays to represent objects, files, or programs.

Hard copy. See *Printer.*

Hard disk. A magnetic disk onto which data is written to or read from. The hard disk is located within the sealed housing of the hard drive (although some hard disks are in self-contained, removable cartridges). The terms hard disk and hard drive are used interchangeably.

Hard drive or hard disk drive. An electromechanical device for reading data from and writing data onto a hard disk. The terms hard drive and hard disk are used interchangeably.

Hardware. The physical components that make up a computer system.

Home Page. Each website has a home page that first appears when a site is entered.

Host computer or host. In networking, typically the host computer is the main, centralized computer that contains data and programs that can be accessed by the other computers in the network.

HTML. Abbreviation for HyperText Markup Language, the language used to produce a document on the Web.

HTTP. Abbreviation for HyperText Transfer Protocol. This protocol is used to transfer HyperText documents across the Internet.

HyperText. Text that can be connected to other information using HyperText links.

HyperText link. A link that connects a word or picture to another piece of HyperText information.

Icon. Small, easily recognized images that symbolize objects, files, or programs.

Integrated. The bringing together of two parts to form one interconnected system.

Integrated circuit. This consists of multiple transistor circuits compressed into a single, commonly silicon, chip.

Interface. The link between hardware and programs, or how software programs appear on a computer screen. See also *User interface.*

Internet. A worldwide network connecting computer networks using TCP/IP protocols.

Internet service provider (ISP). A business that provides connections to the Internet for companies and private individuals. Using a personal computer, subscribers can send and receive e-mail and access the WWW.

Intranet. A private Internet within a corporation or organization. A corporate intranet has Web documents that can be accessed only by the network users.

Joystick. An input device used to move the cursor. It is used with some CAD programs (and computer games).

Keyboard. A set of keys used to type characters, numbers, and symbols and to alter data.

LAN (Local Area Network). The linking together of two or more microcomputers, often called workstations, to each other and sometimes to a minicomputer, a mainframe, or a common printer. A LAN normally serves a small geographical area.

Machine language. A computer's basic language that consists of a series of 1s and 0s. Every microcomputer uses a specific machine language designed for its CPU to execute.

Magnetic tape or tape. A plastic ribbon of tape for magnetically storing data.

Mailbox. An electronic mailbox to store incoming and outgoing e-mail messages.

Mail merge. A word processing function that enables a form letter to be sent to a number of individuals with each letter containing, for example, the specific name and address of each recipient.

Mainframe. A large and powerful computer that can accommodate many users simultaneously executing many programs.

Memory. Refers to the capacity to store data; the parts of a computer in which storage occurs.

Menu. A list of commands or instructions to aid interaction with computer programs.

Microcomputer or personal computer (PC). A small, powerful microprocessor-based machine usually designed for a single user. Microcomputers come in desktop and smaller portable models.

Microprocessor. A chip that is the central processing unit (CPU) of a microcomputer (or is a stand-alone device in household appliances, telephones, alarm systems, and automobiles).

Minicomputer. A midsize computer that can accommodate many users simultaneously operating many programs.

Modem. Acronym for modulator/demodulator. A data communication device that translates digital information into analog signals that can be transmitted over telephone lines and then translated back into digital data.

Monitor. A box-like device that contains a screen used to display computer data.

Mouse. An input device used to move the cursor on the computer screen. It can be used to select programs, commands, and text.

Multimedia. The computer integration of text, graphics, animated images, video, and audio.

Multitasking. The capability to simultaneously run more than one program or task on a computer.

Multiuser.   The capability for a computer system to be simultaneously operated by more than one user.

Natural language.   The spoken or written language that people commonly use.

Network.   Microcomputers can be connected together in a local area network (LAN) or a wide area network (WAN) and may have connections to the Internet.

Neural networks.   A computer model designed to process information in a self-learning manner that simulates the way the neurons of the human brain work.

Online.   This term means connected, activated, or switched on.

Online service.   A commercial service that is accessed via a telecommunications network. Using a personal computer, subscribers to the service can access the Internet, send and receive e-mail, participate in online conferences, and connect to various third-party information providers.

Operating system.   The software for controlling the microprocessor and functioning of a computer system.

Optical disk.   A portable storage device on which large amounts of data can be stored using lasers. A CD-ROM is an optical disk.

Optical scanner.   A device that uses light to scan text and graphic images from paper and digitizes them for input to a computer.

Packet switcher.   See *Router.*

Password.   A sequence of characters that authorizes access to a computer system, a program, or a file (and is usually kept confidential).

Peripherals.   Devices that are attached to or built into a microcomputer.

Personal computer (PC).   See *Microcomputer.*

Portable computer.   May be a laptop, a slightly smaller notebook, or an even smaller handheld or pocket-size device, including a palm-top computer or personal data assistant (PDA).

Printer.   A device used to print text and graphics on paper. (The printout is sometimes referred to as the hard copy.)

Program.   A set of instructions that, on execution, directs a computer to perform specific functions.

Programming language.   A set of rules designed to instruct a computer to execute specific instructions. Examples of these languages are BASIC, COBOL, FORTRAN, C, C++, and Pascal.

Protocol.   Standard communication rules for transferring data across networks.

RAM.   Acronym for random-access memory. Memory in which information is temporarily held and accessed randomly (random in the sense that any portion or byte of data can be arbitrarily accessed).

Real time.   A term referring to the viewing and recording of events as they actually occur (in contrast to events being viewed and recorded using only snapshots of a video image).

ROM.   Acronym for read-only memory. Memory in which instructions are permanently held and can only be read.

Robotics.   An outgrowth of artificial intelligence is robotics. Robots are computer-controlled machines engineered to perform specific human tasks.

Router or packet switcher.   A computer on the Internet that directs packets of information to their appropriate destinations via the most suitable route.

Run.   See *Execute.*

Scanner.   See *Optical scanner.*

Scroll bar.   In a GUI, a scroll bar consists of a horizontal or vertical bar located at the bottom or side of a window and can be used to determine, using arrows, which portion of a document appears in the window.

Server.   The main computer that serves all the other computers in a network.

Software.   As defined in *The Road Ahead* "a comprehensive set of rules that tell a machine what to do, that 'instruct' it, step-by-step, how to perform particular tasks."

Sound card.   An adapter that gives a computer the ability to process sound.

Storage device.   A device in which data can be stored. It may be on the hard drive that is usually located within a computer (data is actually stored on the rotating hard disk that is located within the sealed housing of the hard drive) and on portable devices such as floppy disks, optical disks, or cartridges (each containing a magnetic tape, a disk, or a memory chip).

Supercomputer.   The fastest class of computers used to carry out vast mathematical calculations for extremely complex programs.

System software or systems software.   Consists of the operating system and other special programs that oversee a computer's operations.

TCP/IP.   Acronym for Transmission Control Protocol/Internet Protocol. The collection of protocols that allows computers to transmit data across the Internet.

Trackball. An input device that is, in effect, a modified inverted mouse.

Twisted-pair cable. A twisted pair of wires used for transmission of data over networks.

UNIX. A popular computer operating system that is both multitasking and multiuser.

URL. Acronym for Uniform Resource Locator. The address of a document on the WWW.

USENET. Acronym for USEr NETwork. Newsgroups on the Internet's bulletin board system.

User friendly. A term that indicates a computer or software is easy to use.

User ID. An abbreviation for user identification (or sometimes referred to as "user name") that, along with a password, allows a person to access a network. The unique user ID usually consists of letters of part of the user's name.

User interface. The point at which a person interacts with a program. See also *GUI*.

Utilities or utility software. Special programs that help to maintain the smooth running of a computer.

Video camera. A camera that produces analog video signals of a viewed scene.

Video capture card. An adapter that converts analog video signals to digital data for processing by a computer.

Videoconferencing. Enables a person to use a specially equipped microcomputer to conduct a conference with another person with similar equipment at another site (or between multiple persons at multiple sites).

Virus. A program that can copy itself into a computer's operating system or onto other user files. By replicating itself it may cause the destruction of a computer's entire memory and files.

WAN (Wide Area Network). A network of microcomputers that are widely separated by distance.

Web browser. Software that helps find and interpret documents on the WWW.

Website. A specific location on the WWW. Each website has a home page that first appears when a site is entered.

Windows. A term that refers to how information is displayed on a computer screen. It is characterized by a graphical user interface (GUI) that can be used to divide the display screen into separate, rectangular areas or windows. Microsoft's Windows and Apple's Macintosh operating systems are built on a GUI.

Workgroup. A group of people that work jointly on a task. In computing, this refers to such individuals linked by a network that supports e-mail and the sharing of files.

Workstation. In a network, a workstation is a computer connected to one or more other computers and sometimes to a common printer. This term is sometimes used to refer to high-performance computers that are more powerful than microcomputers.

World Wide Web (WWW or Web). Defined by the *Random House Personal Computer Dictionary* as "a system of Internet servers that support specially formatted documents. The documents are formatted in a language called HTML (HyperText Markup Language) that supports links to other documents, as well as graphics, audio, and video files."

22

*Statistics as a Security Management Tool**

A key tool to successful operational management is the understanding and proper use of statistical information. With respect to security management, statistics are used in a variety of capacities to broaden management's vision and increase its effectiveness with a wealth of information. Statistics are used in many of the effective Security Manager's functions including:

- Budget requests and justification
- Security incident analysis
- Crime analysis
- Risk analysis
- Program monitoring
- Program evaluation

As such, the effective Security Manager uses statistics in all aspects of the position, from mundane administrative functions to advanced program evaluation tasks. From an administrative perspective, the most common statistical information used by Security Managers is the budget from which all organizational resources flow. This flow continues through the Security Department to fund personnel, capital expenditures, and operational costs.

In the operational arena, Security Managers use statistics to ascertain security needs and evaluate program effectiveness. Typically, internal security incident reports are used to determine security weaknesses and problem areas, as well as to select crime countermeasures, calibrate countermeasure effectiveness, and consider future budget needs. Crime statistics, available from local law enforcement agencies, are also utilized extensively in determining concrete security risks. Although internal security reports and police crime data may overlap, it is incumbent on the Security Manager to consider both in determining a facility's true risk.

---

* By Karim H. Vellani, CPP, CPO

PLANNING FUTURE SECURITY NEEDS

Statistics are most commonly used within a security organization to assist in the planning for future security requirements. The use of information regarding crimes and other security incidents helps the Security Manager plan, select, and implement appropriate security measures that address the actual, rather than perceived, risks of the facility. This, of course, assists in making budgetary decisions because the Security Manager, after assessing the crime problem, will have determined the most effective countermeasures including the cost of implementation and maintenance. Budget justification is also accomplished through the use of statistics because effective security measures will reduce the risks and a return on investment (ROI) will be realized (see ROI later in chapter). Ideally, crime and security statistics will guide the security survey, help in the selection of countermeasures, measure program effectiveness, and alleviate the risks and the associated costs of those risks.

The Security Manager need not be a mathematician to fully utilize statistical information; rather he or she needs only a basic understanding of the various methods to use such data along with a touch of personal computer and spreadsheet software knowledge. Statistics are often seen as boring and subjective and may be manipulated to meet the needs (and wants) of an organization. Despite these criticisms, the effective Security Manager uses the best available data to assist in decision making. In seeking to meet this objective, Security Managers should carefully scrutinize the sources of statistical information and use only those that have a proven track record and are acceptable in court (in case of a negligent security lawsuit). Having made this admonishment, it will be helpful here to demonstrate by example how statistics can be used in the security function.

A common application of statistics in the security arena is the use of security reports (Figure 22.1) and crime data to determine the risks to a facility, including its assets and personnel. The effective Security Manager analyzes security and crime reports (statistics) to answer the who, what, when, where, and how questions about security infractions. The analysis may be quite superficial or may dig deeper to determine exact causes of incidents and crimes.

Taking the example of a shopping mall suffering from a rash of car burglaries and auto thefts, a thorough analysis of the crime and security reports will reflect the types of cars that are targeted (the *who*) and what is being stolen, be it auto parts, electronic equipment, or the car itself (the *what*). Digging deeper through the details of the reports, the effective Security Manager will learn the most frequent times the burglaries and thefts occur (the *when*) and the location of the incidents within the parking areas (the *where*). The last piece of the puzzle may be more difficult to establish. The *how* question is often answered postmortem, after the incident has taken place.

ABC Security Team Security Incident Report		Date	Incident ID No.	Site No.	Page
					of

Incident Information

Incident Type	Incident Code	Location	Site Diagram

Date & Time Reported	Date & Time Occurred	Reporting Officer	Supervisor

Complainant/Involved Persons Information

Name	Pseudonym	Sex	Ht	Wt	DOB	Age	Hair	Eyes

Street Address	City, State, Zip	Employer	Employer Address

Home Phone	Work Phone

Witness Information

Name	Relationship	Home Phone	Work Phone

Street Address	City, State, Zip	Employer	Employer Address

Narrative

Follow Up Information

Disposition	Supervisor Name	Supervisor Signature	Quality Control

Law Enforcement/Fire/EMS Information

Responding Agency	Responding Agent	Report No.	Disposition

Figure 22.1 Security incident report.

The effective Security Manager inputs the data into a spreadsheet format for easy analysis, allowing him or her to easily sort information, track trends and patterns, and prepare reports for the security team (Figure 22.2). With the data in this format, sorting by date, time, and day of week will reveal any trends and patterns in the crimes. If, for example, the statistics reveal that car (the who) burglaries and thefts (the what) occur in the parking lots (the where) primarily between 1600 and 2000 hours during the summer months on Tuesdays and Wednesdays (the when), the effective Security Manager can allocate additional resources to this problem to help thwart future incidents. In an attempt to apprehend the criminals, the Security Manager decides to post mall security officers on the rooftop where they will have the advantage of seeing the perpetrators approach the target cars and summon security and/or police officers to stop the criminals. As the perpetrators are caught, police may interview them to determine their methods of operation (the how).

As seen in the previous example, the Security Manager is able to effectively use statistics to:

- Determine and track common security issues at the facility
- Discover security lapses
- Select security countermeasures
- Implement the security plan
- Assist police in apprehensions
- Reduce risks without large costs

Other types of data are often helpful in security decision making. Overall, the most useful are statistics that come from law enforcement agencies and internal security reports; however, security lapses may sometimes be determined from other sources depending on the scenario. Other statistical information, such as point-of-sale (POS) data, can also track internal crime losses and times and frequency of loss and assist in determining which, if any, employees are dishonest.

The use of statistics extends beyond planning security at an existing facility. Statistical data may also be used to select and plan security at new facilities. For example, the real estate department of a company may provide the Security Manager with a list of potential new sites, one of which will be selected based on, among other things, the risks posed at the location. The Security Manager will serve as an advisor to the real estate department by conducting statistical analyses of the areas surrounding each site as well as perform security surveys (see chapter on security surveys) of each site to select the location that poses the least or a tolerable level of risk. In this scenario, the Security Manager will gather and analyze crime data for similar businesses in the area surrounding each site to determine the security problems. The sites that have the least crimes can be evaluated further by means of a security survey. After the sites have been narrowed down by risk and

Incident ID	Police Report No.	Site ID	Crime	Date	Time	Location	Victim	Other Info
ABC00001	990096021	ABC 021	Robbery	11/07/99	21:53	Unknown	Person	Purse Snatching
ABC00012	000007508	ABC 021	Robbery	01/29/00	11:21	Parking Garage	Person	Car Jacking
ABC00018	000019098	ABC 021	Robbery	06/10/00	21:51	Parking Garage	Person	Car Jacking
ABC00007	010044058	ABC 021	Robbery	06/16/01	18:33	Main Lobby	Person	Purse Snatching
ABC00008	010065546	ABC 021	Robbery	10/22/01	15:17	Inside - First Floor	Bank	Aggravated Robbery
ABC00002	010007145	ABC 021	Aggravated Assault	07/26/01	4:15	Outside	Person	Unknown Assailant
ABC00017	000004717	ABC 021	Burglary	02/11/00	0:41	Maintenance Room	Business	Spare Keys (Masters)
ABC00023	006154893	ABC 021	Burglary	06/05/00	0:14	Law Firm - 21st Floor	Business	Laptop Theft
ABC00016	010011316	ABC 021	Burglary	04/12/01	12:00	Law Firm - 21st Floor	Business	Laptop Theft
ABC00019	992155844	ABC 021	Theft	12/21/99	5:45	Parking Garage	Person	Burglary of Motor Vehicle
ABC00011	000032307	ABC 021	Theft	04/29/00	21:45	Parking Garage	Person	Burglary of Motor Vehicle
ABC00013	000032790	ABC 021	Theft	05/01/00	19:48	Parking Garage	Person	Burglary of Motor Vehicle
ABC00020	000753584	ABC 021	Theft	05/07/00	6:21	Parking Garage	Person	Burglary of Motor Vehicle
ABC00015	000050523	ABC 021	Theft	08/25/00	21:36	Parking Garage	Person	Burglary of Motor Vehicle
ABC00022	013987942	ABC 021	Theft	05/31/01	18:52	Parking Garage	Person	Burglary of Motor Vehicle
ABC00006	010037956	ABC 021	Theft	06/02/01	0:12	Parking Garage	Person	Burglary of Motor Vehicle
ABC00009	010034597	ABC 021	Theft	06/22/01	0:04	Parking Garage	Person	Burglary of Motor Vehicle
ABC00014	999000906	ABC 021	Auto Theft	09/06/99	0:08	Visitor Parking	Person	Chevy Truck
ABC00010	000055947	ABC 021	Auto Theft	01/27/00	1:01	Visitor Parking	Person	Chevy Truck
ABC00021	013256486	ABC 021	Auto Theft	07/11/01	17:46	Parking Garage	Person	Chevy Truck
ABC00004	999001345	ABC 021	Assault	09/07/99	21:17	Near Trash Dumpster	Person	Unknown Assailant
ABC00003	000001244	ABC 021	Assault	02/04/00	14:20	Smoking Area	Person	Interpersonal
ABC00005	010020956	ABC 021	Assault	04/04/01	19:45	Parking Garage	Person	Interpersonal

Figure 22.2   Crimes at site ABC021, 1999–2001.

surveys completed, the Security Manager has the necessary information to advise the real estate department.

INTERNAL STATISTICAL ANALYSIS

There are a number of statistics that can be used to measure internal crime at a facility including:

1.   Confidential employee questionnaires
2.   Security reports
3.   Industry research

The use of employee questionnaires (Figure 22.3) may bring to light a number of crimes and security incidents that go otherwise unreported and will shed new light on security issues from an employee's perspective. Employees from the various company departments are valuable for determining security lapses as they operate in very specific areas during their workday. Employee questionnaires should be conducted using the most confidential methods available. Security reports also assist in measuring the extent of internal crime. This may be passive (all security reports are analyzed for elements of internal crime) or active (security reports contain fields that address internal crime methods specifically). Industry research, specifically in the retail industry, also assists in determining the degree of internal crime. Although this information is not site specific, it does help the Security Manager gain an understanding of internal crime's contributing factors.

The most successful use of internal statistics that I have seen occurred in a large, multibuilding apartment community. After spending more than $40,000 on fencing and access control systems to reduce the high level of auto thefts at the apartment complex, the apartment manager was distraught that the auto thefts continued at the complex despite these measures. As a consultant, I was asked to analyze the situation and determine additional measures to be implemented to thwart the problem. After analyzing the crime and verifying the extent of auto thefts, a review of the apartment's resident screening policies was conducted and it was learned that management was not carrying out criminal background checks on prospective tenants as required by policy and leases.

Apartment management immediately conducted the checks and learned that three convicted auto thieves were living in one unit of the complex. This information was corroborated by analyzing the auto theft data for the complex that showed that, although auto thefts occurred in all areas of the parking lots, they were concentrated around the particular apartment building where the three men lived. Because the men lived on property, they had full, authorized access to the complex and its parking areas.

Employee Security Questionnaire

Directions: Please fill out this questionnaire and deposit in any internal mail box. Do not write your name, employee number, or any other identifying material on this questionnaire.

Date:

Department (optional):

1. Have you gone through the building's security training?

2. Did you find the security training useful?

3. Please describe any security problems in your department?

4. Have you experienced unnecessary delays while passing security checkpoints?

5. Do the security officers treat you courteously?

6. Are you aware of any security problems in the parking garage?

7. Are you aware of any security problems in the outside common areas?

8. Have you ever used the building's security escort service?

9. If you could change anything about the building's security, what would it be?

10. Have you ever been victimized while on the job? If so, please describe.

Thank you for your time and assistance in making your security team more valuable!

Figure 22.3 Employee security questionnaire.

Management proceeded to have the three men evicted for failing to pay their rent on time and soon after the eviction was finalized, the auto theft problem disappeared. This example shows the importance of following security policies and procedures as well as analyzing the crime statistics and other internal data thoroughly.

EXTERNAL STATISTICAL ANALYSIS

Analysis of external crime data has many uses, including the discovery of specific security problems; selection of countermeasures; justification of budget requests; and evaluation of security programs, policies, and procedures. The sources of external crime data include:

1.   Security reports
2.   Law enforcement data
3.   Victimization information
4.   News reports
5.   Industry standards

Among these, the primary sources are security reports and law enforcement data. Victimization studies provide useful insight into the characteristics of victims and also contributing factors that criminals use to select victims. News reports and industry standards are used to establish general trends in a geographic area and in particular industries. Demographic information, although not mentioned previously, is a secondary source of information because it is problematic on its own and should only be used in conjunction with security reports and crime data.

Law enforcement data for a facility is relatively easy to obtain from local law enforcement agencies. It normally comes in the form of calls for service (dispatch logs) and offense reports that are written, collected, and maintained by the law enforcement agency. This information is considered less subjective, as it is collected by an uninterested third party who has little reason to manipulate the information for a particular site. Most importantly, it is recognized by the courts as a tool for establishing reasonable security levels and defending against claims of negligent security.

METHODOLOGY

As mentioned previously, the methodology that is used to conduct crime analysis should, at minimum, coincide with case law on issues of foreseeability so that claims of negligent security can be quashed. Most states use crime data to determine if crime was foreseeable (predictable) and if management is on notice of crime. If management is found to be on notice of crime in the area, they often have a duty to protect against it. Although a foreseeability analysis is a good place to start the process of crime analysis, it is certainly not the end. To be more proactive, Security Managers require more data and analysis to reasonably track security lapses and implement effective responses.

The best method for learning the true risk at a facility is to analyze internal security reports and verified police data that have been input into a computer spreadsheet program. Once this information is in a usable format, a number of basic and advanced statistical analyses can be performed. The effective Security Manager will adapt the analysis to best meet the needs of the organization. Among the statistical tools available to the Security Manager are forecasting, temporal analysis, spatial analysis, and pattern analysis.

- *Forecasting* is a useful technique that allows the Security Manager to mathematically project future crime by using the facility's crime history. Forecasting can project specific crime concerns as well as the times, days, and locations of these future crimes.
- *Temporal analysis* is the consideration of time periods when crimes occur (Figure 22.4). It allows the user to effectively allocate scarce security resources during peak time periods to reduce costs.
- *Spatial analysis* is also used to assist in the implementation of scarce resources but focuses on the locations within the facility where crimes are likely to occur.
- *Pattern analysis*, like forecasting, is used to look for emerging crime trends from which security measures can be applied to end the trend or pattern. Both law enforcement data and security reports provide the necessary data pieces to conduct these advanced statistical techniques.

Once the various statistical analyses are complete, the Security Manager is well equipped to make decisions about future allocations of security resources. The crime analysis results should be disseminated among as many departments in the company as feasible to obtain feedback and possible solutions. Most important, the information should be distributed to line security officers and supervisors so that they are aware of the threats and can work toward reducing the opportunity of these crimes. Obviously, the information should be as specific as possible to enhance the detection and protection function with which the security force is charged.

INFORMATION FOR RISK ANALYSIS

Information is the backbone of security surveys and risk analysis. In addition to asset (target) assessment, statistics such as crime information and security reports set the scope for a security survey. Before conducting a

Time Period	Total per Period
0000 - 0359	4
0400 - 0759	19
0800 - 1159	18
1200 - 1559	83
1600 - 1959	105
2000 - 2359	31
Total	260

Figure 22.4 Temporal analysis—crimes and security incidents by time period, 1999–2001.

security survey, the effective Security Manager will have a thorough understanding of the crime and security incident history of the facility. This information guides the Security Manager as he or she conducts the survey and looks for the crime opportunities that can be blocked with security measures (Figure 22.5).

For example, an office building Security Director concerned with a flood of thefts of employee wallets and purses may conduct the survey with an eye toward the opportunities that are available in the office suites. As the Security Director walks the offices, he or she may find that purses and wallets are readily visible from office doors and windows, thus providing the opportunity for criminals to see the target property. A simple and cost effective solution to this problem is to institute a "clean desk" policy whereby employees are encouraged to lock their personal belongings in their desks or a company locker.

A more serious security problem that the manager may face is that of assaults and robberies in the parking garage adjacent to the office building. If the statistical information indicates that the assaults are occurring on the upper floors of the garage and the victim does not know the perpetrator, the Security Manager will assess the security weaknesses of the garage. He or she may find that there are numerous hiding places and unlit areas that may provide the necessary cover for robbers. By applying relatively low cost measures such as mirrors and lighting, the manager will likely reduce the opportunity for criminals to hide.

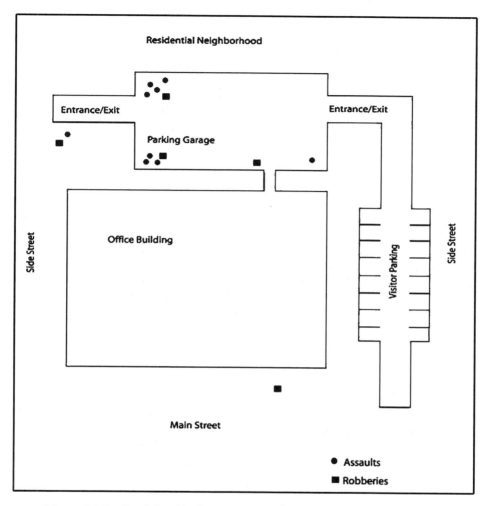

Figure 22.5   Spatial analysis map—assaults and robberies, 1999–2001.

RETURN ON INVESTMENT

In today's corporate environment, it is important for all departments to show bang for the buck, and this philosophy commonly applies to the security organization because often their budget is among the first to be cut. Showing a return on investment (ROI) simply means that security measures are either paying for themselves or better, adding to the bottom line. ROI is important because it helps the Security Manager justify costs and obtain future budget monies. Some security programs will not pay for themselves, whereas others actually become a profit center.

For example, crime analysis almost always pays for itself because it helps the Security Manager select the most appropriate security solutions for specific problems. Without it, the effective Security Manager has little to guide him or her toward effective solutions. More expensive countermeasures such as closed-circuit television (CCTV) systems and personnel are harder to show ROI; however, over the long run these measures become relatively inexpensive when compared to the financial turmoil that can occur from just one indefensible claim of negligent security.

SUMMARY

Statistics are a key tool for achieving successful operational management. Statistics are used in many of the Security Manager's functions including budget requests and justification, security incident and crime analysis, risk analysis, and program monitoring and evaluation. Both internal and external statistical analyses are important for effective security management. The two primary sources of external statistics are security reports and law enforcement crime data. Statistics form the basis for security surveys and assist the security manager to gain an ROI.

REVIEW QUESTIONS

1. What are the uses of statistics for security management?

2. What are the two main sources of data used by Security Managers?

3. When conducting an employee security survey, what method should be used?

4. Define temporal analysis and its benefits.

5. Explain return on investment.

IV
PUBLIC RELATIONS

23

Selling Security within the Organization

Good sense dictates that there is an ongoing need to "sell" the necessity and importance of the security function to the company as a whole. Employees at all levels of the organization must first be made aware of, then understand, and finally come to appreciate that the security function is a viable and integral part of the business, whatever that business or industry may be, and as such contributes to its overall success.

Why is there an ongoing need to sell security? Turnover of employees, including those in the managerial ranks, is one reason. A second reason is a result of the selling effect itself; that is, as security is understood and accepted, its role expands or takes on new internal dimensions (as discussed in Chapter 3) that require new selling.

A final reason is the ever-changing external factors that necessitate change in the security function. For example, race riots occurred in American cities in the 1960s, followed in rapid succession by civil rights demonstrations, antiwar and general antiestablishment demonstrations, airplane hijackings, executive kidnapping and hostage ransoming, and "hackers" accessing corporate computers—all having a dramatic impact on the private as well as the public sector. Then we had new threats such as "home-grown" terrorists and bombers and violence in the workplace, again expanding the dimensions of protection responsibilities. The impact in the private sector, of course, fell directly on the security forces. Shifts in security procedures and new security requirements to meet new challenges require selling. Decade following decade brought new threats and concerns, and today we're dealing with the specter of international terrorism striking in the United States.

Someone must stay abreast of these ever-changing conditions and ensure that management is aware of their potential to organizational and personal safety. Someone must also convince the Chief Executive Officer that, today, he or she and his or her family have a sufficiently high public profile that overseas enterprise activities could provoke terrorist retaliation here as well as abroad. That someone is security management.

Selling security, then, is indeed an important security management responsibility.

HOW TO SELL SECURITY

Security First

The security executive cannot sell the necessity and importance of the security function to others if his or her people do not understand it. More often than not, the average Security Department employee has a rather limited view of the security function, seeing it only as it relates to his or her particular assignment. They do not see the bigger picture. This "tunnel vision" has a predictable influence on one's attitude, and one's attitude affects one's job performance and relationship with others in and out of the department.

The single most important aspect of retail security is shrinkage or inventory shortage. Inventory shrinkage, the difference between the inventory of merchandise on the books and the actual physical presence of goods confirmed by an inventory count, is the one tangible measurement of a Security Department's effectiveness in protecting assets.

In one retail organization, for example, the shrinkage percentage figure, causes of shrinkage, and goals are discussed on posters, in handouts, and in the Security Department's own publication. However, at a recent training meeting in the main office and warehouse facility for security officers assigned to that location, not one officer, including those with years of service, could explain the process whereby the company identifies the shrinkage percentage. Not one officer knew what the shrinkage percentage meant in terms of dollars. They were staggered when told that the company, like all major retailers, suffers an annual loss of millions of dollars. When they were told how important they were in the overall efforts to protect merchandise, the light of comprehension seemed to come on. The company's error was in assuming the employees understood shrinkage and assuming that they knew how important their respective jobs were. Today these security officers are thoroughly convinced of the need and importance of the department as well as of their respective jobs.

New Employee Inductions

There is certainly no better opportunity to sell security than that afforded at new employee induction sessions. Not only is there a "captive" audience but it is an audience eagerly receptive to information about their new work environment.

Some believe that the presentation of security issues during the induction program should be made by a member of line management. Even with a prepared script, however, managers tend to deviate from the material, emphasizing those things that they think are important (which may not be) and omitting information that they feel is better left unsaid because it is distasteful, such as the consequences of internal dishonesty.

Consequently, to ensure that new employees are exposed to the information deemed necessary and appropriate, it must be presented either by a security employee or by way of some form of audiovisual media.

The personal presentation is by far the better technique, if—and that is an important if—the security employee is a personable, interesting, and effective speaker. The higher the rank of the employee making the presentation the better. Ideally, such presentations should be made by the Security Director. The further down the chain of command this task is delegated, the lower the priority it will be given by the inductees. Then the very objective of the exposure—to stress the necessity and importance of security within the organization—is defeated.

In a very large organization, spread over a wide geographical area, the Director's personal appearances may necessarily be limited to special events such as the opening of a new facility. Under such circumstances, the use of audiovisuals is a good alternative. Three of the most commonly used audiovisual formats are the slide/tape programs (35-mm color photographs projected on a screen with accompanying audiotape), a voice message on audiotape, and videotape. All three can be used effectively to orient, educate, and sell security.

Slide/tape and PowerPoint programs are inexpensive and relatively easy to put together. This particular medium can be used to explain to employees in a graphic and colorful manner what the Security Department does. Such programs can tolerably run 8 to 12 minutes, long enough to develop an interesting message for general personnel education as well as for new employee induction sessions.

Audiotape programs should be shorter, probably not exceeding 4 minutes. For this reason they are more practical for inductee consumption exclusively.

Video is unquestionably the most effective medium. One of its advantages is that it tends to personalize the guest or speaker so that people can identify with him or her—a feature not available in slide/tape or audiotape programs. Thus video comes closest to a live personal appearance.

These media can, of course, be combined in a presentation. Slide/tape or audio programs might conclude with a videotaped interview with the Security Director for added personal impact.

More Audiovisuals

The use of audiovisuals in selling security is not limited to new employee orientation presentations. One large hotel and restaurant chain uses the media described and, in addition, short motion pictures produced in-house to dramatize security and safety problems and procedures, ranging from the handling of bomb threats to fire prevention.

One retail organization has made effective use of an audiotape of an interview between the Security Director and a professional shoplifter, who consented to the interview in return for dismissal of a case pending against him in the local courts. The original tape was a high-quality reel-to-reel recording, later reproduced many times on cassette tapes for wide distribution throughout the company.

The shoplifter responded frankly to questions about his trade and skills as they applied to the company. The crook was unquestionably a ham, but his precise answers and his obvious knowledge of the company's merchandising techniques, methods of presenting goods, use of fixtures, floor layouts of individual stores, exact location of stores, one store's laxity in following a given policy compared with another store, what he liked about stealing from this organization, and what he feared had a hypnotic impact on employees listening to the tape.

"Capturing" this thief on tape has made the threat of shoplifting truly credible to the people who can do the most to thwart such activities. He has made literally thousands of employees conscious of their role in preventing shoplifting. He has helped to sell the necessity and importance of security.

There are also a wide range of commercially produced 16-mm motion pictures and videocassettes aimed at industrial and business consumers. Even films that do not specifically apply to the work scene and Security's role there can help sell security—for example, a film on rape prevention presented by the Security Department for the education of female employees.

Finally, because of the increasing use of multimedia, any kind of security presentation can use a combination of PowerPoint type programs and videotape and be made available through company local area network as well as wide area network systems.

Executive Orientations

It is as important, if not more so, to deliver the security message to the management team as it is to the line employees. To ensure this, one organization requires all new incoming middle-management hires to come through the Security Department for a 2-hour orientation (which contrasts with the average 1-hour appointment in other departments). Their visit with Security, usually within their first month on the job, is part of an overall company orientation. The new Controller or Unit Manager thus becomes acquainted with department heads and their philosophies. This is certainly not an innovative practice, yet Security is not always included in this type of executive orientation, and it should be.

Consider the impression made on the new executive. He or she meets the Security Director in the latter's office, where, after light conversation, he or she is given an organizational overview of security. The executive is provided with an organizational chart on which he or she can fill in the names of key supervisors and their phone extensions for future reference. He or she is asked about the security function of his or her previous employer and, using that as a comparison, the Security Director emphasizes the differences, pointing out the merits and virtues of the new company's program over what the new executive is accustomed to. Following that, the executive is introduced to an assistant, who spends time discussing operational practices and problems. Then the executive is introduced to the balance of the department's staff personnel and is given a tour of Security offices.

These new managerial personnel are partially convinced of the importance of security when they arrive, due to the importance attached to the orientation schedule and the 2 hours devoted to security. There is no question in their minds when they leave Security offices that the security function is in the mainstream of the business and has a vital role to play.

Security Tours

Tours of the Security facility are a dramatic way to sell security at all levels in the organization. The behind-the-scenes look is intriguing to most people, comparable to the fascination capitalized on by the television and movie industry in "cops and robbers" entertainment.

To take a class of line supervisors out of their Supervisory Training School and give them a tour of the Security Department usually proves to be a highlight of their entire program. Seeing the proprietary alarm room, the communication center, the armory, the fraud investigators at their desks, and the banks of files and indices referred to in background investigations makes a lasting impression on employees.

Bulletins

An important aspect of selling is advertising. The power of a strong ad campaign is well known. Advertising copy has to be directed toward its market, must be interesting, and must have some regularity or consistency in terms of exposure. Given these criteria, the Security Newsletter for Management discussed in Chapter 13 constitutes part of the Security Department's ad program.

This four-page monthly publication not only keeps company management informed of what contributions the security organization makes but it is also used as a source document for meetings and loss prevention discussions.

This type of bulletin is a natural selling and communication tool. People are curious about crime and the unusual (look at your newspapers and contents of the evening television news), and when such events occur in their neighborhood or workplace, their interest is intensified. Unless the dissemination of security events compromises security, why not share interesting aspects with other employees? Doing so highlights the necessity and importance of the security function.

Meetings

Visibility and the opportunity to speak and answer questions about security during company meetings is a powerful way to sell the organization. Because security usually has an impact, to some degree, on every aspect of company life, the Security Department has something of value to contribute to meetings of any department of the company.

The objective is to achieve visibility and a piece of the meeting agenda. As a rule the person who is calling or conducting the meeting is receptive to enlivening the agenda, and the change of pace and interest that a Security Department representative brings almost guarantees time. There is always an issue to speak to, depending on the composition of the group; for example, at a meeting of the Human Resource Department, Security could talk about recent bond and application falsifications and the importance of Human Resources and Security working together to ensure that only the highest quality applicants be brought into the company.

The Security Director and Security Manager should participate in these meetings but not exclusively. It is important to delegate this function down through all levels of the security organization to the first-line supervisor. This not only helps security supervisors grow but it establishes an unofficial "speaker's bureau" and thus greater exposure. If there is reluctance to permit supervisors to speak for the department (usually out of fear they will say something that does not meet with management's approval), then canned presentations should be prepared and practiced in your own training session.

Security's involvement in company meetings can take many directions. In one retail organization, for example, that participation included the following:

1. *Regional Store Managers' Meeting*, comprising store managers and key staff personnel from one region of the company. During this meeting the security agent in charge of security within that region asked for and received 15 minutes on the agenda, during which he reviewed the policy of scheduling fitting room checkers and related budgetary considerations. Questions and discussion revealed that the topic was timely. The security agent left the meeting with a sense of accomplishment. Later feedback indicated that the agent made an impressive presentation and that there had been good dialogue.

2.   *Human Resources Managers' Meeting.* The Security Director asked for 30 minutes to discuss recent conflicts between Personnel and Security over employee disciplinary decisions. The essence of the message was: "By virtue of our different responsibilities, we are bound to find ourselves from time to time on collision courses. Why collide? Why must we have a win-lose relationship? Instead, if the matter cannot be resolved to the satisfaction of both sides, refer the issue up to the next highest level for a decision." It was a positive and constructive meeting, and the Director's time was expanded to 60 minutes.

3.   *Department Managers' Meeting.* The Security Manager met with department managers responsible for high-loss areas in the business. He discussed contributing causes and suggested ideas on how they could combat such losses. The meeting was small and there was a great deal of attendee participation. The loss area under discussion was not due to theft but to "paperwork errors," yet Security's presence and interest was a plus; in the department managers' eyes, the Security Manager had stepped outside his traditional role and was assuming a different managerial dimension. He helped sell security because of that, as well as coming across as a pleasant and intelligent person who was interested in their problems.

4.   *Dock Workers' Meeting.* A security line supervisor attended a meeting in the warehouse for dock employees. A videotape of a commercially prepared motion picture on internal theft was exhibited. The security supervisor answered questions following the film. This is a tough situation, to stand up and be willing to take any questions, and the dock workers knew it. Following is an exchange at one of those meetings:

Dock Worker: Is it really true you use spies — undercover agents?

Security Agent: That's true.

Dock Worker: And you use them here?

Security Agent: Yes.

Dock Worker: Would you answer this then? How many you got? (Tittering runs through the group.)

Security Agent: It fluctuates, but probably right now, somewhere in the neighborhood of six (almost an audible gasp from the group).

Dock Worker: Six. Wow! Would you answer this question then? What are their names?

Everyone, including the dock worker and the security agent, howled with laughter. That worker sat down and another stood up and changed the subject with an entirely different question. There was a good feeling about that meeting and it helped, again, to sell security.

Involvement Programs

Programs or activities that bring nonsecurity people into personal contact with the Security Department, with a common goal, tend to cement good relationships.

At one university, for example, students have worked with the Campus Security Department as volunteers. The volunteers are furnished a security bicycle and two-way radio for shift patrol work. A similar program exists at another campus, where students voluntarily patrol wooded areas of a large eastern university on their own horses. They provide this service to the security organization in exchange for the facilities for keeping their horses on campus.

Not only does the personal involvement have a positive impact on the individual but his or her involvement, if visible to other employees of the company, serves as an example. The logic is simple: If students see other students patrolling areas of the campus, then they realize there must be a need for security, and if security is necessary, it is important.

Selling security within the organization sets and maintains a climate of understanding, appreciation, and support for the department's objectives. Some of that support comes in the form of budget dollars.

SUMMARY

There is an ongoing need to make all employees in the company aware of the importance of the security function. Security employees should understand the importance of the security function and of their respective jobs.

Induction sessions for new employees offer an opportunity for presentations by the Security Director or another representative of the department. Audiovisual materials such as slide/tape programs, Power Point programs, audiotapes, videotapes, and motion pictures can be used effectively.

All newly hired middle-management personnel should undergo an orientation session with the Security Department. During this visit the new executive learns about the department's structure and function, meets the staff, and tours the Security facility.

Bulletins such as a security newsletter can be used to inform management of the Security Department's contributions to the company. Company meetings offer security representatives a chance to talk about their department's functions and answer questions. Security's relationship with other departments can further be improved by involvement programs that bring nonsecurity personnel into contact with Security.

REVIEW QUESTIONS

1. Discuss the advantages of having new company managerial personnel come through an orientation session in the Security Department. What are some of the subjects that might be discussed in this session?

2. Discuss how each of the following can contribute to the task of selling security within the organization: new employee induction sessions, company department meetings, bulletins, audiovisual materials, and tours of the Security Department.

24

Relationship with Law Enforcement

All law enforcement agencies in the public sector are "security" organizations of one type or another, and many Security Departments (in the traditional sense) are actively engaged in the purest of law enforcement responsibilities, such as crime prevention, detection, apprehension, and prosecution. The key difference between public law enforcement and private security is that law enforcement is a product of and serves the public sector, whereas Security is a product of and serves a given segment of the private sector.

Policing, then, is a responsibility of both public and private police. The distinction between the two is found not so much in the organizational responsibility and objectives as it is in the master they serve. There is an absolute necessity for both—and a mutual dependency. The degree of harmony with which the two interact is affected by many variables, but the relationship can and should be one of effective cooperation rather than friction or competition. In the words of the *Report of the Task Force on Private Security*,

> Ideally, public law enforcement and private security agencies should work closely together, because their respective roles are complementary in the effort to control crime. Indeed, the magnitude of the Nation's crime problem should preclude any form of competition between the two. Rather, they should be cognizant and supportive of their respective roles in crime control.[1]

An interesting relationship existed between the private and public sectors in a mountain community in central California, a town inhabited by employees of a very large utility company headquartered many miles to the south. The company's Security Department was represented in the form of a resident Special Agent, affectionately referred to as "Sheriff" by residents for miles around (not only those who were employees of the utility company). The Special Agent was provided with a company car equipped

---

[1] *Private Security: Report of the Task Force on Private Security.* (Cincinnati, OH: Anderson), p. 19.

with a radio for communication with the County Sheriff's Department based in the valley below the mountain range. Except for during the summer months, there was an unwritten agreement that the "law" was represented by the resident Special Agent. In matters ranging from accidents to criminal offenses, the agent invariably was the first responder and subsequently turned the matter over to the county. Although a representative of the private sector, he served the interests of the public sector as well.

Whether the line between Security and law enforcement is fine or fuzzy, there is a great deal of movement back and forth over that line. There is a continual flow of retirees leaving the public sector and entering the security industry. There are law enforcement aspirants who launch their careers from the security industry. A growing number of "Security Degree" options are being offered in the Criminal Justice, Police Science, and Administration of Justice programs at the community and state university levels. All point out the simple fact that the two career paths run parallel.

The strongest link between Security and law enforcement is usually at the investigative and administrative levels, and the relationship there is one of mutual respect for the contributions each makes to the successful completion of the task, be it a stolen credit card case or plans for protecting a foreign dignitary. As a rule, the poorest or weakest relationship is at the lowest organizational end of both groups—the police patrolman placing the security officer at the bottom of the "pecking order" (the FBI is best, then Secret Service, State Trooper, City A Police over City B Police, etc.).

Focusing, then, on the relationship at the investigative and administrative levels, let us analyze what the public sector does to assist the private sector and vice versa.

SERVICES OF THE PUBLIC SECTOR

Provide Information on Individual Criminal Histories

Formerly, this was the most actively pursued aspect of the relationship between security in the private sector and the police. The police had the criminal records or access to state and federal records. Conscientious security investigators needed that information. Depending on the jurisdiction in terms of state and local laws and depending on the administration, the records of police departments might be wide open and accessible to security investigators or "sealed" and officially unavailable. Years ago the process of obtaining criminal history information ranged from (1) making a phone call to the Police Records Division and asking for a name check, to (2) actually paying a police officer a pre-set fee for name checks, (3) securing the necessary check through acquaintances or friends in the police department, or (4) having security investigators in the reserve or auxiliary ranks of the police department so that they had some access to criminal record files. Later, because of "privacy" legislation, some of those tactics became a crime in and of itself!

The fast food chain that is about to place an employee or prospective employee in a position of trust in their finance division cannot go to the local police and ask them to "clear" the applicant. They would be laughed out of the station. If the police did provide such services (which indeed would be a true service to the business community and certainly would reduce criminal conduct and white collars crimes that affect the community as a whole), they would soon be inundated with requests. Therefore, they could not provide such services even before there were legal privacy barriers. The need for access to criminal conviction records caused a grand dilemma in the private sector.

Fortunately, the pendulum of accessing information is swinging the other way. Some states, like Hawaii, allow those in the private sector to access, via computer, criminal conviction records. Investigators in the private sector can now go to "information brokers" on the Internet and pay for various search efforts of private as well as public sector databases, including court records, which will disclose background information of a candidate. Bearing in mind, then, the private sector is responsible for the consequences of its hiring decisions, there's no excuse for the private college to hire a campus security officer who has been convicted of sexually molesting children.

The irony of this present condition is as follows: The public sector would not dream of hiring employees into positions of responsibility or trust without examining their backgrounds and assessing any records of criminal conduct—but the private sector does have some limitations. However, the courts have held that the employer is responsible for the conduct of its employees despite the limitations. Many "negligent hiring" lawsuits involving guards raping or stealing have been (and will continue to be) processed through the courts, more often than not because the security officer had a criminal history of assaults against women or a history of theft but had never been convicted. The guard company was unquestionably limited on obtaining that history, whereas if the guard was employed by the public sector, the hiring agent could access that data. (In some states legislation now requires the licensing and fingerprinting of armed guards, but even that remedy is limited and still falls short of being the solution.) The civil actions brought against the guard companies oftentimes are fruitful.

The best hope this country has today in its efforts against criminal attacks lies in preventing crime, not in apprehending offenders after their criminal acts. One technique or prevention is to analyze risks based on information (intelligence). Without intelligence there is nothing to analyze.

Provide Information on Possible Criminal Attacks

Through their own system of informers, the police and other law enforcement agencies regularly gather intelligence that aids them at their work. It is not uncommon for police to pass on to a security organization information that specifically affects a given firm or industry. For example, the police department in a large city may learn that the jewelry department of a department store chain with many local stores is targeted for a holdup within the next few days. The greater metropolitan area includes a multiplicity of police jurisdictions, and therefore no single agency could handle the case. Due to the large number of stores, police robbery surveillance teams simply could not be provided. Acting on the intelligence gained from the police, the department store Security Department can provide its own surveillance.

On a more general basis, local law enforcement provides Security with information on counterfeiting operations, check passing and fraud money order scams, the presence of professional boosters (shoplifters), credit fraud gangs, and a host of other similar intelligence that the security industry needs in its daily efforts to protect the industries it serves.

Provide Traffic Control Support for Special Events

The type of industry and its influence on vehicular traffic will determine the relationship with local law enforcement in the area of traffic control. In some cases, the only traffic impact may be predictable minor congestion when employees arrive in the morning and leave in the afternoon. This usually can be regulated with signals rather than manpower.

In other cases, such as the grand opening of a new shopping center, the anticipated traffic could be a major concern not only to the merchants, whose interests are defeated if traffic is snarled and customers cannot get into the center, but to the police as well, who do not want a major traffic jam within their jurisdiction. Thus the experienced security administrator, anticipating traffic problems at an upcoming opening, will sit down with the local police and outline the probable traffic control needs, usually based on his or her experience at a previous grand opening in another police jurisdiction. As a rule, the police handle the traffic on the dedicated streets and Security provides the manpower for the traffic control on the private roadways and on the parking lots.

Poorly coordinated efforts or the total absence of any coordination—and both do occur—result in monumental traffic jams (in one case the freeway off-ramp that serviced the street in front of a shopping center was backed up for over a mile and the State Patrol had to announce a traffic advisory). Efficiently coordinated efforts move vehicles expeditiously into and out of an area.

Accept and Process Crime Reports

The police accept and process crime reports from firms that have security personnel and from those that do not, as well as from private citizens. Why, then, is this a special relationship with Security? If there are no security personnel involved, the police will conduct some inquiry into the facts and details surrounding the alleged crime. Once the proper relationship with Security is established, however, the police will in most cases accept on face value the report from a Security Department. In fact, they will usually accept the completed investigative report from the Security Department's report form and attach it to their own forms or have the information transcribed from the security report form onto their own form, word for word.

There are two reasons why the police will accept security reports: (1) They recognize the professionalism (only of deserving organizations, of course) and respect that professionalism. (2) The report's content could be beyond the investigative expertise of the police (e.g., computer manipulation or a cycle variance in accounts receivable).

Coordinate with Security on Special Enforcement Projects

"Special enforcement" in this context means efforts directed against a particular criminal problem, rather than investigation that concerns specific suspects. When the proper relationship is established with the local authorities, a variety of joint projects of mutual interest and benefit may be undertaken. Such projects could include the following:

1. Because of a series of thefts of autos and auto parts and thefts of packages from cars in a shopping center's parking lot, the Security people can set up a surveillance from the roofs of stores and communicate by radio with plainclothes police down in the lot.
2. Because of complaints received that homosexual acts are being solicited in the public restroom at an amusement park or a hospital, a coordinated effort can be effected to detect and arrest such offenders.
3. Because of a series of indecent exposure incidents on the grounds of a local college, Campus Security and police can set up stake-out teams as well as set "bait."

Coordinate with Security on Major or Important Investigations

There are occasions when a criminal case would be impossible to conclude successfully without the cooperative effort of both the private and public sectors. A dramatic example of such a case occurred in Los Angeles. Investigators for a chain of department stores learned that a large number of employees and nonemployees were working together in a concerted effort to remove merchandise from the department store's warehouse. Most of the participants were identified, motion pictures were taken of some of the theft activity, and an undercover agent was successfully placed in the midst of the group by the Security Department to provide a flow of intelligence. The department store then went to the local authorities (in this particular case, the District Attorney's office) for assistance.

In a coordinated effort, the following occurred: A small electrical supply and service store was obtained about 2 miles from the warehouse. It was wired for voice recordings. A panel truck equipped with a 16-mm motion picture camera (before the sophisticated video cameras we have today) was parked behind the store. Two investigators from the District Attorney's office posed as owners of the store and one manned the camera vehicle. Department store investigators secretly marked the kind of merchandise the undercover agent had indicated would be stolen the next day. Through the undercover agent, word was passed to the thieves that there was a new "fence" in the area (the electrical supply store). The department store provided the money to buy the goods. In a short time, regular trips were being made to the back door of the "fence," and investigators were buying stolen merchandise marked by other investigators the night before. The transactions were recorded by the hidden camera, as well as audibly.

Results: A grand total of 27 culprits were either indicted and arrested, arrested and referred to juvenile authorities, or, in those cases in which a public offense could not be established, discharged from the company.

A case of this complexity and magnitude could not have been resolved so successfully had it not been for the cooperation between private security and law enforcement. Criminal investigations provide frequent opportunities for this effective interaction.

Provide Intelligence on Radical or Political Activists

Advance information about planned protest marches, demonstrations, rallies — in terms of location, time, who is gathering, their objectives, the route they will travel, their specific plans (such as tying up traffic) — is vital information to a security organization in the vicinity of these often socially disruptive activities. The intelligence can be even more crucial to a company that could be the object of attack, as in the case of a major department store whose travel bureau sold excursion tickets to the former Soviet Union. The Jewish Defense League demonstrated at the store, disrupting normal operations and blocking the doorways by sitting down and joining arms. Advance information could have allowed time for planning a defensive strategy and a course of action.

Good planning based on good intelligence pays off quickly. For instance, a major department store in Los Angeles was alerted to a planned Chicano rally at police headquarters, about a half mile from its downtown store. The store's security force was beefed up. The rally was dispersed by police, sending hundreds of protesters (and hooligans, who tend to join such activities) fleeing down the main avenues leading away from the police facility. Groups of these youths broke hundreds of plate glass windows of stores lining the streets in their escape route. The department store lost five huge plate glass windows, but because its security personnel were in force, no merchandise was looted from the displays, and plywood panels (prefabricated for just such an event) were quickly erected for temporary security.

The absence of this type of intelligence from law enforcement agencies would put the security administrator at a marked disadvantage, if not in a hopeless position. The flow of such information is directly related to the relationship of mutual trust and respect that has been established.

Provide Protection during Labor Disputes

Without question, the Security Department is the enforcement arm of management. As a consequence of that reputation and profile, its peace-keeping capabilities during a labor dispute are nil. Typically, only the police can maintain any semblance of order on the picket lines, and even they have their grief because strikers tend to view them as protectors of management and management's property. Security's role is limited to a perimeter defense line on the company property. Police assistance is necessary in terms of keeping the peace; preventing or at least reducing violence against "scabs" or supervisory and managerial personnel; and preventing the blockading of access roads, sidewalks, and driveways. Without that type of regulatory order, dangerous situations might escalate out of control.

SERVICES OF THE PRIVATE SECTOR

The security industry's relationship with—or, perhaps more aptly stated, the industry's contribution to—the general law enforcement picture includes the following factors.

Contribute to the Local Criminal Statistical Data

The annual Uniform Crime Reports published by the Federal Bureau of Investigation are based on data generated at the local level. The statistical tracking of the number of various types of crimes in a community, the number of arrests, and the variety of unsolved crimes serves a number of purposes, including possible budget justifications.

On first observation it might appear that the volume of criminal acts and arrests reflects police activity only. However, a percentage of theses statistics reflect the activity of the security forces in the community— particularly in certain crimes such as larceny. The percentage could be quite small or substantial, depending on the community and the composition of the local police and security forces. The private security force responsible for maintaining order on a large college campus, for example, might often process as many offenders through the "booking" procedure as does the local police agency. In this circumstance, the community served by the private security agency might actually be larger than the one within the jurisdiction of the public law enforcement agency.

The published criminal statistics, then, reflect to some degree the joint effort, but more often than not the independent efforts, of both the public and private sector.

It should be pointed out that the index reflects only "known" crimes, that is to say, crimes known to the police. Actually there is a great deal of crime known to the private sector but for a number of reasons never reported to the police—such as petty shoplifting cases and large internal larceny matters in which the best interests of the company are served in a recovery of the loss instead of a prosecution, with its delays, costs, and doubtful outcome.

Provide the Community with "Tax-Free" Law Enforcement

The Security Department of a single department store in Los Angeles in 1 year will arrest and prosecute in excess of 2000 offenders for such crimes as theft, burglary, forgery, credit fraud, counterfeit passing, and indecent exposure. Add up all the department stores, plus chains stores; add all supermarkets and drug stores; add all the discount stores (including only those retailers who support security forces); and project their combined efforts. Such a projection suggests a conservative figure of 50,000 arrests by security forces in the greater Los Angeles area each year, and the number is growing. Bear in mind that these figures apply only to the retail industry (which represents that segment of the private sector most actively engaged in crime/arrest activities). If the burden of that criminal behavior rested on the police, imagine what it would mean in terms of tax dollars!

Provide Liaison Between Law Enforcement and the Business World

The vast pool of intelligence and resources needed on a daily basis by the police is readily available through the various security organizations serving business and industry. In some cases the intelligence needed is available within the Security Department by virtue of the type of organization—such as an investigator for a telephone company with high technical skill levels needed in some local, state, or federal investigations. In other cases the need can be filled only by a security investigator because the security person has access to intelligence—for example, current or background information on a present or former employee.

Public sector law enforcement personnel would be first to agree that many doors would never open without a court order if it were not for the intercession of the security organization. Many companies, by written policy, will not release any information to any governmental agency but will refer such agency to their Security Department. If the Security Department agrees to the release of information, it is released; if not, it is not released.

Pages could be filled with examples of the relationship between the public and private sector in this area of liaison. The following single example will serve as an illustration, not only of this aspect of cooperative effort but of the thrust of this entire discussion of the complementary roles of private security and public police.

A young police officer took an elective course in security while pursuing his bachelor's degree in Criminal Justice. A local Security Director taught that class. Some years later, that officer was a homicide detective working on a puzzling death. The only thing found in the deceased's pocket was a cash register receipt. Recalling his earlier studies, the detective called his former teacher. Examination and interpretation of the impressions on that receipt provided a wealth of information that led to solution of the case. The receipt was the purchase of a specific classification of merchandise on the date of death. It provided information on where the purchase was made in the city (by store identification number), when during that day the purchase was made (by transaction count), and who sold the merchandise to the deceased (by employee ID code). Armed with that intelligence, and following an interview with the employee that was arranged by Security, the detective resolved his case.

The relationship between the private ad public sector in this case, as in virtually all cases, served the professional interest of law enforcement specifically and the welfare of the community generally.

SUMMARY

The functions of private security and public law enforcement often overlap; the two career paths run parallel. The relationship between security and law enforcement is usually one of mutual respect and cooperation at the investigative and administrative levels.

Law enforcement formerly provided the private sector with criminal history information to assist in background investigations. In recent years, legal decisions on the individual's right to privacy have restricted this service, although some new resources are becoming available. Police often pass on to security organizations intelligence concerning possible criminal attacks or civil disturbances. The police can offer traffic control support for special events. The police accept crime reports from professional security organizations. The police may assist security in special enforcement projects concerning general criminal problems. Major investigations often require the coordination of police and security efforts. Police assistance is usually required to maintain order during labor disputes.

The private sector assists law enforcement by contributing criminal statistical data. Private Security Departments arrest and prosecute many offenders each year, providing a form of "tax-free" law enforcement. Security Departments can serve as liaison between law enforcement and the business community, providing intelligence ad expertise as needed.

REVIEW QUESTIONS

1. Briefly explain six services that law enforcement can provide private security and three services that private security can provide law enforcement.

2. Discuss the controversy surrounding law enforcement's providing criminal history information to security investigators.

25

Relationship with the Industry

No matter how successful or effective a security function may be or appear to be, there is always room for improvement. There is always a better way. Only the manager isolated from the security community is satisfied with his or her operation. The need to grow and to reach out for ways to improve is the mark of a progressive and enlightened security professional.

Where does one reach? The administrators must reach out into the security industry and its vast reservoir of resources and experience. Never before have we better understood the impact of today's shrinking world on industry, especially in view of September 11, 2001. It is a fascinating fact that one administrator's problems in New York City today may be identical to another's in San Francisco or Dallas tomorrow. Perhaps more fascinating, the latter administrator's solutions to such problems may be better than the former's.

In the private sector, comparable industries or businesses are competitors in all things—with the exception of protection. In the case of neighboring universities, one institution competes with the other for academic standing, scholastic achievement within the faculty as well as the student body, success of athletic teams, funding, enrollment, percentage of graduates continuing on in graduate studies, and so forth. Despite that climate of competition, the security heads of those same institutions meet and discuss common problems in a spirit of mutual cooperation, sharing ideas and information for the purpose of improving their efforts to protect their respective institutions.

A department store vigorously competes with its counterpart at the opposite end of the shopping mall in the timing, frequency, merchandise mix, and price-points of sales, as well as other gimmicks to attract customers, such as in-store promotions around public figures and drawings for such prizes as new autos or ocean cruises. Competition is so fierce that if one store extends the hours it is open to the public, the other immediately follows suit. However, the Loss Prevention staffs work cooperatively, advising or warning one another of potential shoplifters, bad check passers, or credit card frauds.

The very nature of the security business demands communication and an effective relationship with the industry. The relationship can be divided into four categories: cooperation, participation, contribution, and education.

EFFECTIVE RELATIONSHIP CATEGORIES

Cooperation

The cooperation relationship within the industry can be divided into individual cooperation and organized (or structured) cooperation.

At the individual level, to establish and then develop personal contacts with peers is an important, if not vital, dimension of the security professional. Although selecting contacts is usually a highly subjective process, commonality of operations and respect for the individual are important. Once established, a professional kinship grows, allowing an honest exchange and sharing of ideas, opinions, and strategies to the mutual benefit of both parties. The key word here is *sharing*. How many times over the years does the typical Security Manager pick up the telephone and call a counterpart across the country or across town with a request for information or assistance! To be denied that capability would be crippling.

Despite the obvious reasonableness, let alone necessity, of maintaining such relationships with others in the business, some have voluntarily maintained very low profiles and could be called "isolationists." Such a posture is undoubtedly based on the false assumption that one must be a very outgoing, sophisticated, and socially charming personality to make professional contacts and friends. Although a good number of professionals are comfortable mixing socially in groups, a surprising number are shy or at least reserved. For many people it is an effort to approach a stranger, even if that stranger is also alone, and strike up a conversation. However, people in the security business do it, mostly because they feel compelled to for the very reasons discussed previously.

Of course, the closest contracts are usually intra-industry—for example, hospital security people are in closer and more constant touch with others in their own area of specialization than with aerospace security people. However, there is a great deal of cross-industry cooperation. In a given period it is not at all unlikely that a banking security professional would be in touch with the utilities people for information on the identity of possible subscribers at a given location, with amusement park security for information on a former employee, or with airlines security for assistance in moving highly valuable negotiable instruments between cities. If the two security counterparts are known to each other, cooperation (if legal and feasible) can be assured. If they are unknown to one another, or have no common denominator such as membership in a security organization, the advantages of mutual assistance and cooperation could be jeopardized.

The candid security administrator today who enjoys any degree of success will freely admit that his or her status is not the result of self-achievement but rather the result of harmonizing all the input from many sources, including the influence of contemporaries in the industry. In sharing experiences, successes, failures, and strategies, we change and grow.

There is a fine line between individual cooperation and organized cooperation, and one tends to weave back and forth over the line. Organized or structured cooperation comes about through associations, societies, or other organized gatherings or relationships of security professionals.

Over the years various "mutual" associations have come and gone in the retail industry. In Los Angeles one was called Stores Protective Association (SPA). SPA exclusively served the retail industry and provided such services as maintaining a database of all known shoplifters and dishonest employees as reported by those companies that were member companies. That database was then used as a screening tool in conducting background investigations of new employees or applicants and was a reliable source to determine if a person being detained for shoplifting, for example, had a history of that kind of conduct. SPA also provided other security-related services such as "integrity shopping," providing some undercover agents, collecting bad checks, processing suspected refunds, and processing civil demands (civil fines for shoplifting). They also published special alert bulletins of importance to security executives.

Other metropolitan areas had similar associations, such as New York City and Houston. Some, like the Los Angeles SPA and Houston's association no longer exist, for a variety of reasons, but the CONCEPT of mutuality is ever viable.

The benefits were obvious: All member stores of the association contribute, on an ongoing basis, the names of all persons arrested for shoplifting and other related retail crimes and the names of all dishonest employees to the master database of the association. Names of new employees are researched against this file, with a predictable percentage of match-ups or "hits." *Example*: A person who is seeking employment with Company A is discovered in the association's database as having been a former employee of Company L and was discharged for theft from that company. The names in this negative database are regularly purged to be relatively current and meaningful.

Today there has evolved a national mutual association called the United States Mutual Association, Inc., whose tag line is, "Providing the Nation's employers with responsible solutions to employee theft." Here is how the USMA works: Member companies report the name and social security number of anyone who has committed a verifiable act of retail theft, employee theft, violence in the workplace, or a drug offense in the workplace. Security incident reports may only be submitted when the dishonesty is documented by such evidence as a signed admission, a signed restitution agreement, criminal conviction, or similar evidence. Each report remains on file for 7 years. More than two-million reports are on file. The USMA operates under the Federal Fair Credit Reporting Act and is affiliated with 10 regional mutual associations.

I have long been a strong advocate for this kind of professional sharing and have lectured, over the years, in such forums as the International Security

Conference (ISC) about the benefit of mutual associations. To this day I still advocate the concept of mutual associations within any given industry, with this caveat: If negative information about specific individuals is shared, that sharing must comply with the Federal Fair Credit Reporting Act.

Some years back I served as the Security Management Consultant to a prestigious golf-resort community in the Cochella Valley (Palm Springs/Palm Desert area) in California. Homes within this community were valued well above a million dollars each. My mission was to redesign the Security Department and its strategies to more effectively deal with and prevent unauthorized access to this gated/walled community that had been experiencing a rash of "hot prowl" burglaries. As my task neared completion, my last recommendation was for the new security chief to call for a founding meeting of all Security Directors of similar private desert communities and host the event. Although there were numerous similar operations, there was no organization, no exchange of information, and no structured way to share data that would be helpful to their common problems. The end result: the creation of a new security organization that met regularly and, between meetings, shared important news and alerts as the occasions presented themselves. Clearly a classic case of structured cooperation.

Participation

The obvious advantage of participation, as evidenced by SPA is that it allows one to go beyond the narrowly restricted and limited boundaries of one specialized field within a wider field (department and specialty clothing stores within the retail industry). Participation in other organizations has other advantages.

Organizations, ranging from local to international, offer the security executive, at one time or another, something in the way of professional growth. Every Security Supervisor, Manager, or Director, irrespective of his or her particular industry, has a variety of professional organizations that he or she may join as a member, visit, call on, or infrequently partake of—all aimed at enhancing knowledge and personal or departmental efficiency. A retail security executive in Los Angeles, for example, would have the following available to him or her:

1. US Mutual Association
2. Retail Special Agents Association (RSAA)
3. Chief Special Agents Association of Southern California
4. National Retail Federation, Loss Prevention Group
5. American Society for Industrial Security
6. International Association of Professional Security Consultants

This list excludes a variety of law enforcement associations (such as the State Peace Officers Association); training or educational organization membership; and other national groups of limited interests, such as the National Computer Security Association or the Business Espionage Controls and Countermeasures Association.

Participation in the groups at the top of the previous list provides the greatest day-in-and-day-out impact on individual and departmental efficiency. As one moves down the list (inserting the excluded organizations where appropriate), the impact becomes proportionately less—but important nonetheless.

An overview of participation in those listed organizations follows:

1. *USMA.* Discussed on preceding pages.
2. *Retail Special Agents Association.* This is a local association of security people of all ranks, with an active associate membership of service and security supply people. The emphasis is on retail in general; that is, not only department and specialty stores but also food, drug, and discount as well. In addition to the fraternal interests, emphasis is placed on outside speakers discussing topics of mutual interest, such as opinions of the bench, pending legislation, governmental practices affecting the industry, and management practices. Concerns are local in nature not national.
3. *Chief Special Agents Association of Southern California.* This group is restricted to security chiefs of major companies, with limited associate membership of number-two people. The association is fraternal, with emphasis on strong liaison with top local law enforcement officers. A significant and very noteworthy contribution to the security community is the publication every other year of a directory of all security and law enforcement organizations in the area and their key personnel. The directory is the only one of its kind and is coveted by all law enforcement as well as security personnel.
4. *National Retail Federation, Loss Prevention Group.* This is a group comprising department, chain, and large specialty store top security administrators who meet annually to exchange retail security problems and solutions, on the broadest possible basis. What is happening in New Orleans could happen in Seattle. Stores in Philadelphia, working with the Chamber of Commerce, are involved in a community-wide effort to reduce shoplifting. That program could work in San Francisco. Similarly, new protection strategies to reduce inventory shrinkage in one company can easily be adopted by others.
5. *American Society for Industrial Security.* This association serves the entire security industry in terms of membership and interest. Local chapters bring together professionals from all industries so that there is a cross-fertilization of ideas and experience. Emphasis is on

upgrading the industry by establishing guidelines and educating members through professionally presented training seminars, workshops, and annual national meetings.

6. *International Association of Professional Security Consultants.* This association is a forum for professional security consultants possessing disciplines concerned with identification, definition, and resolution of security-related problems. One objective is to establish standards of conduct and promote professional ethics for the security consulting profession as well as to provide professional certification for security consultants. It should be noted that there is a trend toward corporate security executives taking on the mantle of consulting; that is, serving as an in-house consultant as opposed to "administering" a corporate program.

The organizations named represent a mix of specific, local, and general industrial interest. The reader of this book—whether student or security practitioner—should substitute or add other relatively comparable organizations in keeping with his or her particular interest or field. For example, in Los Angeles there is a Downtown Security Manager's Association that meets regularly to discuss problems being experienced in commercial office buildings. This allows for networking and sharing of information regarding crimes that are common to such facilities. Similarly, the security chiefs of hotel-casinos in Las Vegas have their own association and they meet regularly to discuss those issues that concern them most, from pending legislation in the state, new court decisions, and new scams in their industry to known cheats and criminals that are attracted to the gaming scene. They have a rapid alert and advisory system with the use of the fax machine. Not surprisingly, they work closely with the Las Vegas Metropolitan Police Department.

Clearly, participation in security-related organizations and their programs brings to the security professional an ever-increasing array of knowledge, insight, and strategy that is otherwise unavailable. Failure to pursue involvement and active participation only brings stagnation and a truly narrow approach to the business of protecting one's company.

Contribution

One facet of participation is contribution. It is a rare man or woman indeed who can participate (belong to and attend) without making some form of contribution. To sit at a round-table discussion and comment does constitute contribution. One-sided participation would be selfish, denying others what the noncontributing attendee seeks. Participation, if open and natural, always serves, informs, and/or enlightens others in some measure.

However, that amount of contribution, important as it is, is not sufficient for the welfare of the security industry. Where would the state of the art be today without textbooks written by security professionals and articles submitted to trade magazines? Someone must give direction to our educational institutions about appropriate curriculum for students now pursuing degrees in security management. Who is talking to the community, to service organizations, and to us about the business deemed so important in the economic health of private industry and business?

Our relationship to the security industry in general, if it is to be constructive and positive, if it is to help upgrade, and if it is to continue to strive for professional recognition of our chosen careers, must have a contributory dimension. Untapped talent surrounds us in our business. A brief examination of some significant areas of contribution, such as book authorship, article authorship, public presentations, and involvement in the educational process, is in order.

Book Authorship

Healy and Walsh, Gallati, Berger, Tyska and Fennelly, Simonsen, Broder, Barefoot, Moore, Vellani, Craighead, and Fay, to name a few, have taken the time and energy to make a contribution to our industry by writing books. Their contributions have been significant and substantial. In most instances, those in the industry who have made literary contributions are not primarily authors. Rather, they are security professionals who are willing to share their points of view, their opinions, and their experiences. In view of the past, present, and projected growth of the industry and the increasing number of colleges and universities offering this discipline, security needs more people who are willing to contribute their experiences by writing books. Here's a unique provoking thought for the reader, something I've said and lectured on for years: Any successful security supervisor, manager, or director can write a book! If you can write a report of an incident, if you can prepare an investigative report, you can write a book.

Magazine Article Authorship

Essentially the same thing can be said about article authorship as was just stated regarding book authorship. At a recent meeting of security executives, one participant was overheard making relatively uncomplimentary remarks about the quality of articles in one of our important trade magazines. How much easier it is to criticize than to contribute! Trade magazines are but a vehicle through which the trade can speak. The publisher, editor, and magazine staff are publishing professionals, not necessarily security professionals. The quality of trade journal content is a reflection of the quality of the trade. The security administrator who considers himself or herself talented but fails to share that talent obviously fails to contribute to the best interests of his or her chosen profession . . . and/or fears the bright light of public scrutiny that often times subjects us to criticism.

Public Presentations

Public presentations, which include in-house talks, presentations before the industry, talks before other trades, or luncheon speaking, tend to give the security function high and positive visibility to the nonsecurity audience and add to the professional growth of those in a security audience. Appearing before the local Rotary Club has little to do with the speaker's relationship to the security industry, except that through the presentation he or she may generate good will for the security cause, with some rippling effect. The same is true with in-house talks and presentations made to other disciplines, such as a Controller's Association.

The real contribution comes in making a presentation to the security industry. No matter how experienced or learned a person may be, there is something new to learn. We learn from others, through their willingness to share—if not in book or magazine article authorship, then at least in their personal presentations. For a person who is considered a leader in the industry or an administrator with a successful track record to refuse to make a presentation before the industry is unfortunately short-sighted as well as selfish. Security professionals have an obligation to contribute to the cause for the good of all. They cannot in good conscience sit back and rest on their laurels.

Involvement in the Educational Process

Teaching in the Security Administration field is a very marked contribution to the industry. Not everyone has teaching skills, of course, so opportunities in this area are limited. However, there is an increasing call to service in terms of participating in college curriculum advisory committees now forming in response to the burgeoning security programs at the college and university level.

Education

The last important category of relationships with the industry is primarily self-serving but in a positive way. The sum total of an active relationship of cooperation, participation, and contribution is self-education. Keeping abreast of the industry—in terms of new technology, new case law, new legislation, innovative concepts, and new trends—is at least as important to the security practitioner and administrator as are the daily operations of the organization.

For those security professionals who failed to complete their college education, now is an ideal time to return to school and earn their degree. Security Administration programs are being established all across the country in response to a demand for formalized education in the security field. When I entered college, only 13 schools in the country offered a degree in law enforcement. Thirteen! There was no such thing as a degree in Security. Today, schools offering degrees in Criminal Justice and Security are common, and a number of institutions are offering graduate degrees.

Interestingly, one's degree need not be in Criminal Justice or Security Administration. Any degree will suffice. Indeed, there are those who support the notion that a graduate in Business Administration will make just as good a security executive as a Criminal Justice graduate. To me, the degree is but evidence of an individual's ability to persevere, evidence of one's self-discipline, and evidence of one's ability to set goals and then achieve such goals; in a word—an achiever. That's what every profession seeks—achievers!

In this business one cannot afford to sit in the backwaters and permit the rest of the industry, in all its vastness, to stream by. Time was when change came slowly in the security profession. Today we are truly in a state of "future shock." Changes are rapid and accelerating. Technical advances in electronics, communications, and computer science is almost overwhelming and bright, progressive people are needed. Opportunities abound!

SUMMARY

In a continuing effort to improve the operation, the security administrator must look to his or her peers in the security industry.

Cooperation within the security industry takes the form of individual and organized efforts. Personal contacts among peers allow an exchange of ideas and strategies. Organized cooperation occurs through the activities of formal associations of security professionals.

Security professionals have the opportunity for participation in organizations ranging in scope from local to national. Participation usually includes some form of contribution. Contributions of the security professional to the field can include book and magazine article authorship, public speaking, and teaching.

Cooperation, participation, and contribution form an important part of the education of the security professional in his or her effort to keep abreast of constant changes in the field.

REVIEW QUESTIONS

1. What are the advantages to the Security Manager of active involvement in the security community?

2. What professional organizations are available for Security Managers in your area and what are their activities?

26

Community Relations

A Security Department's involvement or participation in community relations activities is directly related to (1) the public's need for information, (2) the need to inform the public, and (3) security management's receptivity to such public exposure.

One might argue that there is really no difference between "the public's need for information" and "the need to inform the public." The distinction is this: The public's need is a demand and a need *they* identified, whereas "the need to inform the public" is first identified by the company.

An example of the public's need for information might well be a community's concern about the safety of a newly constructed nuclear power generating station, or the public's concern over a rumor that the community's water supply is vulnerable to terrorist attack. The utility company's Security Director could be an effective representative and speaker at local civic and business organization meetings because there's a public perception that security and safety are one in the same. Indeed, in some instances that's true.

In some cases local concern has taken the form of organized demonstrations, hostility, and violence. When business or industry moves into a new community, they may meet with some resistance. Today there is much concern about the impact of industry on the environment, which includes everything from atmospheric emissions, traffic congestion, noise pollution, light pollution, and architectural blight on the landscape to the killing of old oak trees. Reaction to such issues is often emotional. Local government is usually sensitive to the feelings of its constituency, and actions by local government such as finding fault with construction inspections, making unrealistic demands to comply with local codes, and delaying the issuance of permits and approvals can often be traced back to an ill-informed public.

Certainly senior management of the company must be visible and carry the brunt of a program aimed at establishing good community relations. The question is, does Security have a role here? Indeed it does, primarily in the form of a security executive who can first establish a relationship with key local officials in public safety and law enforcement departments and then, through those officials, with community groups. Such a spokesperson, if he or she is involved in the new business project from its early stages, can help allay fears and at the same time build goodwill for the company — depending, of course, on his or her public speaking skills.

The need to inform the public is a challenge to the retail industry, for example, with its constant problems of shoplifting, particularly juvenile shoplifting. For security representatives to go out into the community and talk about the personal consequences of theft and the impact of losses on retail prices plays an important role in educating an otherwise ignorant and apathetic public.

Security management's response (as a whole) to these needs is usually traceable to the head of the security organization. For example, if the Security Director is gregarious, outspoken, and a confident public speaker, then the department will usually enjoy a high profile in terms of community relations. Not only will the Director have public exposure but others on the staff will be encouraged to represent the organization.

On the other hand, if the Director is uncomfortable or dislikes public exposure, he or she will avoid it altogether or at least minimize it, regardless of the public's or the company's needs. It usually holds true that if the Director maintains a low profile, so does the staff. It is simple for the Security Director to avoid or minimize community relations activities; he or she just passes the need or the challenge to a peer in the industry, to some other Director, or to another executive in the company—someone on the legal or operations staff, perhaps, or the public relations people. It is a rare but strong Security Director who will refer such public exposure to a subordinate, because the subordinate's high profile and public recognition as a speaker could be considered threatening.

Ideally, the Director will have public poise and will respond positively to the needs of the community. The company should be supportive of the Security Director's participation in community events, and—by virtue of his or her sensitivity to the department's role—will actually go out and help identify needs that can be addressed through a good community relations program.

Community relations, for our purposes, includes the following:

- Public speaking engagements
- Print media interviews
- Radio interviews
- Appearances on television
- Participation in community-oriented projects
- General public contact

PUBLIC SPEAKING

The luncheon speaker, after-dinner speaker, guest speaker between the women's business meeting and "social hour," and the classroom or auditorium speaker are very much part of the American scene, not only in his or her very presence as a vital part of the social context in which he or she appears but also in the trappings and traditions that surround the speaking engagement. The process begins with the advance announcement of the program and build-up of the speaker's credentials and the topic. It continues as seating arrangements at the head table are made, as the speaker sneaks last-minute looks at cue cards or typed text, and as he or she is introduced by the program chairman and is greeted by applause. The speaker's opening comments aim at a bit of humor to "break the ice." Later comes the final, second round of applause following the presentation, expression of appreciation, and the inevitable little circle of people who surround the speaker after the meeting has been adjourned. All of this is somehow a natural and expected occurrence in our culture.

If the speaker does poorly—and many do—it is so noted and quickly forgotten. What was most important was that the process was right. Interestingly, even mediocre presentations contain some new and or interesting information. Conversely, if the speaker did well, there tends to be a lingering sense of goodwill about him or her, the message, and the organization. In short, there is little risk in public speaking of incurring ill will, but there is a great opportunity for developing genuine goodwill.

As stated earlier, the need of the public (or any segment thereof) for information and the company's need for the public to know represent the two legitimate reasons for a public speaking appearance on the part of a security executive. Something less than "legitimate," then, could be an appearance when there is no need to know. That could well be a church's Women's Auxiliary or the local PTA, depending on the prospective speaker. For example, what is the legitimate need for a hotel security presentation to a club of Vietnam veterans confined to wheelchairs? Perhaps one could make a case for the presentation on the basis that such vets do travel from time to time, and security tips could be helpful.

More importantly, if an organization calls on, invites, or asks for a presentation, that request in and of itself represents a need that can be filled. More often than not, filling that kind of need automatically brings about a great deal of goodwill.

Goodwill, then, is the common denominator and underlying theme, not only in public speaking appearances but in all community relations activities, although the specific objective of any one such activity is informative in nature. Rare is the company that is not interested in goodwill. The Security Department, by virtue of its unique role and image, is in a position to generate goodwill for the organization as a whole, if it is willing to.

Some administrators called on to speak worry unduly over the topic selected by the requesting group because they feel inadequate to speak on that specific topic. Guest speakers should understand that the topics requested are usually only suggestions. The group frequently is uncertain about what they want. The negotiability of topics gives the prospective speaker latitude to direct the topic and remarks to areas in which he or she is more comfortable or that are more appropriate to the occasion.

Put another way, the speaker, more often than not, can select the topic to be presented.

Ideally the presentation should be tailored to appeal to the audience and have some constructive application for that audience—even if the presentation is principally meant to develop goodwill. In the case of the veterans in wheelchairs, the hotel security administrator could not only entertain but could provide the audience security- and non–security-related advice concerning hotel accommodations and services for the physically disadvantaged.

This is an important point: The security executive must recognize that he or she is a spokesperson for the industry, be it hotel management, transportation, manufacturing, and so forth, as well as a security spokesperson. To talk in terms of the industry and as a member of its management adds polish and dimension to the presentation befitting his or her professional position. Gone are the days of the cigar-chewing security chief who did not know—or, for that matter, care—what the company's objectives were, what they were doing, or where they were going.

Figure 26.1 suggests possible speech topics for a number of different security functions that might be appropriate for four different types of audiences. The list of security functions, the variety of audiences, and the wider variety of topics could consume pages.

PRINT MEDIA INTERVIEWS

My experience with the press has been that if you are wrong, the press will ensure that the public is clearly so informed, and if you are right they will serve as a powerful ally. The distortions that do creep into newsprint tend to be impartial—that is, there is as much favorable distortion as there is unfavorable.

Response to requests from the press for specific news, general news, or feature material is, or should be to some measure, controlled by the Public Relations Department of the company, which can aptly serve as a buffer between Security and the press, if need be. A sound practice and policy is to require that all press contacts be cleared through the public relations people first. This accomplishes two things: (1) the people charged with the release of information to the press officially sanction the subsequent dialogue between Security and the press and the release of information and (2) such sanctioning gives Security natural "protection" against criticism that can be inspired by distortions or by releases that come as a surprise to management.

Press releases can include the appointment of a new director or manager, significant criminal attacks, significant successes, or unusual achievements (such as winning in a national or local security competition).

	Local Business and Civic Groups (e.g., Rotarians)	School Civic Classes and PTA	Church Groups	Professional Groups (e.g., Controllers Association)
Hotel Security	· Orientation of the industry · Interesting loss statistics · Humorous anecdotes · Tips for the businessman who travels	· Career opportunities in hotel management · Humorous anecdotes · Examples of a hotel detective's day's work	· Combination of the civic and school presentation	· Case studies of internal losses · Systems modifications resulting from internal loss cases
School/Campus Security	· Need for community support for school bonds · Security costs · Examples of loss	· Vandalism problems and how they affect the quality of school life · Why the need for security	· Overview of security problems and the need for moral leadership from the church	· What's new in combating vandalism and losses, in terms of strategy and hardware
Aerospace Security	· Discussion of possible application of security technology to local businessman's problems	· A look into the future · Interesting cases and problems · Career opportunities in the industry	· As the church's goal is one of peace, so is the industry's · Examples of attacks against that effort	· Unique problems or demands connected with present or new contracts and projects
Utilities Security	· Security measures aimed at protecting resources, the community, and the consumer	· Youth's role in conserving resources · Examples of youth's acts of vandalism and attacks	· Importance of home and church's influence in conserving resources and energy · Example of problems	· Security auditing procedures · Examples of delaication case in payment processing center
Retail Security	· Discussion of threat and problem of internal dishonesty and ways for small businessman to detect and prevent same	· Statistics on juvenile shoplifting · Consequences of theft	· Overview of shoplifting and how the losses affect prices · Need for leadership in setting moral standards and values	· Examples of recent credit and EDP frauds and prevention efforts in those areas
Transportation Security	· Industry losses and impact on insurance and freight charges	· Transportation's role in community and economy · Attacks against the industry · Consequences of attacks	· General information, similar to that given to the schools	· Hijacking frauds and techniques to detect such frauds

Figure 26.1 Suggested speech topics for various audiences.

Feature articles on a Security Department and its responsibilities provide interesting reading and favorable publicity for a company, particularly if slanted as an "inside look" at protection.

RADIO INTERVIEWS AND APPEARANCES ON TELEVISION

Radio talk shows or "spot" commentaries can serve in essentially the same way as public speaking engagements; that is, informing the listening public of those things they need to know about security. One successful technique has been the recording of a retail security professional's remarks while talking with a radio reporter. One-minute sections are then excerpted from the prerecorded interview for hourly airing in support of a community's anti-shoplifting campaign during the holiday season.

Radio as well as television exposure depends a great deal on the size of the community and the sophistication of network and local broadcasting programming, coupled with the community's need for information or the considered human interest aspect of a given Security Department. I recall one particularly interesting radio call-in show in which I answered listener's calls into an Ohio radio station with the aid of my speaker phone while sitting in my office in California. Some callers phoned from their cars. The interest in and response to my answers made for a lively and informative show.

The important thing here is for Security Managers to recognize the potential of these two important community communication media and to seize on those opportunities when they present themselves.

PARTICIPATION IN COMMUNITY-ORIENTED PROJECTS

Some community projects, whether sponsored by the Junior Chamber of Commerce, local government, or the efforts of a private organization, deserve if not demand support and participation of security professionals. An example would be a community-wide campaign to reduce auto thefts by encouraging drivers to lock their cars.

Depending on the campaign's organizing group and contact points in the community, the security executive could be the intermediary between the campaign and senior management of the company. Consequently he or she would be instrumental in obtaining funds for the effort. Ideally, Security would be in this position.

Furthermore, those Security Departments that have public parking facilities, such as amusement parks, hospitals, museums, sports events facilities, shopping centers, and so forth, could help the cause by distributing literature or notices supporting the campaign on vehicles parked in their areas. Such notices could be in the form of 4-by-4-inch red cardboard octagonal "stop signs" that say "Stop Auto Thefts . . . Please Lock Your Car," or some similar message.

Such programs also provide the opportunity for radio and television interviews with security professionals supporting that campaign. Interviews of this sort provide excellent visibility for the company and demonstrate its concern for and support of community-wide programs that really benefit the public.

A recent community-wide project in the Los Angeles area involved the preparation and distribution of a booklet, entitled "Probable Cause," on the state's antishoplifting law. Funding for the publication of this booklet came from four major department stores, although the real benefactors of the publication were the small or independent stores, which have little or no security. Acknowledgment of such support was printed on the back of the booklet.

Other community as well as statewide antishoplifting campaigns have marshaled the support and expertise of retail security executives, with, in some instances, a profound impact on the general public—certainly a positive contribution to the community as a whole.

Again, funding, expertise, distribution, personal appearances, and radio and/or television interviews are all viable ways to participate and contribute to community projects that serve not only the best interests of the community but the interests of the Security Department and company as well.

GENERAL PUBLIC CONTACT

Perhaps the most overlooked area of good community relations is the day-in and day-out Security Department contacts with the general public. Courtesy, good grooming, business demeanor, and the individual attitude of each member of the department can—and do—have an impact on the company's image and reputation of community goodwill. The power of a smile is always impressive.

SUMMARY

The Security Department's involvement in community relations activities is related to (1) the public's need for information, (2) the company's need to inform the public, and (3) security management's receptivity to public exposure. Ideally, the Security Director will respond positively to the needs of the community and will take an active part in identifying needs that can be addressed through a good community relations program.

Methods by which the Security Director can inform the public and create goodwill include public speaking appearances, press appearances and interviews, radio interviews, and participation in community-oriented projects such as campaigns to reduce auto thefts and shoplifting.

The Security Department's day-to-day contact with the public also contributes to the company's image and goodwill.

REVIEW QUESTIONS

1.   List six types of activities that enable the Security Department to establish a good community relations program.

2.   Suggest several possible topics for a Security Manager addressing a local civic group, a high school class, and a women's club.

3.   Give several examples of community-oriented projects in which Security might participate.

V
MISMANAGEMENT

27

Jackass Management Traits[1]

The management process of achieving organizational goals by working through other people is as much an art as a science. Those in leadership roles, irrespective of the level of responsibility, affect the lives of every subordinate in a very dramatic and emotional way—far more than many leaders suspect. What a manager says or doesn't say, or does or doesn't do, is highly visible to subordinates and is carefully scrutinized. Flaws as well as strengths in one's management style tend to be exaggerated. By virtue of the manager-subordinate relationship, the exaggerated flaw becomes dominating and overshadows or otherwise neutralizes good qualities.

Now a blunder committed in ignorance is forgivable. Theoretically, once the error is understood the manager will correct it. However, there are those who understand their past mistakes, yet, for whatever reasons, persist in exhibiting the flaw in their daily managerial style. These flaws then become unforgivable and hereinafter are referred to as "jackass management traits."

It only stands to reason that employees who are resentful, disgusted, disappointed, feel cheated or abused, or are angry with their bosses are not going to do their best. However, there's another dimension to this whole problem of poor managerial practices. That dimension is employee dishonesty. Social science researchers have established a relationship between theft (as well as other deviant behavior) and an employee's perception of the employer and supervisor. Clark and Hollinger, researchers with the University of Minnesota, state:

> [T]he dissatisfied employee was found to be more frequently involved in employee theft. This was especially true among the younger members of the work force. The most consistent source of dissatisfaction seemed to be the supervisor and the employer. Where the supervisory personnel were viewed as unhelpful, incompetent, and unconcerned, higher theft was detected. Where the integrity, fairness and ethical quality of the company were questioned, more theft was found.[2]

---

[1] This work originally appeared in the *Protection of Assets Manuals* published by the Merritt Company and Tim Walsh in 1980 and 1981.
[2] Clark, John P., and Hollinger, Richard C. Theft by Employees. *Security Management Magazine*, September 1980, p. 108.

Michael Geurts, Associate Professor of Marketing with Brigham Young University, writes the following regarding employee dishonesty:

> Retaliation is [another] reason for theft. The store has been offensive and retribution must be made, . . . and, . . . the employee who is insulted by [the] supervisor will often seek revenge by stealing.[3]

Such findings and conclusions come as no surprise to the professional security/loss prevention practitioner. It is, however, refreshing as well as encouraging to have professionals outside our industry document, in empirical terms, what we've known for some time.

The question is: Are we in security management aware of, and sensitive to, the possibility of jackass traits existing within our own security organizations? Security people react to supervision and management styles (and flaws) the same as nonsecurity people (albeit with a little more toleration). It behooves us then to eradicate jackass traits from the security pyramid by educating, training, and being examples ourselves, before we go into the greater organization and discuss causes of deviant behavior among employees. Put another way, we must practice what we preach and put our own house in order.

During my research in preparation for writing this fourth edition, it was suggested that my jackass characters be somehow indexed for quicker reference. The suggestion is a good one. Hence, the following is a quick reference to the different kinds of donkeys that find their way into positions of leadership:

Jackass Characteristic	Character No.	Page No.
Acts Before Thinking	18	348
Abuses Rank	31	362
Blind	28	359
Behind the Times	16	346
Can't Trust	13	343
Cowardly	12	342
Despot	27	358
Hires Family Members	23	354
Ignores Complaints	8	338
Ignores Training	4	334
Jailer	10	340
Knows Everything	2	332
Lifeguard	19	349
Likes to Fire People	29	360
Mechanical Heart	22	353
Moody	20	350
Makes All Decisions	3	333
Negative about Everything	25	356

---

[3] Geurts, Michael. Inventory Shrinkage in Retail Stores: Costs and Causes. *Retail Control*, August 1980, pp. 43–44.

Plays Favorites	15	345
Punishes	11	341
Racist	32	363
Rules of Company Are Holy	5	335
Sexist	24	355
Steals Ideas from Employees	26	357
Secretive	9	339
Stingy	6	336
Slave Driver	17	347
Snob	7	337
Shames Others	30	361
Too Busy to Manage	21	351
Undecided	14	344
Wants to be Popular	1	331

1. THE MANAGER WHO SEEKS TO BE "LIKED" RATHER THAN RESPECTED

Everyone wants to be liked. Being liked gives us confidence and a sense of well-being. However, the manager who strives to be "one of the gang," or wants everyone to like him or her, gets trapped into avoiding unpopular

Figure 27.1 The Popularity Kid.

decisions and ignoring disciplinary problems. Generally, people prefer to work in a well-ordered environment. They don't really want the boss to always be a nice person. Managers who avoid saying "no" or "don't" simply make the work load more difficult for everyone else. Employees aren't looking for a buddy in their boss. They know that too much socializing can lead to a compromised leader. What they do look for is a fair, impartial, predictable, honest administrator or leader who sets and maintains standards. Those qualities gain respect, which is far more important in leadership than being liked.

2. THE MANAGER WHO IGNORES THE OPINIONS AND ADVICE OF SUBORDINATES

One must wonder if the "know-it-all" really believes he or she knows it all and is that smart or if such a manager is actually insecure and is fearful of subordinates discovering that he or she doesn't have all the answers all the time. There's nothing wrong with not having all the answers all the time. There's nothing wrong with saying, "I don't know."

What really turns many employees on is to be asked, by the boss, "What do you think?" They think plenty! It's amazing how smart many people are,

Figure 27.2   The Know-It-All.

and it's equally amazing what they can do in terms of solving problems and coming up with creative strategies and ideas. To ask individuals such questions as, "What do you think?" "What are we doing that we shouldn't be doing?" and "What are we not doing that we should be doing?" invariably brings out startling food for thought. To deny oneself that input is to operate with one arm tied behind the back. After all, the collective wisdom of the group or department must exceed that of even the most brilliant managers.

The manager who can create the climate in which employees have some voice in the things that happen and in which they participate or somehow contribute to the operation as team members will get the most out of employees. They're on the team and want the team to succeed! A successful team reflects favorably on its leader!

3. THE MANAGER WHO FAILS TO DELEGATE PROPERLY

The true art of delegation includes giving responsibility with commensurate authority and then holding the subordinate fully accountable for his or her use of that authority. The primary mistake made by managers is that they give a subordinate a task (responsibility) but fail to give the necessary

Figure 27.3   The Judge.

authority to discharge that task. Put another way, the manager keeps strings attached to the assignment in terms of insisting it be done his or her way, not the subordinate's, and reserves for himself or herself the final (as well as many intermediate) decisions.

Two key conditions develop with this managerial flaw: (1) the manager becomes mired down in nitpicking relatively unimportant decisions, making everything "his" or "hers" and undermining the whole point of delegation and (2) subordinates lose "heart" because they know the boss will arbitrarily change their plans and decisions in favor of his or hers. They say, "What's the difference what I do? He'll change it anyhow." Not only is it demoralizing but it's a poor utilization of managerial time and the potential talent of all parties.

4. THE MANAGER WHO IGNORES THE TRAINING AND DEVELOPMENTAL NEEDS OF SUBORDINATES

This is the manager who attends his or her favorite training courses, seminars, and conventions but wouldn't dream of spending the money to send subordinates. As a rule, the manager knows most of the information and data that will be presented at a seminar, so he or she is quoted as saying, "The only value of these seminars is the contacts you make and maintain, and what you pick up as news and hints during cocktails." The pity is, subordinates could learn a great deal, even if the boss can't! However, when a

Figure 27.4 The Stifler.

training seminar comes to town he or she can't seem to find the funds for subordinates to attend or feels that other demands of the organization have priority. This is the same manager who resents the training department's requesting or requiring that his or her people attend company-sponsored programs, because their attendance at these programs takes time away from the job.

Employees with potential and ambition thirst for education and training to help them grow. Denying them that opportunity stunts their growth, fails to maximize their latent talents, and creates resentment. After all is said and done, the greatest resource any organization has is its people. However, this manager isn't sensitive to that.

5. THE MANAGER WHO INSISTS ON DOING EVERYTHING "THE COMPANY WAY"

Cynical humor has it that there are three ways to do a task: (1) the right way, (2) the wrong way, and (3) the company way. There really is a fourth: a better way.

The manager who's a stickler for compliance with the "book" (the company way) and who's more concerned about the means than the end result is the one who blocks enthusiasm, interest, creativity, and motivation. Some flexibility in standard procedures on the part of the manager can result in reduced costs and increased production. This kind of manager, who is

Figure 27.5 Moses.

compliance-oriented and avoids risks, typifies the person who has peaked out careerwise.

6. THE MANAGER WHO FAILS TO GIVE CREDIT WHEN CREDIT IS DUE

Nothing is more deflating, disappointing, or demotivating than having the boss ignore or overlook an achievement. A sincere "Job well done" or "Thank you" goes a long way. A note or brief memo from the manager expressing appreciation for a task well done is treasured by the deserving employee! Even a desk-side or hallway expression of thanks means a great deal. Thoughtlessness is a mark of stinginess. Interestingly, the boss that appears to be blind to achievement more often than not is the same boss that has the eyes of a hawk when it comes to recognizing mistakes. Slow to praise, quick to criticize. Everyone can spot this jackass a mile away. People expect praise and recognition when it is earned and expect constructive criticism when it is due. That's the way it should be.

The manager who's stingy with words is usually also stingy with salary increases. It's the nature of the beast.

Figure 27.6   The Miser.

7. THE MANAGER WHO TREATS SUBORDINATES AS SUBORDINATES

Employees are people first and employees second. Each person is the center of his or her own universe. Gather a group of employees in a room and pose this question, "After all is said and done, when you get right down to it, who is the most important person in this room at this very moment?" After an awkward silence someone will speak up and say, "I am," and that's right!

The manager who looks on or treats employees as inferiors stabs their very sense of self-esteem. However, he or she fails to kill it, and that wound never heals but rather, at the sight or thought of the arrogant boss, festers and smolders with resentment. Wounded people may remain on the job out of necessity and always say, "Yes, sir" or "Yes ma'am," but their heart—let alone their real potential, energy, or loyalty—is not there, even though their bodies and minds are. There are some who bide their time to return the stab in an innumerable assortment of ways. It's better to hurt a person's body than his or her pride and ego.

Figure 27.7 The Snob.

8. THE MANAGER WHO IGNORES EMPLOYEES' COMPLAINTS

Not listening is a luxury only jackasses and dictators can afford. How many companies today are unionized because employees' complaints went unheeded? Employees don't vote for unions, they vote against management. What kind of management do they vote against? That management that ignores employees' problems, real or imaginary. That's the very heartbeat of a union organizing effort. The union, in effect says, "We hear you, even if your own management won't. Vote us in. We'll represent you and then, and only then, management will listen. They'll have to!"

Not only should a manager listen, he or she should find ways to encourage employees to get things off their chests, to point out unfair practices, and to complain about dirty restrooms or poor cafeteria food. Long gone are the days when the employee stoically accepted what management had to offer. The manager who ignores employees' complaints today is the kind of jackass that should have been put out to pasture at the close of the 1950s.

Figure 27.8   The Deaf (and Dumb).

9. THE MANAGER WHO DOESN'T KEEP PEOPLE INFORMED

Whenever you hear employees say, "You never know what's going on around here," you've got a problem. Ideally, employees should not have to ask the question "Why?" because the question should have been answered before it was asked. People spend more of their waking hours on the job than at home or anywhere else. It's a big and important part of their lives. It's big for their families, too, because the job puts food on the table, pays the rent, buys the all-important automobile, provides the medical insurance, and so forth. Thus the job and the company (and the two are so intertwined they're hard to separate) are the source of the employee's sustenance and that of his or her family.

Thus everything that happens on the job is important and is scruti-nized with keen interest. When someone is transferred, promoted, resigns, retires, comes aboard, goes on medical or maternal leave, or is laid off, in one way or another it affects someone else. The same is true with organiza-tional realignments, benefit changes, and new shifts or hours. These changes should be explained to all employees at the earliest possible time.

Frequently an official notice is prepared for distribution. However, the typical company distribution system is very sluggish. The line employees who type or prepare the notice know what's happening. Before the notice

Figure 27.9 The Secret Agent.

gets out officially, those in the know leak news and it gets distorted. On top of that, depending on the kind of communication system in use at the company, many news items don't even get to line employees. They arrive on the desks of supervisors or managers who are supposed to inform their subordinates but don't.

To further magnify the frustration, you find the secret agent jackasses whose philosophy is, "Don't tell anyone unless there's a need to know," thus shrouding in mystery any changes and activities within their own pyramids.

This whole problem of poor communication, or no communication, breeds suspicion among the troops, and frequently more time is spent speculating over changes than is spent on the work itself.

10. THE MANAGER WHO HOLDS HIS OR HER ASSISTANT BACK

Every manager should be developing his or her assistant to take over the manager's job, as soon as possible. At the same time that manager should be preparing for a higher level of responsibility in or out of the present pyramid. Most employees want to move up the organizational ladder, and the effective manager fosters this healthy "bubbling-up" climate.

Figure 27.10   The Jailer.

Now there are two types of managers: One has the desire and ability to move up, while the other has no desire and/or ability to move up. In the latter case, it's grossly unfair to keep a promising assistant from advancing somewhere else in the company just to have a backup in the event of an emergency, such as a heart attack or sudden illness, in one's own office. The end result in such circumstances is that the assistant, who's obviously bright enough to make the assistant level, in due time will see that he or she is being kept on ice for emergency reasons and will simply leave the company for opportunities elsewhere. There goes a valuable and expensive investment.

11. THE MANAGER WHO VIEWS THE DISCIPLINARY PROCESS AS A PUNITIVE ACTION

Punishment isn't good discipline. In fact it's the worst of discipline, because it's negative in nature. Regrettably, many managers equate discipline with punishment, and they're off base.

The word *discipline* is derived from the Latin *discipulus,* which means "learning." The word *disciple* comes from the same root (as, the early Christian "disciples" were "students" of Christ). Today, when understood

Figure 27.11   The Whipper.

and seen as a constructive tool, "discipline" means the training that corrects, molds, or strengthens an employee in the interests of achieving organizational goals. Punishment comes after all else fails. Punishment should be a means to an end that should be organizational, not personal.

Here's a way of looking at discipline that you should never forget: The effective disciplinary process condemns the act, not the person. The approach is, "You're OK, but what you did is not OK." By attacking the performance (or performance failure) rather than the person, the whole process takes on a constructive dimension and is palatable to everyone. The manager who says, "Can't you get it through your thick skull . . . ?" is condemning or attacking the person instead of the person's performance and consequently isn't going to get satisfactory results. That manager is doing things backwards, which suggests that perhaps the manager has a thick skull—similar to that of a jackass.

12. THE MANAGER WHO FAILS TO BACK UP HIS OR HER PEOPLE

What a way to lose the support and respect of subordinates—hang them out to dry when something goes amiss! Employees under this manager know

Figure 27.12   The Coward.

where they stand when trouble rears its ugly head. They stand alone, because the boss disassociates himself or herself from anything that goes wrong. After washing his or her hands of any guilt, he or she attempts to fix the blame on someone else, rather than to fix the problem.

This fair-weather manager has an insatiable appetite for organizational successes—achieved, of course, by subordinates. He or she accepts full honor and glory for all the good things, even while letting shine forth a noble hint of modesty. This manager is indeed a winner. Never makes an error and takes all the credit. This jackass actually has the traits of a pig.

13. THE MANAGER WHOSE WORD CANNOT BE TRUSTED

The pretender is a slippery character with an almost uncanny ability to cloud up issues and renege on earlier promises or statements. Subordinates walk out of the office confused and baffled after a session with this kind of manager. A subordinate may walk into that office to inquire about a promised early performance review (with a possible increase), but the manager pretends he or she is confused about any earlier promise and then suggests the subordinate must be confused. To cap off this tragicomedy, this kind of boss righteously points to the very source of his or her wisdom and

Figure 27.13 The Pretender.

power, the sign on the wall that reads: "I know you believe you understand what you think I said, but I am not sure you realize that what you heard is not what I meant."

Talk about tragedy. This kind of manager loves the pretender style, believes it's inspired in heaven, and believes the style contributes to the overall success of the organization. The truth is that this manager is viewed with suspicion and disdain, not only as a manager of people but as a human being. What a tragic work climate this manager creates!

14. THE MANAGER WHO AVOIDS MAKING DECISIONS

Nothing can be quite as exasperating as waiting for the boss to make a decision. If a project poses a critical question, until the decision is made the project remains motionless. Nothing happens.

Some flaws in management styles never leak beyond a given subpyramid, but this particular flaw has a way of becoming widely known and snickered over. This is true because sooner or later "Ol' Undecided" will be faced with a decision that will affect the entire company and not just his or her department. How many times has the following occurred? Employee A asks employee B, "What's the status on the new proposal for intercompany transfers?" Employee B answers, "It's sitting on Harry's (The Undecided) desk." Employee A just rolls his or her eyes back.

Figure 27.14 The Undecided.

The unwillingness to make decisions clearly reflects a lack of self-confidence or fear of making the wrong decision (an error!). A key leadership responsibility is to give direction. Decisions give direction. Failure to act, let alone act in a timely fashion, is a serious deficiency that breeds frustration and a "don't-give-a-damn" attitude among subordinates.

15. THE MANAGER WHO "PLAYS FAVORITES"

Showing partiality to one or more employees at the expense of others quickly generates hostility toward the "favored" and resentment against the manager. The manager has no choice but to discharge his or her office in an objective, impartial manner. Anything less than that is blatantly unfair. It causes problems in such institutions as schools, government, and the home. It invariably leads to organizational disharmony.

A manager may well harbor personal likes and dislikes for various employees, but if he or she has any class or a sense of professionalism, no one will ever know. Of course, jackasses lack class.

Figure 27.15 The Bestower.

16. THE MANAGER WHO FAILS TO STAY CURRENT IN THE FIELD

Keeping up with the "state of the art" in terms of new technology; new concepts; new studies; changing laws; and changing attitudes, trends, and needs is a personal as well as professional requirement, especially for those in leadership roles. To discover that the manager is "behind the times" or is computer illiterate is a source of wonderment to subordinates, one that ultimately leads to a credibility gap. There's no way to bridge that gap once it has developed, except of course to become current. Catching up is an awesome task when one considers that the reason behind the need to catch up is only that the manager is too lazy to stay current. That very laziness is like a disease that accelerates in its crippling growth. Reversal is rare.

A manager can't just reach the top of any given plateau and rest on the laurels of that accomplishment. If you don't grow vertically then at least grow horizontally; that is, stay abreast of your business, keep learning, keep improving, and keep growing.

Absolutely nothing remains constant or static, except the intellect of a jackass.

Figure 27.16   Rip Van Winkle.

17. THE MANAGER WHO ENJOYS "POURING ON" MORE WORK THAN A SUBORDINATE CAN HANDLE

No useful purpose is served by inundating employees with more work than they can handle. Invariably quality is sacrificed for quantity, and desperation over too much to do in too little time leads to compromises that can include deception and destruction of assignments. Most people enjoy their work and find satisfaction in the achievement of a job well done. To purposely overload subordinates "just to be sure they're kept busy" directly contributes to high turnover, mental fatigue, some physical disabilities with resultant lost time, and general resentment and frustration. This jackass categorizes those who stay home ill as malingerers and those who object to the way work is assigned as "lazy." The manger is so dedicated to getting the maximum work out of every employee, that coffee breaks, lunch breaks, holidays (particularly birthday holidays), and vacation breaks are resented. This jackass is happiest when people come in early, work late, and come in on their day off when such extra time is off-the-record and without compensation.

Only a jackass is blind to the fact that maximum production and organizational efficiency come from employees who enjoy their work and produce willingly.

Figure 27.17 The Slave Driver.

18. THE MANAGER WHO ACTS OR OVERREACTS TOO QUICKLY

This manager would be dangerous if armed—leaping before looking, acting before thinking, and shooting without aiming (always from the hip). Making on-the-spot decisions without the facts is another characteristic of this kind of manager. This jackass also changes subordinate's plans without the benefit of discussion. Those who are in charge of executing the manager's plans are never given any notice if the plans are changed. This managerial type reacts to normal problems as though they were crises. When the smoke clears, others are blamed for the mess this jackass caused.

People resent taking the blame or being criticized for conditions created by the boss. That leads to secrecy. The boss can't react to something unknown. Employees say, "We'll handle it ourselves and the boss will never know the difference." What a breakdown in communications! The result is that this jackass becomes suspicious, goes on the prowl, and in the end reacts that much more irrationally. It becomes a vicious circle that causes an unhealthy work environment.

Figure 27.18   Hair-trigger Harry.

19. THE NEWLY PROMOTED MANAGER WHO BELIEVES HIS OR HER MANURE IS ODORLESS

Now that this jackass received a promotion and is taking over the department, everything will now be OK. All the problems are in the past. All the earlier failures will be corrected. Everything will be changed for the better. How poor everything was before. The new manager arrives like a knight in shining armor who is going to "clean house" and get this organization on its feet and moving forward again.

Talk about a dumb jackass. Doesn't the new boss realize a lot of people were quite happy under their old boss (who they were sorry to see go but pleased about the promotion) and honestly believed the department had been doing an effective job before the change? Even if an effective job was not being done, only a jackass would come in and make a lot of noise about how bad things have been. It only alienates the staff.

Newly appointed managers should heed the warning given to little children when taught how to cross a railroad track: Stop, Look, and Listen.

Figure 27.19 The Lifeguard.

Who's to blame for this kind of jackass? The jackass's boss! That boss failed to prepare the new manager for this new venture, this new level of responsibility. The new boss was told: "You're the best candidate, you have all the qualifications, I have great confidence in you, now go in there and do one helluva job!" This kind of pep talk creates giant egos, leaving anyone giddy from the rapid elevation. The new manager must be the best and the only one to save the sinking ship. If anyone is in deep—and hot—water, it will be the newly promoted manager. However, with such a swelled head, the new boss probably won't go under.

20. THE MANAGER WHO'S MOODY

Everyone who works for this jackass speculates, on a daily basis, what kind of mood the boss will be in today. Those who indulge in moodiness tend to have a fascinating array of personalities: cheerful, mean, silly, argumentative, sullen, aggressive, charitable, condescending, and magnanimous, to name a few. Sometimes the same mood will last for two consecutive days, which of course prompts a great deal of discussion among the ranks. The key to all activity in a given day is this jackass's secretary who everyone counts on for relating the "mood of the day." "Barbara," they'll say on the phone, "is it safe to come up to discuss a budget revision?" "Oh no, not

Figure 27.20   Ol' Unpredictable.

today," she may answer, particularly if she likes you. God help you if Barbara doesn't like you because she could send you into the lion's den, a hapless victim.

This managerial style doesn't breed respect, it breeds cynical disdain for those who indulge in the usurpation of authority. Managers must be predictable and consistent. They should be available to advise, counsel, assist, and work with all employees when the need surfaces. The very idea of having to throw your hat into the office to see if it'll be stomped flat and thrown back out, or if you're welcome to enter, is juvenile. Perhaps this is an immature jackass.

21. MANAGERS WHO FAIL TO PLAN AND PUT PRIORITIES ON THEIR WORK

The difference between a fire chief and a firefighter is that the former directs the efforts of the firefighters who make up the company or battalion and the firefighter extinguishes the flames. When you hear a manager say, "All I did today is put out fires," that's telling you the manager abrogated his or her authority as a leader and inserted himself or herself into the line activity of

Figure 27.21   The Fire Fighter.

the organization. Now there are occasions when absolutely everyone must pitch in to get a job done, but jackass fire chiefs are consistently in the smoke. There are several explanations for this. First, they failed to plan their day's activities and/or failed to stick to the plan. Second, they either failed to put priorities on their work (first things first, etc.) or didn't know how to identify their tasks in descending order of importance and then attack those tasks. Third, they find problems surfacing that they choose not to delegate to subordinates (and delegation is the key to good management) and get in there to resolve the problems themselves. Fourth, they are comfortable with and love fires and putting them out.

There are four problems with these managers: (1) they are not properly managing; that is, they are not getting the job done through others; (2) they are not discharging their responsibility to plan, organize, budget, control, direct, staff, and delegate; (3) subordinates are denied the opportunity to perform; and (4) they are not available as leaders because they are up to their shins in cinders.

The need for managers of people to be available to subordinates cannot be overstressed. Employees look for, expect, and need leadership. If subordinates need assistance or advice or have work or personal problems, and the boss is not in, where do they go? They go into a state of frustration, that's where they go! Where does frustration lead?

22. THE MANAGER WHO LACKS EMOTION AND EMPATHY

I want you to reflect back over the years and recall the person who you would designate as "The Best Boss I Ever Worked For." Everyone has one! Now recall "The Worst Boss I Ever Worked For." Everyone has one of those, too. The difference between the two? One was warm and sensitive, and truly cared about you as a person. The other was cold, indifferent, and cared less about you. For which of these two bosses did you give your all? With respect to the poor manager, is it not true you harbored some resentment against senior management for supporting such a manager, a manager with a mechanical heart?

The interrelationship between people is a very dynamic and emotional process. The jackass that functions like an inanimate robot turns people off emotionally. An organization is not a chart with blocks, lines, department names, and ranks. It comprises people—people with human needs and feelings. On the job a primary feeling is one of self-worth. This need for self-worth spans the entire organization from the chief executive office to the lowest paid, entry-level position. The manager who is sensitive to that value of worth, who genuinely is concerned about each employee, evokes a reciprocal feeling—as does the unemotional, cold, oblivious manager.

Regrettably, too many managers are simply sharp technicians. They excel in understanding the workers' tasks and tools. Good managers under-

Figure 27.22   The Iceman Cometh.

stand and excel (or at least try) in dealing with people who perform the tasks, use the tools, and bring profitability to the enterprise.

23. THE MANAGER WHO HIRES RELATIVES INTO THE ORGANIZATION

To bring members of one's family into the organization is a no-win situation for everyone. Such family members are not fully accepted by the work force. Employees feel, right or wrong, that relatives have an unfair advantage, and the boss's decisions on every aspect of internal affairs that affects relatives is viewed with suspicion and criticism. That's why many enlightened organizations prohibit this practice.

Why are family members not accepted by the staff? There are three reasons: (1) As a rule, employees resent others getting a job through "connection"; (2) most employees refuse to believe that relatives who are promoted earned that promotion; and (3) most employees suspect relatives are a "pipeline" and funnel information to the boss. The end result is employees are resentful and guarded.

Figure 27.23   The Nepotist.

Only a jackass would opt for the problems incurred when hiring relatives.

24. THE MANAGER WHO VIEWS WOMEN AS BEING LIMITED TO PLEASURE, BREEDING, AND MENIAL FUNCTIONS

This jackass is from a herd that's slowly dwindling but is not yet extinct! It's absolutely archaic to believe that all women should be subdued, lovely, barefoot, pregnant, and in the kitchen. Gender has nothing to do with one's intellectual capacity, leadership potential, or administrative and executive skills. Discriminating on the basis of sex is a hangover from a society and culture now in the distant past. Today we're in a fast moving, highly technical, computer-oriented, sophisticated business and industrial era in which pure talent should be the only criteria for advancement into positions of greater responsibility. More women than ever before are in the work force. In many industries the percentage of women to men is significant. What a marvelous pool of talent! Only a jackass would purposefully kindle discontentment and resentment in the work place by engaging in sexual discrimination! The mainstream of commerce today is maximizing those

Figure 27.24 The Sheik.

human resources represented in the female work force. This jackass isn't in the mainstream but still watering in a stagnant billabong.

25. THE MANAGER WHO FAITHFULLY PRACTICES THE ART OF PESSIMISM

This manager sleeps under a wet blanket and throws cold water on every innovative, creative, new, or different idea or strategy. Consistently pat answers include: "We can't." "It won't work." "We tried that before and it didn't work." "No way!" "We can't afford it." "I'd look stupid trying to sell that." "Management won't buy it." "It's not in the budget." "Too risky." "We're not ready for it." "Where the hell did you come up with that idea?" "Let's not make any waves." "Don't rock the boat." And, of course, "No."

This manager is flawless in terms of predictability and is unequivocally insurmountable. Enthusiasm within the department is effectively blocked, causing creative employees to grind their teeth in resentful frustration. Subordinates just marvel at how this "loser" holds the seat of power.

Ol' Negative is also pessimistic about future plans, the future of the company, the skills of subordinates, the future of the country, and probably believes the Apocalypse is just around the corner. Worse yet, this pessimism

Figure 27.25   Ol' Negative.

is contagious. Just 10 minutes around Ol' Negative and you're depressed too. That's why this manager is avoided like a jackass afflicted with the plague.

26. THE MANAGER WHO STEALS SUBORDINATES' IDEAS

The following is a four-act play. As the curtain opens on Act I, Mary Clark, the subordinate, is seated in front of her boss's desk. She's talking with her boss, Harry the Pirate. "Harry," she says, "I have what I think could be a dynamite suggestion for our marketing campaign on the XL4300." Harry's interested and asks Mary to spell out her suggestion. When she's done, Harry says, "Well, let me think about it, Mary. I'll get back to you later. Thanks."

Act II. The curtain opens and we see Harry the Pirate sitting in his boss's office talking to Walt Big. "Walt, I've been giving a lot of thought to our marketing strategy on the XL4300. Let me bounce this idea off you, for your reaction." Harry then reiterates Mary's suggestion. When he's done, Walt jumps up and says, "Harry, you've done it again! By God, that's one helluva idea. How long would it take you to flesh-it-out and formalize it on paper, I want to take it upstairs." Our Harry, who's now beaming with modesty replies, "You know I'm up to my ears on the Big B project. Tell you what I can do. I'll get Mary Clark to pull it together. We've talked about it

Figure 27.26 The Pirate.

already. I'll have her get it up to you before the day's out. She does good work." "Great," says Walt, unsuspecting of Harry's sleight-of-hand act of theft.

Act III. Mary has been called back into Harry the Pirate's office and Harry is talking to her. "Mary, the more I think about the XL4300 suggestion, the more I'm convinced you should go ahead and formalize it. Drop everything else, pull it together, and take it up to Walt's secretary." "Oh, that's exciting," says Mary, "I'll do it right away," and out she goes, unaware she's been victimized.

Act IV takes place the following day in the employee cafeteria, where Mary is having lunch with coworkers Tom and Dick. Tom says, "I overheard Walt Big's secretary telling some of the girls how Chairman Grand came down to Walt's office, all excited about a new marketing strategy that came from Harry." "Why, that wasn't Harry's idea. That was mine!" exclaims Mary, almost in tears. "The use of the word *was,* past tense, is correct, my dear," says Dick. "It is now Harry's. You do the work and he takes the credit. It's his style, you know!" "That's dishonest," says Mary. All nod in agreement as the lights dim and curtain closes.

27. THE MANAGER WHOSE STYLE AND AUTHORITY ARE BASED ON ABSOLUTE POWER

There's no joke about the fact that despots still exist in management circles today. They're formal, officious little dictators. Interestingly enough, most *are* of small stature. They know best and the subordinate's role is to do as told without questioning why.

One can't help but think this jackass is indeed playing a role on stage because it's so much in contrast to modern practices, but they're still around. They tend to intimidate everyone around them and love to have people speak in hushed tones in their presence, as well as step aside as they move straight ahead. To them the organization is like a supreme "state," and it's their sacred duty to rule with an iron hand. A strategy they share in common with one another is to call subordinates to their office to make them sit outside, agonizing over why they were called.

In the early twentieth century, such despotism characterized the usual managerial/supervisorial style and was accepted as a way of organizational life. Today despots are despised with a passion. No one will ever know how much theft, arson, sabotage, and successful union organizing efforts can be directly attributed to this strutting jackass.

Figure 27.27   The Despot.

28. THE MANAGER WHO SEEMS OBLIVIOUS TO WHAT'S HAPPENING

Managers of people don't have the freedom to pick and choose what they want and don't want to see. However, there are those who seem to have blind spots when it comes to certain acts or people within their pyramid. The visual impairment runs a range from "spots" to "tunnel vision" to "total." If effective and professional managers came on the scene, they would be horrified to find the chaos that occurs when a supervisor chooses not to see unchecked behavior that's not acceptable in the organization. The truth is, if one member of the staff starts "getting away with murder," it becomes common knowledge among the troops and others will follow suit. Many times blindness comes from a fear of taking corrective action—not wanting to be disliked or considered "mean."

When employees "goof off" it's not because they prefer that conduct over productive work. It's because productive work is not necessarily rewarding in a poorly disciplined environment. Most of us tend to gravitate to where the rewards are. If rewards don't come from the boss but come from peers instead, then such rewards are sought. Lone workers who keep their nose to the grindstone in this kind of workplace will probably be ridiculed. Better to be rewarded than ridiculed, right? If you can get away with making

Figure 27.28 The Visually Handicapped.

long-distance personal phone calls and taking company postage stamps, what else can you get away with?

29. THE MANAGER WHO LOVES TO "SACK" EMPLOYEES

There are those jackasses that take absolute delight in firing employees. They'll diligently monitor a likely prospect, allowing correctable failures to mount and accumulate, so that the killing blow will not be deflected by some do-gooder human resource representative or otherwise rational executive. When that prospect receives walking papers, the headhunter goes about, unproductively, selecting a new victim. One suspects these managers notch the edge of the desk with each "kill" (little notches if on probation, big notches if past probation).

The truth is that it's relatively easy to terminate someone compared with working with a marginal employee and salvaging the initial investment that goes into the recruiting, selecting, processing, orienting, and training. Most employees are salvageable and want constructive criticism and guidance to achieve acceptable company standards. Headhunters are easy to spot because they tend to sneak about, noting observations in little books from behind pillars. Although they're loathed, they wear the mantle proudly

Figure 27.29 The Headhunter.

because they perceive their mission as one of purging the impure from the organization.

The tragedy here is some fall victim to this jackass and their termination is unfair. When managers and organizations are perceived as "unfair," the variety and magnitude of subsequent consequences can be costly.

30. THE MANAGER WHO EMBARRASSES SUBORDINATES IN THE PRESENCE OF OTHERS

Discipline, corrective action, constructive criticism, or reprimands constitute a necessary and ongoing activity in every organization. Good managers know when and where to conduct such activity. Jackasses don't! Every employee understands and should expect correction, if warranted. However, they have natural expectations as to how, when, and where that correction will take place. If handled in the privacy of an office, in the context of a discussion about performance (or nonperformance) rather than a personal attack, more often than not the employee will listen to what's said and correct the questionable performance.

However, employees who are tongue-lashed, shouted at, or are "chewed out" in the presence or earshot of others are embarrassed and humiliated. They focus and dwell on the humiliating experience. They profit or learn nothing constructive or positive from the correction but rather shift

WHAT A STUPID MISTAKE!

Figure 27.30   The Humiliator.

guilt, as it were, from their performance to the equally wrongful performance of the Humiliator. Not only does the victim harbor resentment but peers who witnessed the public display identify with the victim, and they too harbor rejection and resentment against the boss.

All this to what good end? No good. Only jackass bad!

31. THE MANAGER WHO FOLLOWS "DOUBLE STANDARDS" IN THE ORGANIZATION

A key responsibility of every manager is to set a proper example. If the work day begins at 9:00 A.M., the manager should be there at 9:00 A.M. Rules that apply to the staff should apply to the boss. If employees are entitled to purchase company goods, products, or services at a discount, the discount percentage for the boss should be the same, not higher. If the company allows employees to travel on business via coach and the boss travels with subordinates, he or she too should ride coach and not first class. If the boss must fly first class, then at least that mode of travel shouldn't be flaunted; he or she should fly a different carrier or different schedule. Certainly rank has its privileges (RHIP). Everyone recognizes that. Privileges in rank are manifested in salary differences, as an example. However, aren't executive salaries usually treated as confidential? If confidential, why? Because obvi-

Figure 27.31   Mr. RHIP (Rank Has Its Privileges).

ously the disparity would only cause problems. Wisdom and common sense dictate that conspicuous disparities be avoided.

The jackass managers who flaunt their privileges by parking in restricted areas, coming in late, enjoying long breaks and lunches, going home early, having their secretary do personal business for them, staying in fancy hotels next to the hotel where their staff stays, bragging about their higher travel per diem, and generally relishing their advantages in open view of subordinates who work shoulder to shoulder with them are inviting problems.

32. THE MANAGER WHO'S A RELIGIOUS OR RACIAL BIGOT

This is a close cousin to the Sheik or sexist who we already identified as a managerial jackass. The difference between the two is the sexist simply feels women have limited value, whereas the Night Rider may be fundamentally opposed to either Jews, Protestants, Catholics, Latinos, African Americans, Asians, or other groups. It's simply ridiculous to categorically state that given classes, groups, or races of people have no executive or managerial potential. Now a simple jackass may take that position. However, an effective and intelligent leader knows otherwise. Identifying and then maximizing individual talent to achieve organizational goals is a requisite and

Figure 27.32   The Night Rider.

responsibility of sound management. I personally couldn't care less if an individual has a religious conviction, social orientation, or skin pigmentation different from mine. My concern is: Can this person do the job, and do it well?

For just a moment, forget managers denying themselves and the organization the full spectrum of talent present in the greatest resource any firm has—the human resources of its employees, prejudice, be it racial or religious, consistently has bred discontentment and confrontation. What else can it breed in organizational life?

SUMMARY

Now we have a grand total of 32 supervisory and managerial flaws found in organizational life. We've chosen to call them jackass management traits. Although it's good to poke fun at some of these otherwise tragic characters, it's sad to consider so many negative traits still existing and, in some cases, prevailing. However, there's good news, too. These failings that exist in the very source of our strength and our economic base are rapidly being replaced with a new breed of leadership that understands and appreciates the values of human dignity and worth. This is not coming from the bottom up, but from the top down. There is a growing recognition among senior management that good leadership inspires self-motivation among the troops, rather than harsh or otherwise insensitive managers prodding employees down the jackass trail.

Appendix A

EMPLOYEE PERFORMANCE EVALUATION

HOURLY AND WEEKLY RATED
NON-SUPERVISORY PERSONNEL

NAME _____   DATE OF RATING _____

JOB TITLE _____   ON PRESENT JOB SINCE _____

EMPLOYEE NUMBER _____   SERVICE DATE _____

INSTRUCTIONS: Read the definitions under each factor listed below and check (√) the box that best describes this employee's overall performance for the past year. To the right of the definitions are various elements for each factor; again check as appropriate. Any BAS rating must be explained in the comments sections.

RATING CODE DEFINITIONS

(O)   OUTSTANDING: Performance of extraordinary or rare nature. Consistently exceeds normal job requirements. Makes substantial contributions to the success of the department.

(AAS)   ABOVE ACCEPTABLE STANDARDS: Performance that frequently exceeds normal job requirements. Makes definite contributions to the success of the department.

(MAS)   MEETS ACCEPTABLE STANDARDS: Performance that meets normal job requirements. There is no evidence of any major deficiency.

(BAS)   BELOW ACCEPTABLE STANDARDS: Performance that is frequently below normal job requirements. Evidence of major deficiencies. Improvement is required to meet job requirements.

PART I

1. KNOWLEDGE OF JOB

The understanding of basic
fundamentals, methods, and
procedures of the job.

O   AAS   MAS   BAS

A. KNOWS PROCEDURES
B. LEARNS WORK QUICKLY
C. KNOWS EQUIPMENT AND
   FORMS
D. KNOWS WHY THINGS ARE
   DONE

O A M B

COMMENTS: _____

_____

2. QUALITY OF WORK

Grade of acceptable work
compared to what might
reasonably be expected.

O   AAS   MAS   BAS

A. ACCURACY OF WORK
B. THOROUGHNESS OF WORK
C. NEATNESS OF WORK

O A M B

COMMENTS: _____

_____

3. QUANTITY OF WORK

Volume of acceptable work
compared to what might
reasonably be expected.

O   AAS   MAS   BAS

A. OVERALL VOLUME OF WORK
B. CONSISTENCY OF OUTPUT
C. EFFORTS TO IMPROVE
   OUTPUT
D. UTILIZATION OF TIME

O A M B

COMMENTS: _____

_____

4. ADAPTABILITY

Quickness to learn new duties and
to adjust to new situations
encountered on the job.

O   AAS   MAS   BAS

A. ADJUSTS TO NEW SITUATIONS
B. QUICK TO LEARN NEW DUTIES
C. FOLLOWS COMPANY POLICY

O A M B

COMMENTS: _____

_____

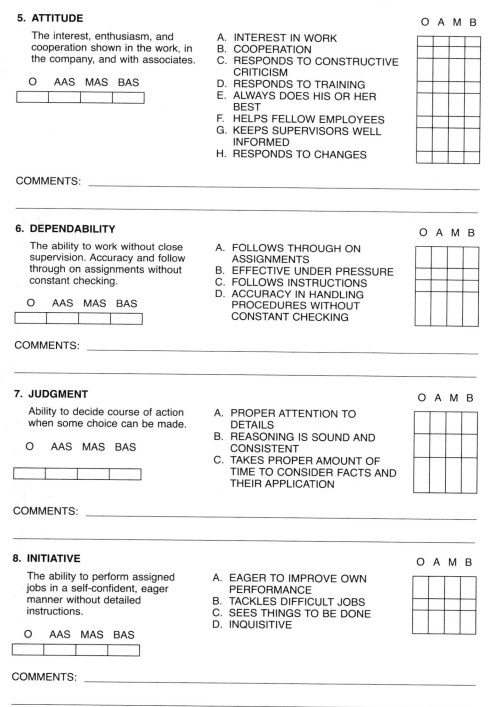

5. ATTITUDE

The interest, enthusiasm, and cooperation shown in the work, in the company, and with associates.

O   AAS   MAS   BAS

A. INTEREST IN WORK
B. COOPERATION
C. RESPONDS TO CONSTRUCTIVE CRITICISM
D. RESPONDS TO TRAINING
E. ALWAYS DOES HIS OR HER BEST
F. HELPS FELLOW EMPLOYEES
G. KEEPS SUPERVISORS WELL INFORMED
H. RESPONDS TO CHANGES

O A M B

COMMENTS: _____

6. DEPENDABILITY

The ability to work without close supervision. Accuracy and follow through on assignments without constant checking.

O   AAS   MAS   BAS

A. FOLLOWS THROUGH ON ASSIGNMENTS
B. EFFECTIVE UNDER PRESSURE
C. FOLLOWS INSTRUCTIONS
D. ACCURACY IN HANDLING PROCEDURES WITHOUT CONSTANT CHECKING

O A M B

COMMENTS: _____

7. JUDGMENT

Ability to decide course of action when some choice can be made.

O   AAS   MAS   BAS

A. PROPER ATTENTION TO DETAILS
B. REASONING IS SOUND AND CONSISTENT
C. TAKES PROPER AMOUNT OF TIME TO CONSIDER FACTS AND THEIR APPLICATION

O A M B

COMMENTS: _____

8. INITIATIVE

The ability to perform assigned jobs in a self-confident, eager manner without detailed instructions.

O   AAS   MAS   BAS

A. EAGER TO IMPROVE OWN PERFORMANCE
B. TACKLES DIFFICULT JOBS
C. SEES THINGS TO BE DONE
D. INQUISITIVE

O A M B

COMMENTS: _____

9. CUSTOMER SERVICE
(As Applicable)

O A M B

Alertness to, acknowledgment of, and interest in the customer.

O   AAS   MAS   BAS

A. IMMEDIATE APPROACH AND ACKNOWLEDGMENT OF CUSTOMER
B. RECOGNITION OF WAITING CUSTOMER, IF BUSY
C. GRACIOUS, COURTEOUS, AND ATTENTIVE
D. GIVES ALERT AND INTELLIGENT SERVICE

COMMENTS: _____

---

10. MERCHANDISE KNOWLEDGE
(As Applicable)

O A M B

Well informed on entire stock in department.

O   AAS   MAS   BAS

A. VOLUNTEERS MERCHANDISE INFORMATION
B. GIVES ACCURATE INFORMATION
C. USES FASHION AND ADVERTISING INFORMATION
D. DEMONSTRATES USE AND CARE OF MERCHANDISE
E. INQUISITIVE

COMMENTS: _____

---

11. SALES PERFORMANCE
(As Applicable)

O A M B

Overall selling performance.

O   AAS   MAS   BAS

A. VOLUME
B. ATTITUDE
C. SUGGESTIVE SELLING
D. CLOSING THE SALE

COMMENTS: _____

---

12. APPEARANCE

O A M B

The overall impression given to the customer. Neat and businesslike or sometimes careless and untidy.

O   AAS   MAS   BAS

A. APPROPRIATE FOR THE JOB
B. IN GOOD TASTE
C. WELL GROOMED

COMMENTS: _____

13. ATTENDANCE

A. NUMBER OF DAYS ABSENT_____SINCE_____
B. NUMBER OF OCCASIONS ABSENT_____SINCE_____
C. OVERALL DEPENDABILITY AS RELATES TO ATTENDANCE AND TARDINESS

COMMENTS:

_____

_____

PART II

SUMMARY RATING
NAME _____

Overall job performance and contribution to the success of the department.

COMMENTS:

_____

_____

☐ OUTSTANDING

☐ ABOVE ACCEPTABLE STANDARDS

☐ MEETS ACCEPTABLE STANDARDS

☐ BELOW ACCEPTABLE STANDARDS

PART III

1. DISPOSITION

IMMEDIATELY PROMOTIONAL TO: _____

_____ PROMOTIONAL IN _____ MONTHS TO: _____

_____ RECOMMEND TRANSFER TO: _____

_____ LEAVE ON PRESENT ASSIGNMENT _____

_____ PLACE ON JOB PERFORMANCE CAUTION OR WARNING 1   2   Final
                                                       ☐   ☐   ☐

_____ TOO NEW TO SPECIFY

2. RECOMMENDATIONS FOR TRAINING OR OTHER ACTION:

_____

_____

_____

_____

3. REMARKS:

_____

_____

_____

_____

_____   _____   _____
RATER DATE   SENIOR RATER DATE   PERSONNEL MANAGER DATE

PART IV

NOTE: Do not conduct interview until Senior Rater and Personnel Manager have signed this form.

1. REPORT OF INTERVIEW

_____

_____

_____

_____

_____

_____

_____   _____
DATE OF INTERVIEW   SIGNATURE OF INTERVIEWER

Employee Comments

_____

_____

_____

_____

_____   _____
DATE OF COMMENTS   SIGNATURE OF EMPLOYEE

Appendix B

SECURITY VULNERABILITY SURVEY

Facility _____ Survey Date _____

Address _____ Facility Manager _____

Telephone No. _____

I. GENERAL FUNCTION

_____ Leased Owned

No. Employees Assnd. _____

Operating Hours: Weekdays   Saturday   Sunday

                      Opens _____ Opens _____ Opens _____

                      Closes _____ Closes _____ Closes _____

Address & Phone of Police Jurisdiction: _____

Area Evaluation: _____

II. BUILDING & PERIMETER

_____ 1. Type of construction?

_____ 2. Door construction (hinges, hinge pins, solid core, etc.)?

_____ 3. Total number of perimeter entrances?

_____ 4. Are all exits & entrances supervised?
        If not, how controlled?

_____ 5. Are there perimeter fences?
        Type?
        Height?
        Distance from bldg.?
        Cleared areas?
        Barbed-wire top?
        Roof or wall areas close to fence?

_____ 6. Are there any overpasses or subterranean passageways?

_____ 7. Height of windows from ground?
        Adequately protected?

_____ 8. Any roof openings or entries?

_____ 9. Any floor grates, ventilation openings?

_____10. Any materials stored outside bldg.?
How controlled?

_____11. Adjacent occupancy?
Comments:

III. VEHICULAR MOVEMENT

_____ 1. Is employee parking within perimeter fence?

_____ 2. Are cars parked abutting interior fences?

_____ 3. Are cars parked adjacent to loading docks, bldg. entrances, etc.?

_____ 4. Do employees have access to cars during work hours?

_____ 5. Vehicle passes or decals?

_____ 6. Are guards involved in traffic control?
Comments:

IV. LIGHTING

_____ 1. Is perimeter lighting provided?
Adequate?

_____ 2. Is there an emergency lighting system?

_____ 3. Are all doorways sufficiently lighted?

_____ 4. Is lighting in use during all night hours?

_____ 5. Is lighting directed toward perimeter?

_____ 6. Is lighting adequate for parking area?

_____ 7. How is lighting checked?

_____ 8. Is interior night lighting adequate for surveillance by night guards (or by municipal law enforcement agents)?

_____ 9. Are guard posts properly illuminated?
Comments:

V. LOCKING CONTROLS

_____ 1. Does the facility have adequate control and records for all keys?

_____ 2. Is a master key system in use?

_____ 3. How many master keys are issued?

_____ 4. Are all extra keys secured in a locked container?

_____ 5. Total number of safes?

_____ 6. Last time combination(s) changed?

_____ 7. If combination is recorded, where is it stored?

_____ 8. Total number of employees possessing combination?

_____ 9. Review procedures for securing sensitive items (i.e., monies, precious metals, high dollar value items, narcotics, etc.).

_____10. Who performs locksmithing function for the facility?

_____11. Is a key inventory periodically taken?

_____12. Are locks changed when keys are lost?
Comments:

VI. ALARMS

_____ 1. Does this facility utilize any alarm devices?
Total number of alarms?

<u>Type</u> <u>Location</u>   <u>Manufacture Remarks</u>

_____ 2. Are alarms of central station type connected to police department or outside guard service?

_____ 3. Is authorization list of personnel authorized to "open & close" alarmed premises up to date?

_____ 4. Are local alarms used on exit doors?

_____ 5. Review procedure established on receipt of alarm?

_____ 6. Is closed-circuit television utilized?
Comments:

VII. GUARDS/SECURITY CONTROLS

_____ 1. Is a guard service employed to protect this facility?

If yes. Name: _____ No. of guards _____ No. of posts _____

_____ 2. Are after hours security checks conducted to assure proper storage of classified reports, key controls, monies, checks, etc.?

_____ 3. Is a property pass system utilized?

_____ 4. Are items of company property clearly identified with a distinguishing mark that cannot be removed?

_____ 5. Review guard patrols & frequency?

_____ 6. Are yard areas and perimeter areas included in guard coverage?

_____ 7. Are all guard tours recorded?

_____ 8. Are package controls exercised regarding packages brought on or off premises?

_____ 9. Does facility have written instructions for guards?

_____10. What type of training do guards receive?

_____11. Are personnel last leaving building charged with checking doors, windows, cabinets, etc.? Record of identity?

_____12. Are adequate security procedures followed during lunch hours?
Comments:

VIII. EMPLOYEE AND VISITOR CONTROLS

_____ 1. Is a daily visitors register maintained?

_____ 2. Is there a control to prevent visitors from wandering in the plant?

_____ 3. Do employees use identification badge?

_____ 4. Are visitors issued identification passes?

_____ 5. What type of visitors are on premises during down hours and weekends?

_____ 6. Does any company's employees other than _____ have access to facility?

<u>List Company Names</u>   <u>Type Service Performed</u>

_____ 7. Are controls over temporary help adequate?
Comments:

IX. PRODUCT CONTROLS (Shipping and Receiving)

_____ 1. Are all thefts or shortages or other possible problems (i.e., anonymous letters, crank calls, etc.) reported immediately?

_____ 2. Inspect and review controls for shipping area.

_____ 3. Inspect and review controls for receiving area.

_____ 4. Supervision in attendance at all times?

_____ 5. Are truck drivers allowed to wander about the area?
Is there a waiting area segregated from product area?
Are there toilet facilities nearby?
Water cooler?
Pay telephone?

_____ 6. Are shipping or receiving doors used by employees to enter or leave facility?

_____ 7. What protection is afforded loaded trucks awaiting shipment?

_____ 8. Are all trailers secured by seals?

_____ 9. Are seal numbers checked for correctness against shipping papers? "In" and "Out"?

_____10. Are kingpin locks utilized on trailers?

_____11. Is a separate storage location utilized for overages, shortages, damages?

_____12. Is parking (employee and visitor vehicles) prohibited from areas adjacent to loading docks or emergency exit doors?

_____13. Is any material stored in exterior of building?
If so how protected?

_____14. Are trailers or shipments received after closing hours?
If so, how protected?

_____15. Are all loaded trucks or trailers parked within fenced area?

_____16. Review facility's product inventory control.

	Loss	Breakage	Returns
Average			
Monthly			

_____17. Review controls over breakage.
Comments:

X. MONEY CONTROLS

_____ 1. How much cash is maintained on the premises?

_____ 2. What is the location and type of repository?

_____ 3. Review cashier function.

_____ 4. What protective measures are taken for money deliveries to facility?
To bank?

_____ 5. If armored car service utilized, list name and address.

_____ 6. Does facility have procedure to control cashing of personal checks?

_____ 7. Are checks immediately stamped with restricted endorsement?

_____ 8. Are employee payroll checks properly accounted for and stored in a locked container (including lunch hours) until distributed to the employee or his or her supervisor?
Comments:

XI. PROPRIETARY INFORMATION

_____ 1. What type of proprietary information is possessed at this facility?

_____ 2. How is it protected?

_____ 3. Is "_____Restricted" marking used?

_____ 4. Are safeguards followed for paper waste, its collection and destruction?

_____ 5. Are desk and cabinet tops cleared at end of day?

_____ 6. Is management aware of need for protecting proprietary information?
Comments:

XII. OTHER VULNERABILITIES

_____ 1. Trash pick ups. (Hours of pick ups, control of contractor, physical controls.)

_____ 2. Scrap operations. (Physical controls of material and area, control over scrap pick ups, etc.)

_____ 3. Other.
Comments:

XII. PERSONNEL SECURITY

_____ 1. Are background investigations conducted on employees handling products?
Handling cash?
Engaged in other sensitive duties?
Supervisory position?
All employees?

_____ 2. If so, who conducts background investigation?

_____ 3. Are new employees given any security or other type of orientation?

_____ 4. Do newly hired employees execute a corporate briefing form for inclusion in their personnel file?

_____ 5. Are exit interviews conducted of terminating employees?

_____ 6. Is a program followed to ensure return of keys, credit cards, ID cards, manuals, and other company property?

GENERAL COMMENTS:

Appendix C

Selected Security Related Organizations

- American Polygraph Association—Organization dedicated to providing a valid and reliable means to verify the truth and establish the highest standards of moral, ethical, and professional conduct in the polygraph field. www.polygraph.org
- American Society for Industrial Security, International (ASIS)—The world's largest security organization that is dedicated to increasing the effectiveness and productivity of security practices via educational programs and materials. www.asisonline.org
- Associated Locksmiths of America—Professionals engaged in locksmithing business. www.aloa.org
- Association of Certified Fraud Examiners—Organization dedicated to combating fraud and white-collar crime. www.cfenet.com
- Association of Christian Investigators—Mission is to integrate the private security investigative profession with Christian values. www.a-c-i.org
- California Association of Licensed Investigators—Association of licensed investigators in California; links to other state associations. www.CALI-pi.org
- Canadian Society for Industrial Security—A professional association for persons engaged in security in Canada. www.esis-scsi.org
- High Technology Crime Investigation Association—Association of high-technology criminal investigators. www.htcia.org
- International Association for Healthcare Security and Safety—Professional hospital/healthcare security management association. www.iahss.org
- International Association of Auto Theft Investigators—Formed to improve communication and coordination among professional auto theft investigators. www.iaati.org
- International Association of Campus Law Enforcement Administrators—Informational website regarding university and college security. www.iaclea.org
- International Association of Personal Protection Agents—Informational site for international bodyguards. www.iappa.org
- International Association of Professional Security Consultants—Members are independent, non–product-affiliated consultants pledged to meet client needs with professional consulting services. www.iapsc.org
- International CPTED Association (ICA)—Crime prevention through environmental design practitioners. www.cpted.net

- International Foundation for Protection Officers—Training and certification of line protection security officers. www.ifpo.org
- International Process Servers Association—An online resource designed to assist process servers, private investigators, skip tracers, attorneys, and paralegals. www.serveprocess.org
- International Professional Security Association—Promotes security professionalism in the United Kingdom. www.ipsa.org.uk
- International Security Management Association—Organization of senior security executives. www.ismanet.com
- International Society of Crime Prevention Practitioners, Inc.—Crime prevention organization. www.crimeprevent.com
- Jewelers' Security Alliance—A non-profit trade association that has been providing crime prevention information and assistance to the jewelry industry and law enforcement since 1883. www.jewelerssecurity.org
- National Alliance for Safe Schools—Organization promotes safe environments for students. www.safeschools.org
- National Association of Legal Investigators—Source for locating investigators nationwide. www.nalionline.org
- National Association of Professional Process Servers—A worldwide organization that provides a newsletter as well as conferences and training. www.napps.com
- National Australian Security Providers Association—Australian industry association. www.naspa.com.au
- National Burglar and Fire Alarm Association—Represents the electronic security and life safety industry. www.alarm.org
- National Classification Management Society—Classification management and information security organization. www.classmgmt.com
- National Council of Investigation and Security Services—Organization for the investigation and guard industry. www.nciss.com
- National Fire Protection Association—National Life Safety codes. www.nfpa.org
- National Society of Professional Insurance Investigators—Membership, education, and recognition information. www.nspii.org
- Security Industry Online—Represents manufacturers of security products and services. www.siaonline.org
- Security on Campus, Inc.—Resource for college and university campus crime safety and security issues. www.campussafety.org
- Society of Competitive Intelligence Professionals—The premier online community for knowledge professionals all around the world. www.scip.org
- Society of Former Special Agents of the Federal Bureau of Investigation—Publications and member information. www.socxfbi.org
- South African Security Industry Associations—Directory listing of South African security associations. www.security.co.za
- Spanish Association of Private Detectives—Spanish organization for private investigators and process servers. www.detectives-spain.org/english

- Women Investigators Association—An association geared to the special needs of women investigators. www.w-i-a.org
- World Association of Professional Investigators—New investigation organization in London. www.wapi.org

Appendix D

Suggested Security/Loss Prevention Reference Sources

BOOKS

Barefoot, J. Kirk. *Employee Theft Investigation.* (Stoneham, MA: Butterworth-Heinemann, 1990).

Berger, David L. *Industrial Security,* 2nd ed. (Woburn, MA: Butterworth-Heinemann, 1999).

Broder, James F., CPP. *Risk Analysis and the Security Survey*, 2nd ed. (Woburn, MA: Butterworth-Heinemann, 2000).

Craighead, Geoff. *High-rise Security and Fire Life Safety.* (Woburn, MA: Butterworth-Heinemann, 1996).

Fay, John. *Encyclopedia of Security Management.* (Woburn, MA: Butterworth-Heinemann, 1993).

Federal, R. Keegan, Jr. *Avoiding Liability in Retail Security.* (Atlanta, GA: Stafford Publications, 1986).

Federal, R. Keegan, Jr. *Avoiding Liability in Premises Security.* (Atlanta, GA: Stafford Publications, 1989).

Fennelly, L. *Handbook of Loss Prevention and Crime Prevention*, 3rd ed. (Woburn, MA: Butterworth-Heinemann, 1996).

Hannon, Leo F., JD. *The Legal Side of Private Security.* (Westport, CT: Quorum Books, 1992).

Horan, Donald J. *The Retailers Guide to Loss Prevention and Security.* (Boca Raton, FL: CRC PRESS, 1997).

Kuhlman, Richard S., JD. *Safe Places? Security Planning and Litigation.* (Charlottesville, VA: The Michie Company, 1989).

Maxwell, David A., JD, CPP. *Private Security Law—Case Studies.* (Stoneham, MA: Butterworth-Heinemann, 1993).

McCrie, Robert D. *Security Operations Management.* (Stoneham, MA: Butterworth-Heinemann, 2001).

Nemeth, Charles P. *Private Security and the Law.* (Cincinnati, OH: Anderson Publishing, 1989).

Sennewald, Charles A., CPP. *Shoplifters vs. Retailers — The Rights of Both.* (Chula Vista, CA: New Century Press).

Sennewald, Charles A., and Tsukayama, John K. *The Process of Investigation*, 2nd ed. (Stoneham, MA: Butterworth-Heinemann, 2001).

Simonsen, Clifford E. *Private Security in America—An Introduction.* (Upper Saddle River, NJ: Prentice Hall, 1998).

Sklar, Stanley L. *Shoplifting—What You Need to Know About the Law.* (New York: Fairchild Publications, 1982).

Vellani, Karim, and Nahoun, Joel. *Applied Crime Analysis.* (New York: Elsevier Science Publishing, 2001).

Zulawski, David E., and Wicklander, Douglas E. *Practical Aspects of Interview and Interrogation.* (New York: Elsevier Science Publishing, 1992).

MAGAZINES

Security Management, Security Design & Technology, Access Control, Loss Prevention, Security Journal, International Security Review, Journal of Security Administration, Police & Security News, Security, Security News, and *Journal of Homeland Security*

NEWSLETTERS

Security Law Newsletter, Security Letter, Premises Liability Report, Corporate Security, Homeland Security & Defense, Private Security Case Law Reporter, IOMA's *Preventing Business Fraud, Employee Security Connection, Security Director's Digest, Security Management Bulletin,* and *Computer Security*

INDEX

Other Books from Butterworth-Heinemann